Getting Away from It All

KAREN STEIN

Getting Away from It All

Vacations and Identity

TEMPLE UNIVERSITY PRESS
Philadelphia • *Rome* • *Tokyo*

TEMPLE UNIVERSITY PRESS
Philadelphia, Pennsylvania 19122
tupress.temple.edu

Library of Congress Cataloging-in-Publication Data

Names: Stein, Karen, 1979– author.
Title: Getting away from it all : vacations and identity / Karen Stein.
Description: Philadelphia : Temple University Press, [2019] | Includes bibliographical
  references and index. |
Identifiers: LCCN 2018046411 (print) | LCCN 2019014555 (ebook) |
  ISBN 9781439918760 (E-book) | ISBN 9781439918746 (cloth : alk. paper) |
  ISBN 9781439918753 (pbk. : alk. paper)
Subjects: LCSH: Vacations—Psychological aspects. | Leisure—Psychological aspects.
Classification: LCC GV186 (ebook) | LCC GV186 .S74 2019 (print) |
  DDC 306.4/812—dc23
LC record available at https://lccn.loc.gov/2018046411

♾ The paper used in this publication meets the requirements of the American National
Standard for Information Sciences—Permanence of Paper for Printed Library Materials,
ANSI Z39.48-1992

Printed in the United States of America

9 8 7 6 5 4 3 2 1

Contents

Acknowledgments

For their careful readings of many early drafts of this book, indispensable feedback, and generous insight, I thank Eviatar Zerubavel, Deborah Carr, Richard Williams, Karen Cerulo, and Christena Nippert-Eng. I am especially grateful to Eviatar Zerubavel for the guidance and support he has given in seeing this project through from its beginning to its completion. I also thank those who offered valuable advice at various stages of this project's development: Andrea Barra, Daina Harvey, Monique Porow, and Elizabeth Williamson. Also, for their ongoing support, I thank Thomas and Kathalina Stein; Thomas and Russell; and Jeremy, Rex, and George Dyer. Last, I thank the anonymous participants in the study, without whose cooperation and time this book would not have been possible.

Getting Away from It All

Introduction

The power of vacations and their role in shaping how people see themselves is evident in the ways individuals play with identity during their time off. When attending the Sturgis Motorcycle Rally held every year in South Dakota, for example, one may temporarily become a motorcycle biker, whether he or she is one the rest of the year or not. At Calgary's annual Stampede, visitors can wear cowboy boots and hats and participate in the rodeo. At fantasy camps, adults can pay to temporarily become a rock star, a New York Yankee, a figure skater, a race car driver, or a television star, among many others. Trends in the travel industry that emphasize playing up or leaving behind particular role requirements from everyday life similarly illustrate the appeal of vacations for voluntary identity changes. "Mancations" offer all-male bonding trips that can include poker, extreme sports, and golf. "Momcations" appeal to women to leave behind their children and husbands and relax with other mothers.[1]

These ideas are also reflected in popular media that depict vacations as a time to bond with family, learn something new, fall in love, or just relax and let loose. The family vacation as bonding experience is caricatured perhaps most popularly in *National Lampoon's Vacation* as Chevy Chase attempts to keep his family together and happy during a cross-country road trip to a theme park. In *Dirty Dancing* the diligent and naive main character Baby learns to loosen up a little and fall in love with a man from a lower socioeconomic status at a family resort in the Catskills, while in *Forgetting*

Sarah Marshall a man travels to a Hawaiian resort to forget about his ex-girlfriend. In *The Hangover* a group of men party to such excess in Las Vegas that they completely forget what happened to them the night before.

There is great range in the types of vacations that people enjoy: a week at the beach with the family, a trip to Disney World, a whirlwind European tour, hiking in a national park, a relaxing weekend at a spa, golfing, a road trip, camping, and so on. The list is as long as peoples' imaginations make it. The possibilities extend to the limits of interest and ability. Vacations signal class and economic standing, and they also reveal aspirations and goals. In this distinct time, set apart from the demands of everyday life, vacations reveal what people choose to do, rather than what they must do.[2] They are opportunities for self-definition. Asking people about their ideal vacation experience is illustrative of the range of activities and desires that people undertake.[3] Some wishes seem to be unusual and substantial changes from everyday life. Others are more mundane, capturing a desire to expand some existing element of the self, work on relationships, or just relax a bit:

> Okay, no kids. First of all, no kids. I mean, maybe if they were older, it would be different. Someplace away, like far enough away. It doesn't have to be on a plane but away. At least an hour away. So I don't feel like I'm at home. Away, warm, nothing to do. (Jamie, midthirties, married, teacher, and graduate student)

> Um, I want to travel. I want to see everything. Europe. I want to go to South America. Just go as far as possible and just *see* things, experience them. Doesn't everyone? [*Laughs.*] (Selena, late twenties, single, graduate student)

> Ha! We'd live with the great-grandkids. We'd go where the great-grandchildren are. (George, late sixties, married, retired)

> Generally, for me it depends on what happens in my everyday life. If it's very stressful, which it has been in the last few years, then my idea of vacation is somewhere in the woods, far away from civilization, with a campfire and a nice cold beer. (Jodie, late thirties, single, physician)

> My ideal vacation would be go to Alaska. Get on a Cessna 182 float plane, fly as deep as I could in the bloody wilderness of Alaska,

with my equipment, backpack, rifle, and knowledge, and just try to work it out for a month or two. (Mark, midfifties, married, shop manager)

The common idea in each of these personal aspirations and popular depictions is that on vacation people can do or be something or someone different from that of their day-to-day experience. One can change for a little while, try to strengthen bonds with family members or leave them behind altogether, or just relax and enjoy the days in ways that the limitations of everyday life do not allow. In this way, while on vacation, people temporarily reorganize the identities and roles that make up the self. Limited to a specific time and situated in a particular place, people may exercise self-definition. In this "time off" people can engage the multifaceted nature of self-identity by taking on new roles or fortifying or diminishing existing roles in a different context.

Vacations are fertile sites for analysis of these temporary identity shifts because they are distinctly bounded and structured to offer individuals an opportunity to put on hold selective features of day-to-day experience or adopt new, favored behaviors. They are specifically built into the structure of the year to allow people time off from select social obligations that constrict and regulate their actions. They are thus a period of enhanced personal freedom that can tell us much about how people choose to construct and enact an identity when social rules and proscriptions are eased, removed, or shifted. This is what defines a vacation regardless of financial, social, or psychological limitations. Individuals create a temporary arrangement that allows for exploration, experimentation, and indulgence and also coheres with the ongoing self in a way that probably would not be sustainable in the long term. Vacations mean different things to different people and activities can range from a trip to the beach, cultural events, or adventure tourism. I argue their significance is not in the specific activity undertaken but is in the temporary relaxation of one's experience of social structure. The vacation, then, is a discrete moment in time that we as a culture have agreed to isolate for mental flexibility about who we are and what we can be.

Vacations address the tension of freedom and constraint in the navigation of identity by offering a socially and temporally bounded space that is disengaged from certain constraining elements of social structure. The people one interacts with on a daily basis, obligations of employment, and even the experience of one's socioeconomic position[4] may be temporarily altered. Since people have more flexibility in who they want to be and what they want to do for this short time, vacations are a moment during which individuals have more agency in steering their identities. Jodie describes the freedom she experiences when she vacations by herself:

> I like it because I like the freedom of the fact that you can just sort of do and be whatever you want to be, if you've got the actor's skill to do that. But I think you can just sort of start with a clean slate. You've got no one with you that you think, "I better behave because that person knows me." I think you do adjust if you've got someone with you that you know. . . . I like not knowing anyone because it gives you an enormous freedom, I think, to just talk to everyone and not feel responsible.

This agency comes from the possibility of opportunities for new, altered, or reprioritized identities. Mona, a stay-at-home mother and wife, sums this up when she talks about one of her favorite vacations:

> My dearest friend in San Antonio has a house in Miami, and we go for a weekend to Miami. And it's just fun, because we can hang out, and, like, I still like rap music. I can go listen to rap music. I can't do that with my kids. So that's fun. But it's a very different trip. Because I'm traveling as myself versus as a mother. You know? . . . I don't have to watch out for somebody. They have to watch out for me.

Vacations, then, allow an examination of what people choose to be when certain limitations of their structured social world are eased and at the same time illuminate how individuals remain tied to identities, either voluntarily or not. Of course, most people cannot truly leave it all behind and escape all the factors that make up their everyday selves. Everyday role requirements and structural constraints intercede in the construction of identity. Income and wealth limit the ability to get away from it all, as do factors such as personal ties to family, especially children, or close friends. People, however, have the agency to moderate how components of everyday life intercede in their vacation time. In this sense mental methods of segmentation and integration[5] become crucial to the negotiation of identity during these breaks, because individuals manage the degree to which their everyday identities and role requirements overlap into their time off, and vice versa. They manage self-identity in part in response to what they let in to or keep out of their everyday experience.

At the same time, connections to home can rarely be cut off entirely. Individuals construct identities that in some way contrast with what they do in everyday life while also negotiating connections to daily experience. Some facets have more pull over us, and we will not or cannot easily put them aside. Most parents cannot forget their responsibilities toward their children for a week or two and probably do not wish to, although many may joke otherwise. Someone very committed to a job similarly may have a hard time putting away the smartphone and not checking in with work, perhaps even planning for some designated work time during the vacation. Sociologists recognize that experiences of freedom and constraint are not the same for everyone and are instead relative.[6] One person's vacation may not be considered much of a change at all to someone else.

Income and wealth certainly aid an individual in successfully getting away from it all, whereas personal ties like family and friends keep us bound to home while away. A stay-at-home mom who goes on a family vacation may find that her day-to-day responsibilities have not changed much at all. People do, however, have the agency to moderate how components of everyday life intervene in their vacation time.

The trade-offs between freedom and constraint and between autonomy and security are among the fundamental ways that people make choices about what they want and at what expense. People are looking for autonomy and freedom in many ways, but throughout the vacation they are voluntarily giving it up for security, comfort, and ease. If people want to be on their own, they must attend to time, closely watching the clock in order to be self-reliant and successful. Otherwise, they can have someone else attend to it for them and give up that freedom as they submit to shared schedules. Similarly, people wish to travel to new locations in space and experience a new place, but they also want escape routes if things go wrong and a comfortable environment to return to at the end of the day. Traveling with others offers support and company in sharing the experience but comes at the cost of using valuable time to do things one might not want to do. Traveling alone can be liberating, but it can also be dangerous, lonely, or boring.

The goal of this book is to understand more than just the identity shifts people make on vacation; it seeks to address how they use such pauses in everyday life to temporarily alter or shape identity and the self. This is a study of flexibility and individuality and the juncture at which self-definition meets social constraint. I examine the spatial and temporal environments in which identities are situated and constructed and how social interactions with others limit or facilitate identity shifts. I also examine how identities are cognitively bounded through the routines and rituals that mentally set this special time apart. Vacations are ideal for such inquiry because they are bounded in time and space, culturally determined, and almost universal to contemporary experience.

They are an event that is central to everyday life. Too often sociology focuses on the unusual, the outliers, or the special cases that reveal the uncommon.[7] These cases may be empirically interesting,[8] but they are not representative of general experience and leave out much of what shapes everyday life. Vacations are not an outlier. As I show, they make up a primary location in which people balance who they want to be with who they are allowed to be.

Identities and the Flexible Self

Individuals today face more options for what and who they want to be than at any other time in history. For the average American, unthreatened by the constraints of absolute poverty, there can seem to be almost unlimited options available, along with a lot of pressure to figure out who to be. The relative prosperity of American life has brought with it the freedom, and then the responsibility, of making choices about the self. In the past, identities were more ascribed. One was born into a particular life, and that shaped the choices available. Most were so burdened by the sheer amount of labor involved in getting through the day that choice or ambivalence over identity was an unavailable luxury. Long workdays on a farm or in a factory, multiple children to take care of, and no modern conveniences made life laborious and exhausting. A person did not really have a choice in who he or she was and probably had no desire to figure it out.[9] There was just not enough time for existential ambiguity. This is no longer the case. The transition away from an agrarian and industrial society also meant a transformation of self. People now have the opportunity and the expectation to fashion a self from myriad options. While structural constraints remain, people make countless choices that shape who they are and how they want to exist in the world.

After World War II, large-scale social shifts began moving people into the middle class. Individuals who previously remained financially bound to certain activities began to experience a loosening of the constraints guiding their actions and identities. As people gradually gained more expendable income and more time, prescriptive mores holding identities in check were relaxed. It was at this time that vacations as we now know them became democratized as well, moving from being an indulgence of the wealthy, who had extra time and money, to being a part of American life for everyone. As people acquired more disposable income, they took more vacations and experienced the ability to get away from the mundanities of everyday life. At the same time, this social upheaval presented a massive shift that restructured the nature of social relations. Life no longer was rooted in communities, long-term relationships became more fleeting, and what were once considered lifelong job opportunities became unstable or temporary.[10] The rise in vacations coincided not just with the increasing prosperity of the country but also with a time when identities became destabilized and voluntary alteration of identity became an option. As people became separated from the ascriptive circumstances that channeled their activities and their attention, they were also provided with expanded opportunities for identity, through both work and play, such as the vacation.

These social changes created a tension between the desire to be a unique individual and the constraints on that desire. Even with the disruption of traditional social order, constraints always remain on who one can be, and at the same time there is great pressure to be oneself. Without strong ties to religion, kinship systems, or communities to define who they were, people were given the task of figuring out who they might be. Discovering self-identity became an individualized project as the authority behind these ascriptive statuses declined and people were given more autonomy to determine how they wanted to live.[11] Selfhood came to be understood as being something essential inside oneself that may be hidden but could be uncovered gradually and selectively with self-exploration. By this belief the true self could potentially contain all kinds of things not being expressed, such as creative abilities, personality traits that run contrary to one's everyday actions, or undiscovered abilities and potential.[12]

Although dating back much further than the present age, the popular trope of travel as self-discovery fits well within this late modern ideology. The link between identity and travel has long been established and is employed by the travel industry. A series of advertisements for the U.S. Virgin Islands, for example, suggest a person could travel to the islands to find a "you unscripted." The ads feature comparisons of what identity facets a person would lose while vacationing there and what they would find in their place. An image of a man exploring a castle is accompanied by the text "Lost: Cubicle Dweller, Found: Time Traveler," another image shows a man on a boat who is "Lost: Sales Manager, Found: Captain of His Destiny," and a woman in a wedding dress is "Lost: Girl Next Door, Found: Goddess."

Tourism research has also looked to these ideas to fashion theories about travel and identity.[13] Tourists are understood as being able to forge a sense of identity through interactions with an "exotic" other, or through a period of separation with the familiar, and in the challenges and opportunities of being in a new place. It is argued that by situating themselves in alternative narratives individuals create "identity claims" that communicate malleable, multifaceted identities. This takes place in a process of intersubjective identity construction occurring from before departure to after return. It would be too far to say, however, that in the present day people can be whoever they choose.

While there is considerable room for freedom in shaping and selecting identities, this process is still fundamentally structured by social location. Friends and family, socioeconomic status, religion, nationality, and so on, all guide who a person will be. From this location in social structure individuals develop a sense of who they are and a self that is defined by roles and responsibilities.[14] Identities are not equivalent to self but are components of it. They can be understood as parts of the self that reflect the roles individuals hold and where they are situated in social relations.[15] Identity is formed by the links between the individual and society, the interplay of agency and structure in that society, and the shaping of the self within the social world.[16]

Self and identity have become highly theorized concepts with many meanings between and within academic traditions. Because of the complex nature of identity and the individual's relationship to society, there are multiple theories and definitions for self and identity and no agreement on a single definition. For this reason it is necessary to briefly outline how I conceive of and use these concepts throughout this book. The interactionist tradition in sociology views the self to be flexible and mutable throughout the life course. Self and identity can change in different situations and over time.

In this book, I follow the interactionist tradition and therefore conceptualize identity in three ways: as situational, social, and personal. These three types make up the web of identities that constitute the self, and all are subject to change at some level.

Situational identities emerge on the basis of face-to-face interactions and mutually agreed-on meanings in a particular context. These identities tend to follow culturally defined role expectations and are therefore constrained by cultural norms. Situational identities can easily change between encounters as people move between different circumstances. Because of their superficial nature, these identities tend to be least associated with an authentic or true self. Examples include a diner in a restaurant, a student, or a commuter.[17]

Social identities, on the other hand, result from membership in a particular group or category of people and are generally considered more lasting or stable. For example, female, working class, Presbyterian, or American could all be considered social identities. They define people in relation to others in their group through a set of shared characteristics and differentiate them from others who do not share those characteristics, such as male and Jewish. Tending to constrain people in how they view themselves and how others view them, these identities are less flexible than situational identities. They tend to cross situations and contexts rather than be limited to particular times and places. Because they are more enduring and often highly salient, they are usually considered essential features of selves.[18]

Last, personal identities are the individualized narratives that people construct for themselves and tell about themselves. These include specific things done during their lives and the attributes that they consider important. Personal identities are thus defined in terms of what makes an individual different from others. Choice is easier to insert into the construction of these identities than in social identities and more meaningful than in situational ones. Because they are based on narratives of self, these identities can and do change over time and with audience, although their highly personal nature ensures they are usually considered an essential or authentic representation of self. Examples are rebel, conscientious student, or activist.[19]

It is also important to disentangle social roles from social identities. Whereas roles are external expectations linked to positions within social structures, identities are more internal. They are composed of internalized expectations and meanings that come from the role or set of roles that one occupies. Although a person will enact a role, he or she may or may not identify with it.[20] Identity is about more than performing for others or taking up an expected set of behaviors. It is about how a person conceives of him- or herself. Identities are formed by the roles that an individual adopts and the sum of the relevant social interactions in which they participate. Roles offer the opportunity to occupy an externally defined part, and an identity comprises some set of roles or role opportunities that a situation presents.

Throughout this book I also refer to self-identity, something more broad than these three types of identities that can be understood as facets of self. Self-identity is the behavior, values, attitudes, and worldview of an individual. It encompasses how a person perceives of him- or herself and performs that perception for others. Self-identity is multilayered and complex and reflects how the social and individual come together through a combination of shared, internal, and performed dimensions.[21] The study of the self, then, entails examining the situations and contexts in which these forms of identity come forward. In this sense, it can be helpful to talk about identifications. People identify with certain situations and contexts, and different identifications are called on and performed in different situations. Identifications do not determine behavior or allow prediction of what a person will do. Rather, they serve as a map to the complex hierarchies people hold for who they are.[22]

In contemporary life, then, with its many commitments and changing circumstances, individuals juggle an array of identities that have varying intensity and different relationships to self and social context. Within this framework, adding, subtracting, shifting, and fluctuating identities are commonplace and to be expected. Identifications are never settled, and for most, these alterations to who they consider themselves to be are taken for granted as expected parts of moving through life. Whether becoming a parent, getting a divorce, graduating from college, moving to a new city, starting a new job, becoming vegan, or eating meat again, the self is always in flux.

Therefore, an essential temporal character structures identities. They have different beginnings, endings, and durations. Their length and character depend on the context of a life and the needs, desires, and interests placed on people by themselves and others. Some of these identities have specific and expected start and end points, either at a certain moment in the life course or at the end of a particular duration; others are expected to be ongoing; and still others transition into other identities. One graduates from high school at age eighteen, and college should then take about four years, transitioning one temporary student identity into another, and then the student identity is most conventionally replaced by a professional identity. If all goes well, being a boyfriend is replaced by being a fiancé—both temporary identities that might be replaced with the more permanent identity of husband, although that also could become a temporary identity if it becomes divorcé. Identities, therefore, should be understood as not being static or fixed but as taking forms that fluctuate over time.

As identities are shaped through social interaction, they are also outwardly expressed through dress, behaviors, mannerisms, and language. People play up, or foreground, aspects of their self that match their social environment, and at the same time they shift other facets of self to the background if they are not relevant to that particular time and place.[23] In this reflexive process individuals communicate to others who they are and how they want to be seen and also reinforce for themselves personal identity and create personal mental distinctions between identities. People use differentiation in clothing, space, language, and timekeeping to create the cognitive distinctions that delineate and define identities.[24]

The flexible self offers the opportunity for and the ability to individuals to play with self-identity by taking on new identities, roles, and personas, leaving others behind, or otherwise reordering, replacing, or scrambling a set of identities. This flexible self is the backdrop on which identities shift or rearrange and submerge or come forward, depending on context. These changes can be abrupt or transition over time. They can be very different or have some overlapping commonalities. The identities that individuals hold will necessarily overlap and compete with each other as people move between the numerous demands and obligations of their everyday lives. Because they intersect and occasionally conflict, identities must be cognitively organized, hierarchized, and negotiated by the individual. People must decide when and to what degree they will embrace a particular identity and everything that comes along with it. Some of this work is done voluntarily, as with a shift to a leisure identity, and some is mandatory, as with a shift from home to work. Identities are organized according to level of salience for the corresponding situation.[25]

Of course, some identities are more persistent than others, and individuals have varying levels of comfort with the degree to which they may overlap. Christena Nippert-Eng identifies two ideal types to better delineate how identities are managed in different situations.[26] "Segmentors" strive to keep certain facets of self separate, setting rigid cognitive boundaries that reduce the opportunity for overlap of one into the other. Segmentors mentally enforce distinctions between identities—for example, keeping separate key chains for home and work. With such a practice, associations of the two would not intermingle. On the other hand, "integrators" allow more fluidity and intermingling of roles and responsibilities. For example, keeping one planner that includes both work and social appointments would combine the two and invite more integration of identities. For either type, this cognitive management of identities is reinforced through daily practices, by organizing one's day-to-day belongings, activities, and social relations so that they reflect and reinforce the desired comfort level in partitioning or combining identities.

Identity can be conceptualized as an accomplishment. Identities are not simply something that someone has; they are things that someone works on.[27] Because an identity is something that is created in interaction, it is the result of effort or intentionality on the part of the individual to craft. In this sense dimensions to identity are manipulated by the individual in different social situations. They do not have a uniform character in all situations. Instead, they have characteristics such as duration, density, volume, and dominance that change in different environments. People spend different amounts of time presenting different facets of identity in different social situations. They put more or less emphasis on aspects of self in a context, and they prioritize an identity in certain circumstances. Time and place, then, are important variables that modify what an individual will identify with, how strongly, and for how long. People play up, or foreground, aspects of their self that match their social environment and shift other facets of self to the background if those facets are not relevant to that time and place. They also raise the relative concentration or dilution of the expression of identity facets at different points in time.[28]

This perspective shows how even essential or enduring identities can change and shift across contexts. A person may choose to present him- or herself as 100 percent of an identity in a situation in which it is fitting to do so. Other identities then fall to the background. For example, someone may be 100 percent Christian in one circumstance, such as at church or on a religious holiday, and dial back on that identity in another context, such as work. Other settings promote the dilution or concealment of identities. The typical office is usually organized as an environment that does not encourage strong displays of personal identity. The work identity is prioritized and others are pushed to the background.[29]

This cognitive effort comes to the fore in shaping identities while on vacation. The voluntary nature of time off means that people may contour the experience to meet their own desires but must negotiate limitations. Despite the adage, most people cannot truly leave it all behind on vacation and break from the factors that make up their everyday selves, but they can selectively moderate how and to what extent components of everyday life will overlap with their vacation. People have the agency to create breaks for themselves by integrating, segmenting, foregrounding, backgrounding, diluting, and intensifying identities during their time off.

The switches and inversions that can be made by anyone on vacation are tempered by external limitations. Socioeconomic position is one of the key limits that shape the experiences one can have and the opportunities to work with for shifting identity on vacation. More resources make it easier to temporarily shift some obligations to the background and foreground others. The larger the shift, the more likely that it will require more resources, such as leaving one's kids at home. The argument of this book is that everyone can create breaks for themselves to some extent, and it is this capacity to introduce change and contrast that allows temporary alterations. Cognitive change makes these shifts possible, and opportunity is not limited to one socioeconomic group.

The examples throughout this book show people making shifts to their identities in two ways: they engage in either identity work or identity play. While "identity work" as a form of identity change or adaptation has been well documented,[30] largely missing from this literature are conceptions of identity as playful or experimental.[31] In identity play, people are altering identity for fun by taking advantage of opportunities that they do not usually have but would not necessarily want to do in day-to-day life. They are doing things for the fun of doing them, not to better themselves or strengthen relationships or get something done but for the sake of doing the thing itself, and in doing so introducing something to their personal experience of self that they otherwise might not encounter or that might have remained underdeveloped.

On the other hand, to work at an identity is to make the effort to achieve some shared expectation of what an identity or role should be and thus gain acceptance or stability. This type of identity shift is often about complying with existing roles and the established rules for enacting and displaying them.[32] Adult behavior during leisure isn't limited to nonserious or frivolous action. The flexibility of this time can also make it an opportunity to work on or build existing identities and relationships. Leisure time may be used to build identities related to significant relationships, such as a parent, spouse, or partner, and therefore comes with expectations for it. For others, a period of sustained leisure can rebuild a relationship and its concomitant identity. One's behavior is then integrated with the overall self, and these types of vacations cannot be thought of as independent of everyday life. The work being done on these trips is more about building or developing aspects of self. It is about self-actualization rather than self-indulgence.

In this book I talk about identity shifts, a concept that encompasses both work and play. People alter identities for various reasons. Sometimes they want to build on an existing identity, develop it into something deeper or stronger, and take that with them into their future self. Other times people just want to experience something for the sake of doing it.

They want to tap into a part of themselves that may go underused or is not practical for everyday life and then put it away again. Vacations allow both types of identity change.

As a set of expectations or responsibilities that come along with a position in social structure, such as mother, teacher, or friend, identities and roles guide social interaction. Everyone has a set that they perform regularly, but this relatively stable grouping does not always meet the needs and interests of the individual. People thus temporarily add to or subtract from their role set. Ephemeral roles are voluntarily chosen and short lived and satisfy needs not met by one's everyday role set.[33] They range from the short to the long term and can include significant change and commitment, such as adultery, playing poker and gambling, doing drugs, or doing "whatever is intense and intermittent and defined in contrast to everyday life."[34] Ephemeral roles provide a temporary release or contrast with the constraints of day-to-day experience. A key aspect is that they are voluntary. A person switches into them because he or she chooses to. Other roles are not so ephemeral. People such as volunteer firefighters, rescue workers, or military members on reserve who leave for one weekend a month to return to training temporarily reorganize their priorities in a way that draws on professional skills and interests but that is not part of their everyday work obligations. The role becomes highly salient for a time, and everyday responsibilities get pushed into the background.

Ephemeral roles offer the opportunity to occupy an externally defined role. Identity shifts, then, often encompass a new set of roles that a situation presents. They are a reflexive expression of internalized roles not expressed within the course of everyday life. In identity shifts people are not just adding new roles that are temporarily accessible; they are also playing with, or working with, existing identities by strategically emphasizing and deemphasizing and by strengthening and weakening them. They are building and changing or adding and subtracting.

The Cultural Construction of Vacations

As I began to conceptualize this study and started talking with people about their trips, I quickly realized that defining the concept of vacation was more difficult than it seemed. The notion covers many expectations, activities, and motivations. They are experiences as varied as the people who take vacations. While this may make them difficult to define, it is also what makes such breaks excellent sites for the study of voluntary identity shifts. Vacations are what we want them to be. They hold an idealized place in our collective consciousness about what we can do and who we can be. In their removal of some limitations of everyday life, they introduce the possibility for something new. The contemporary word "vacation" derives from the Latin *vaccarre*, meaning "empty" or "lacking." The time set aside for a vacation tends to be thought of as more lax, an empty time, when certain rules and norms that structure and delimit everyday life are eased.[35] Today, the *Oxford English Dictionary* defines "vacation" as "freedom, release or rest from some occupation, business or activity."[36] Other vacation researchers have defined vacations as "a cessation of work, a time when a person is not actively participating in his or her job."[37] These definitions do not refer to duration, location, or activities, only that a vacation is a period of freedom, a respite from something.

When asked what a vacation means to them peoples' definitions have two central dimensions. For some a vacation is about which everyday identifications can be taken away; for others it is about which can be added. Emily summarizes the first view: "Usually vacations are to get away from your job, or away from your family, or something back home." Blake shares this view: "For me a vacation is just getting away from your stresses. A vacation could be in your own backyard for all you care about. As long as I don't have to deal with the day-to-day activities that I would normally do." Blake and Emily define vacations by the absence of something they identity with in their everyday lives, usually something that introduces stress or responsibility. In contrast, Jodie defines her vacations in terms of the opportunities they give her to engage in desirable experiences and do something new:

> I do very different types of vacations. Depends on where the next whim takes me. It'll be camping, backpacking, driving a thirty-foot RV, doing volunteer work, run a marathon, doing a hiking trip. Just going away for a chill-out weekend. Girly weekends with friends. It's very, very different depending on what's the next thing I want to discover or do.

Vacations are both freedom from and freedom to—freedom from the strictures of daily routine and freedom to do new things. Contrasts to everyday life are achieved through both these means. People selectively eliminate some kind of obligation that ties them to everyday responsibilities. Often this responsibility is work, but it can also be family relations, a particular space or environment, or a rigid daily routine. Alternatively, they also create difference by bringing in novelty. Trying new activities, going to new places, and indulging oneself create contrasts with routine. It is in these contrasts that vacations are defined.[38] What is important about the experience, what ties them all together, is the select release from the everyday social structures that define, order, and delimit the identities individuals hold. For this reason a vacation can be very far away, in a city, in the countryside, or literally in one's own backyard. What is important is how people introduce breaks into experience.

A culturally based structure of social forces mediates ideals and desires even during time off and leads people toward particular destinations and activities based in contrast with everyday life. Popular vacation activities follow a cultural logic in making desirable certain types of break from modern life. For example, in the American context of postindustrial, work-intensive urban life, the camper going back to nature is a contrast with a person in the industrialized city,[39] the paradise a beach vacationer visits contrasts with modernity and overdevelopment,[40] and road trips promise a feeling of adventure, autonomy, and spontaneity that contrasts with the proscribed monotony of settled life.[41] The "vivid scenarios"[42] for what a desirable vacation should be seem to be the result of individual desires but are instead the well-defined product of socially and historically contingent meanings that have developed over time.

A brief examination of the history of vacationing in the West, primarily the United States, shows how people have come to conceive of particular notions of vacations and how they can provide opportunities for manipulating self-identity. It also shows how vacationing and travel, an important component of a "good" vacation, have long been linked with ideas of selfhood. Over time, vacationing has been established as a means of self-improvement and traveling as a method of self-development. While elites have always made use of their time and wealth to enjoy time off and recreation, it was not until the late nineteenth century, when this luxury was extended to the middle and working classes, that the practice became an institutionalized part of American and European life and a popular way to explore the possibilities of identity.

The concept of vacation in the United States and Europe grew out of a distrust of leisure. In the United States, the Puritan influence of valuing work as the key to success led people to see work as a blessing and play as a threat. In a social order whose main division was between the few of the wealthy aristocrats and the many of the working class, the majority of people did not have the time or resources to enjoy extended periods of leisure anyway. Gradually, as the spoils of hard work and rewards of market capitalism began to pool into a nascent middle class, the number of people with the material security and the aspirational motivation to take time off for extended periods of leisure increased. Opportunities for travel and time off broadened, and the capacity to signal status through leisure activities spread.[43]

While work was still valued, the advantages of play in providing relief and respite were increasingly acknowledged. Leisure came to be seen as necessary for the well-being of individuals and of society as a whole. Both doctors and ministers advised taking time off from the rigors of work to replenish one's energies. This led to a dilemma for the new middle classes of how to enjoy their leisure without compromising their commitment to work or giving in to the temptations of idleness that were not in keeping with religious sensibilities.[44] Too much time off was not just unproductive; it was seen as potentially dangerous. In the United Kingdom this tension between the benefits of leisure and its potentially corrupting influence was met by "rational recreation." Starting in the first decades of the 1900s and employed as a form of social regulation by wealthier classes, controlled time off for personal enrichment and relaxation was seen as a source of "moral improvement" for the working classes.[45] Guided by this philosophy, people pursued pleasure as a reward for hard work and only as it could contribute to their well-being and growth. On one hand, leisure was associated with setting an example that encouraged personal responsibility and improvement, moral regulation, and education for the public about health and nature. On the other, the possibility of too much leisure time caused a fear of idleness, drug and alcohol abuse, and potentially subversive thoughts and antisocial behavior. People needed to have some free time, but if they had too much they would get up to no good. It was believed that too much free time would lead to free thought and then questioning of the unequal distribution of society. Properly sanctioned uses of time off had to be encouraged to keep that in check.[46]

In the United States and England vacationing thus became tied with using leisure time for self-improvement. The pursuit of pleasure was encouraged primarily as a reward for labor but only as it could contribute to the well-being and edification of the individual. Time off was necessary for relaxation, especially so that one could return refreshed and ready for more hard work, but it could still have a utilitarian purpose. Methodist campgrounds in the United States turned into religious resorts where people could relax without the lures of drinking, smoking, and sexual temptations present at the lax beach resorts available to the more wealthy. Other self-improvement vacations that combined recreation with personal enrichment became a popular way to fill the time. Educational camps like Chautauqua, where people could attend lectures and classes as well as participate in vigorous recreation, were successful.[47]

Resorts and retreats were not new, however, having long existed as hideaways for wealthier classes to challenge and subvert restrictive norms. The opportunities of vacation time to play at and challenge norms and structures can be seen here. At secular resorts bathing suits became increasingly revealing, sexual norms could be tested, young men and women flirted beyond parental controls, and vices like alcohol and gambling were indulged. What made such places so threatening to middle-class respectability and religious regulation was also what made them popular among people looking for a break from restrictive social life. The resort culture of the early nineteenth century gradually spread to the middle class as vacation time became democratized, which helped loosen Victorian propriety in the society as a whole.[48]

Although it was considered appropriate to challenge social limitations at resorts and similar vacation spaces, they still mirrored many structural aspects of society, including discrimination and prejudice. Non-Christian and nonwhite clientele were often excluded and formed their own vacation destinations and cultures. Jewish residents of New York, for example, created a "resortland" throughout the Catskill Mountains that was shaped by their urban culture, including imported music, humor, vaudeville revue style, culinary customs, language, and worldviews.[49] These accommodations ranged from the elite, like Grossinger's, to low-cost bungalow colonies. The Catskill resorts were easily accessible by train and automobile from New York City and offered a respite from crowded, hurried urban life. Beyond being a family escape, they also functioned in finding partners for unmarried youths who traveled to the mountains with their families for the summer and flirted and experimented with relationships and sex.[50] Not only young people challenged social norms on sexuality. As with other resorts and summer colonies where women stayed through the season and men left during the workweek and returned on weekends, the relaxed atmosphere offered the opportunity for flirtations and challenges to conventions for adults as well.[51]

In addition to religion, vacation destinations were also sharply separated by race. Segregation and discrimination made travel difficult for African Americans well into the twentieth century. Black travelers in both the north and the south had to negotiate de jure segregation, intimidation and violence, inflated fees, and long distances to access recreation areas. Especially before desegregation, African Americans faced impediments to free mobility while en route to recreation areas not typically encountered by the white motorist. Hostile neighborhoods and lack of amenities often meant not being able to make routine stops. Segregated gas stations, motels, hotels, restrooms, and restaurants eliminated much spontaneity or freedom during travel because routes had to be planned and scheduled in advance. If something went wrong or off schedule, black travelers could be left without a place to stay or a source of assistance.[52]

The establishment of black-owned businesses and travel guides helped circumvent such obstacles. In states that had large black populations, African Americans created thriving resort communities like Idlewild, Michigan; Oak Bluffs, Massachusetts; and Atlantic City and Belmar in New Jersey.[53] Other black institutions, like the summer hotel at the Tuskegee Institute, offered self-improvement-style vacations where people could attend edifying courses and lectures during their time off.[54]

Into the twentieth century leisure increasingly came to be seen as necessary for the well-being of individuals and of society as a whole. While work was still valued, the advantages of play in providing relief and respite from the challenges of day-to-day life and work were increasingly acknowledged. A rested and relaxed worker was a more productive one, and business owners realized that allowing a limited amount of time off for employees could improve their performance. Employers thus led the way to the institutionalization of the vacation as they started to voluntarily give their workers paid time off, following the rationale that allowing more leisure time would increase productivity and efficiency. They later continued this trend when they offered vacation time to nonunion workers as an incentive against organizing.[55]

It was not until the period of post–World War II affluence that the family vacation became institutionalized as a widespread practice among the American middle class. In a consumption-oriented postwar America this served several purposes.[56] A regularly scheduled vacation communicated to others that one could afford to spend the time and money required for a trip away from home that was taken only for leisure. It also appealed to middle-class values as a way to educate children through the opportunities provided by travel. Camping, a road trip, or visits to cultural-heritage sites were seen as a way to educate children in life skills and in how to be good citizens. At the same time, vacations were idealized as strengthening family togetherness. A week or two spent only with family and away from other obligations was considered an effective way to reinforce family bonds and thus an acceptable, beneficial use of time off.

Camping was also considered an effective means for people to get away from the hustle of city life and to avoid idleness during their vacation.[57]

Campers left behind the pressures of civilization and urbanized living and enjoyed the benefits of fresh air and outdoor living, although also possibly filling leisure time with a significant amount of effort and discomfort. Camping also became established as a ritual of American masculinity, especially for fathers and sons, with its associated hunting, fishing, boating, and outdoor sports.[58]

Camping gained popularity in the United States before the rest of the world primarily because of the widespread ownership of automobiles in this country. Cars made taking vacations much easier for the middle and working classes and expanded opportunities for what people could do and where they could go during their time off. An automobile-based infrastructure of motels, rest stops, and trailer camps soon developed in response to and to encourage car travel.[59] Before cars, the primary mode of long-distance transport was trains, which were expensive and limited to particular routes. Automobiles expanded not only the destinations available but also the distance that could be traveled. With access to an automobile a family could travel farther from home during limited time off and then sleep in the car or at a campsite. Cars thus offered expanded opportunities for travel and exploration during leisure time to those who, in the past, could not go far.

Modern vacations, for the most part, rest on the ideal of the benefits and opportunities of travel—not just tourism in a narrow sense of the word but movement to other places more generally. In an American mythology that links mobility with freedom,[60] vacations and travel fit together as a means of achieving autonomy. Travel on vacation is not just a trip to Europe but also a family trip to Washington, D.C., a camping trip to Yellowstone, or a road trip to explore the country. Travel is viewed as a source of cultural capital and educational experience for those who undertake it and has become a fundamental part of a vacation for many.

Initially, travel was limited to aristocrats and scholars. Although it could be unpleasant (the root of "travel" comes from the Latin for "travail," to toil or labor), it was considered indispensable in the education of the elite.[61] The Grand Tour, the progenitor of modern tourism, sent wealthy English youth through continental Europe to acquire experience and cultural knowledge. Between the fifteenth and eighteenth centuries, the basics for how one should travel became stylized in ways that guide performance today. Travel was established as an art. Modes of traveling, conventions, and norms were created that determined what to visit, how to get there, how to look at it, and what to wear and carry while doing so.[62]

This period is also when travel became associated with ideas of the self and self-making. It was believed to lead to an accumulation of wisdom and experience that broadened the mind and developed personality.[63] This itself was a romanticization of the voyages of discovery that go back even further in antiquity. Self-making and learning have been intertwined with the notion of travel throughout history, from Homer and Gilgamesh to Captain Cook and Jack Kerouac.[64] The Grand Tour also linked notions of travel and absence from home with indulgence. Wealthy English youths took advantage of the opportunities of being away from home and the potential for release this provided. Although idealized as being about education and self-improvement, a good deal of their activity while away also centered on debauchery, drinking, sex, and consumption.

These ideas of self-improvement and development by seeing the world have carried over into modern travel and leisure. Studying abroad or a summer spent backpacking or traveling Eurail, in an echo of the grand tour, for young adults is considered an investment in middle-class youth to make them more cosmopolitan and self-confident.[65] With Road Scholar or a package tour, older adults can achieve a dream of seeing the world or exploring their cultural heritage in a comfortable and relatively low-risk environment. Although modern travel, and especially the institutionalized tourist experience that has grown with the package tour, lacks much of the adventure and interaction with the unknown experienced in earlier times, it is still romanticized as an opportunity for self-discovery and exploration possible only outside the confines of everyday life.

Travel not only is used in the development of the self; it is also used as a signal to others to communicate something about self. Vacations and travel, particularly to faraway places, signals status. Over time, travel itself has come to be a "performed art" in which people act in stylized ways that reflect the norms, technologies, institutional arrangements, and mythologies of their social world.[66] Travel is a skill, and people develop that skill and signal status to others through more travel. Tourism is highly valued for its snob appeal because destinations and practices signal to others one's predispositions and preferences. Destinations with a connotation of intellectual or cultural worth are popular for this purpose, especially locations perceived as less traveled or more authentic because they set one apart from the many.[67] These differentiate the traveler from the tourist. Such practices amount to repertoires of high-status cultural signals.[68]

As the number of people who travel continue to rise and as travel gets easier and more convenient, the definition of what is considered exotic or interesting enough for self-development has changed. Destinations outside Europe are growing increasingly popular. *Let's Go*, a popular budget-travel guide aimed at college students, lists the top five study-abroad travel destinations for 2011 as China, India, South Africa, Chile, and New Zealand.[69] As more Americans travel internationally, people must travel farther and wider to claim the same benefits for cultural capital accumulation and self-development as in the past.

Such travel is also defined by the elusive search for the authentic.[70] Seeking out and achieving an authentic experience is a method of drawing distinctions.[71] While a search for authentic experience can occur in something as seemingly mundane as the nightlife of one's own city, others travel long distances to find authenticity in exotic cultures. In doing so they aim to find the typical, everyday worlds of other people delivered via a credible or sincere performance.[72] In view of tourism as a commodity spreading across the globe and savvy travelers becoming more cynical about what they experience, authenticity becomes ever harder to find and forms of tourism change. Practices of experiencing authenticity have altered with the expansion of travel. No longer content with just observing and sightseeing, tourists increasingly interact with their visited environment. Volunteer and ecotourism, bicycle tours, culinary tours, and wine tasting tours, in addition to activities like learning to speak a little bit of a new language, allow embodied interaction with a location, such as scenery or local food or drink, through touch, taste, and smell to gain a more fully authentic experience.

Outline of the Book

To investigate vacations I broke them down into three typical experiences that follow this culturally and historically patterned use of time off. I focused on three sites for in-depth interviewing and observations. In the first half of the book, I examine the particularities of these three main research sites. I examine each as an exemplar of a particular form of vacationing and in how it undergirds identity shifts: rest and relaxation, tourism and travel, and staying home. In the second half, I focus on the commonalities of form among these types and the similarities of how identities are shaped and rearranged across circumstances. That people employ similar mechanisms regardless of the type of vacation they undertake underscores that these cognitive patterns of identity formation persist across substantively different situations.[73] Participating in established patterns before, during, and after the occasion affirms the experiential foundation of constructing an internally coherent and externally discernible identity. I also include a narrative analysis of vacation blogs to identify properties shared among a broader range of vacation sites and further expand the experiences and perspectives I found among my interviewees.

In choosing my research sites, I first made a distinction between people who vacation for rest and relaxation and people who seek edification or to explore difference through travel. While many vacations combine at least some elements of the two, I treat these as ideal types. To capture the first group I spent four months of my research at a beach resort in Hawaii. I completed in-depth and key informant interviews with vacationers, and I augmented these self-reported accounts with ethnographic observations of behaviors. The resort and surrounding neighborhood attracted a diverse group of people, and I was able to speak with families, couples taking a break together, singles looking for fun, and people combining work travel with some time off. Chapter 1 discusses the work people do in establishing a vacation as a break from everyday life for release, relaxation, and play. As a part of this, staff members in hotels, resorts, and other vacation sites play a critical role in allowing and enabling others to inhabit the identity they desire. They both design and share the spaces in which identities are situated. They shape the experience as they help create the frame for the identity shift.

To capture the second group of vacationers who choose travel and tourism I spent three months of my research in China with volunteer tourists. Volunteer tourism is the most recent form of tourist inclination to achieve authenticity and self-enrichment through travel. I was able to live and explore with fellow tourists and experience their trip along with them. In addition to participant observation, I completed in-depth interviews with my cotravelers, who included college students looking for edifying fun, parents looking for educational trips with their kids, and adults on their own looking for adventure with the security of a group. Chapter 2 discusses these efforts at shaping identities in new environments, seeking authenticity, and doing tourism correctly while also dealing with the challenges of travel such as homesickness and at times an overwhelming amount of new stimuli. The importance of travel as a learned skill emerges as people negotiate a challenging new environment and draw on personal resources to navigate the situation.

Not all vacations involve travel, however. Between 2008 and 2010, when I was collecting data for this book, the Great Recession brought popular attention to the idea of nontravel vacations, or "staycations." While not an unusual experience, the idea of staying home had to be reintroduced to a middle-class American audience grown accustomed to equating "real" vacations with travel and consumption. This group provides an excellent example of people trying to shape identities based in difference without leaving the physical space of everyday life. Drawing from in-depth interviews with people who recently completed a stay-at-home vacation, Chapter 3 examines how people negotiate mobility and stasis in their identity shifts. Reasons for staying home include not having the resources for an extended trip away, not wanting or feeling able to stop working and step away from everyday responsibilities, and not wanting to deal with the hassle and added effort that travel can introduce, especially with young children. These vacationers must tackle the compromise made between the promise made of mobility and freedom and the practical advantages of staying put.

While each of these styles of vacationing can seem very different, formal properties of the identity shifts bridge them. Chapters 1 through 3 examine the differences between vacation styles, and Chapters 4 through 6 explore the similarities among them. In addition to interviews and participant observation, I also use narratives drawn from vacation blogs to inform the remaining chapters, because I am looking for similarities across a range of experiences. Using the lenses of time, space, interpersonal experience, and boundary making, I demonstrate how individuals use breaks in social structure to alter identity. Examples are drawn from each group of vacationers to demonstrate how these patterns transcend content. I examine how components of environments shape identities and the organization of the self.

To set aside a break for identity shifts, a vacationer must first negotiate the mental boundaries within which the experience will be situated. Because these breaks exist as a disruption in a set of ongoing, shifting, and overlapping identities, they must be cognitively demarcated. The second half of this book explores the distinctions people make with respect to their vacation time that make it special or set it apart from the usual. It also explores how the realms of home and away may overlap, either voluntarily or involuntarily. Individuals manage connections to day-to-day experience to selectively include and exclude reminders, influences, and obligations from home. From before leaving until returning home, people engage in established routines and activities that create an experiential foundation for identities that are externally validated and internally coherent. Respondents often find themselves both pleased and challenged by negotiating reminders of home, including contacting friends and family, receiving and returning emails and phone calls, and buying gifts and souvenirs.

Chapter 4 examines the objects that surround vacationers and the ways these things help them craft an identity shaped in difference from everyday life, as well as maintain connections to home. The objects people interact with help construct and project identity. Clothes, equipment, souvenirs, cameras, maps, and guidebooks are intentionally brought on a vacation and often introduce an element of change, while the ephemera of everyday life that move with a person bring the everyday along. Together they facilitate identity shifts by propping up the performance of a particular facet of self.

When asked to define what a vacation means to them, people usually name two criteria: a change in place and a change in routine. This indicates that such a break has a distinct spatial and temporal character. People interact with and make sense of their world through the arrangements of space and place. Settings, as well as the other people who occupy them, both channel and encourage the identities of the people in them. Chapter 5 examines how people modify identities in response to space and place. The organization of environments hosts different experiences of identity, from exaggerated and specialized to diffuse and submerged, while soliciting certain role performances and muting others. In the context of vacations, the introduction of the travel and tourism industry to a location changes meanings of place in ways that support or inhibit role performance for the traveler. At the same time, the mental construction of distance from everyday life is used strategically by vacationers to create a sense of break whether they travel many miles or stay close to home.

Chapter 6 examines the complementary role of temporality in identity construction. Time, as a constructed and constitutive element of people's social environment, shapes identity through the ordering of roles. Schedules, routines, and timetables influence what roles are performed when and for how long. Definitions of duration and frequency are normative and determine how long and how often a person may inhabit a role or engage in an activity. The temporal orientations of different environments demonstrate that social organizations of time are not universal and that even people in the same environment can have very different experiences of temporality depending on their standpoint. In some instances, structures of time can be altered by others to support identity shifts, and in others people must shape their experience to the dominant form of social time.

This book coincides with a time when vacations have a diminished role in American society. In 2017, 43 percent of Americans reported that they were not planning to take a summer vacation, most because they could not afford it or because they could not take the time off from work. In the same poll, of the three-quarters of respondents who answered that they are given paid time off at their job, about half reported that they do not use all, or even most, of the vacation time they earn. Just 34 percent of full-time employees who receive paid leave reported that they used all their vacation time.[74] In 2018, Americans collectively forfeited 212 million unused vacation days, or the equivalent of $62.2 billion in lost benefits.[75] In some sense, these workers can be considered the lucky ones, since without any legally mandated paid time off in the United States, almost a quarter of all workers get no paid leave at all, particularly low-wage, part-time, and small-business employees.[76]

Compared with Europeans, we vacation much less and work much more and seem to accept this as satisfactory. Whereas the United States does not legally require employers to offer paid time off, the European Union mandates that member countries provide a minimum of four weeks or twenty days of paid vacation time, and several European countries require even more.[77] While as a culture we tend to value work and productivity, it is worth considering what we are losing with this emphasis. We are already aware of burnout, the exhaustion that comes from working steadily with little reprieve. But what do we lose when we do not discover, do not indulge, and do not take the time that we need to explore and develop facets of our self? This is tied with the question of why this topic is worth pursuing in a book. What is the importance of vacations, and why should we advocate for them and make room for them in our lives? My intention in this book is to demonstrate that vacations are more than just taking time off to relax and rejuvenate, more than just having some time to do the things that people enjoy doing. They are also about who we are, who we want to be, and what we can be.

1

At the Beach

Relaxation and Release

Jack and his wife had had big plans for their trip to Hawaii. They planned out all the things they were going to do, making a long list in advance of leaving for their trip. Instead, as they come to the end of their week-long vacation, they have spent the last five days sitting on the beach, Jack with his white socks pulled up past his ankles to protect from the sharp coral, people watching and drinking beer. He laughs and says, "Everyone's thinking, 'Look at that redneck.'" But really he does not care and has done nothing to change his activities the whole time he has been here, except buy some plastic shoes designed to give better protection from the coral. When I ask if he gets bored sitting around all day and doing nothing, he gives me a look as though it's the strangest question and replies, "Maybe when I'm bald, and fat, and ninety years old, it will be boring," but for the time being it is all the entertainment he needs. He comments on how different it is here in Hawaii, both from his hometown in Oregon and from other beaches he has visited in the mainland United States. The weather is different here, where it does not rain all the time, and the people are different and smile and say hello instead of ignoring you. He did interrupt his lazy beach time one afternoon to visit the Pearl Harbor memorial, commenting, "You gotta do it. As an American."

There are two basic kinds of vacationers. There are those who travel to a new place to move around and explore and those who travel to

somewhere new to stay in one place. The latter is a kind of residential vacationer, in contrast with the peripatetic tourist. The purpose of such a
trip is not to keep moving and seeing new things but to stay in one place,
to relax and enjoy one's environment to the fullest extent. Usually, the
setting itself is the draw: the beach, the mountains, a lake. The beach vacation is the epitome of such a trip.[1] Frequented by millions of vacationers
each year, beaches evoke a topophilia in their visitors. Most people love
beaches. They are often beloved places where people can relax and enjoy a
change of pace in a scenic setting. Language suggesting renewal of the self
is common when discussing such vacations. Words such as "recharge," "re-
store," "rejuvenate," and "replenish" are used. The idea is of renewing or
replenishing a sense of self left denuded by the travails of modern life,
including the demands of work, family, and urban living. Going to a pleasant environment, preferably stripped of some of the stressful cues of the
city or the suburb, provides the opportunity for rejuvenation. This type of
vacation is set in an environment promising a break from everyday life, a
total change from a stressful daily milieu. A destination promising sea,
sun, sand, and sex is promoted as the model for such time off.

Hawaii is perceived as an ideal destination for this sort of escape. The
islands have been marketed to mainland Americans as a destination
promising "Edenic regeneration" for the last century.[2] The natural environment and the local population have historically been presented as
timeless and unchanging in an intentional contrast with the modernity
of visitors' lives. People travel to Hawaii in search of relaxation and natural beauty set in a cultural landscape of friendly yet exotic Polynesia without leaving the United States. Not only do they get a peaceful, exotic vacation in modern accommodations; they also do not need to deal with
passports, foreign money, or language barriers.

Romanticized imagery of the islands goes back to the nineteenth century when writers such as Robert Louis Stevenson, Mark Twain, Jack London, and Herman Melville began traveling in the Pacific and recounting
what they observed. With their reporting and short stories, they helped
popularize an exoticized version of Hawaii.[3] The result was that large
numbers of American tourists looking for rest, relaxation, and a bit of the
unusual were attracted to the islands, and by the late 1920s tourism had
been effectively established there as a lucrative industry. By this time an
effective infrastructure of hotels, travel companies, a tourist service bureau, tourist publications, and aggressive marketing had been put in place
to lure visitors from the mainland and place them in comfortable Polynesian surroundings.[4]

Being part of the city of Honolulu, Waikiki is not particularly rural, although it is often praised for its natural beauty. Instead, the beach is lined with large hotels and resorts, shops, restaurants, and bars. Souvenir shops and convenience stores are on almost every corner, where people can buy what they need for a day at the beach or a night out in the city, including inflatable toys, suntan lotion, towels, snacks, beer, and liquor. They can also stock up on cheap souvenirs such as novelty grass skirts and tiki dolls. People walk up and down the main streets of Kalakaua and Kuhio Avenues in island attire, some outfitted in bright, bold aloha-print shirts or dresses, and those on their way to the beach wear bathing suits and cover-ups. Others, in boots, visors, and khaki shorts, look ready for a hike out in the nearby mountains or up Diamond Head, the extinct volcano that frames the end of Waikiki.

The days follow a predictable rhythm. While the sun is out most of the action is on the crowded beaches, where people spend hours playing in the water, surfing, snorkeling, and lying in the sun working on their tan. Once the sun goes down, people shift from the beach to the streets. Music can be heard coming from bars and restaurants along the main strip where cover bands, guitar players, and hula dancers perform. A singer playing happy hour on the beach sums up the laid-back attitude that is actively constructed to induce this sensation in vacationers in Waikiki: "You know how they say, what you do in Vegas stays there? Well, what you do here we forget in ten minutes because we're going swimming. We're just so happy to have you all here." After dark, buskers come out to line the streets of Kalakaua Avenue: ukulele players, a saxophone player who paints himself silver, fortune-tellers, a man who will take your picture with his pet parrots on your shoulder, and men who weave baskets and other small souvenirs out of palm leaves. Later in the evening, after all the families and couples have gone back to their hotels, their place is taken by prostitutes looking to entertain tourists who have other than family-friendly interests.

The atmosphere of Waikiki is festive, laid back, playful, and affluent. It is an effect positioned between an upscale leisure retreat and the kitschy old Waikiki of hula dancers and tiki statues. A good deal of effort is put into manufacturing this for visitors. During the four months I was in Waikiki there was a parade almost every week. Regular festivals celebrating Hawaiian culture showcase local music, dancing, food, and crafts. The Hilton Hawaiian Village, a megaresort, sets off a fireworks show every Friday night. Hotel employees throughout this strip are ever vigilant, trimming bright green lawns, collecting trash, and polishing every visible piece of metal down to the fire hydrants. Palm trees lining the streets are carefully trimmed so that a coconut does not fall on someone's head. In the evenings tiki torches light the streets of Kalakaua Avenue and along the resort grounds where men wearing "traditional" Hawaiian attire of a loin cloth travel from torch to torch blowing on a conch shell before lighting them. People take sunset catamaran tours in boats painted to look like Polynesian canoes from which the sound of rhythmic drumming on the shore can be heard. Tour groups regularly shuttle around the city in trolleys painted to look like historic Honolulu transportation, and periodically the loud sound of engines bounces off the tall buildings from brightly painted convertible novelty cars that tourists drive through the streets.

Because of the sunny days, moderate temperatures, and relatively little rain, most buildings are designed with an open-air layout. Lobbies are not enclosed and doors are left open, inviting the warm air to circulate through interior spaces. The hotels of Waikiki where most tourists lodge follow this layout, usually designed around a large open lobby. These areas of most of the large resort hotels function as a quasi-public space with a mall-like atmosphere. People are welcome to walk in off the street and enter the numerous shops, restaurants, and bars inside. Each holds a set of shops: a Hawaiiana store, a ukulele store, a store selling swimwear and beach articles, and a convenience store.

For four months I worked behind the bar at a coffee shop in the lobby of a large resort hotel in Waikiki. Living and working in Waikiki offered the benefit of twenty-four-hour immersive contact with the study site but also the opportunity to view the vacation experience from the outside perspective of someone who works to provide the experience for others. The hotel offered attractions to visitors typical of the large complexes that line the beachfront in this area of Honolulu. On the grounds were multiple pools, restaurants and bars, shops, and conference facilities, and courses were offered in Hawaiiana, including lei making, hula dancing, and playing the ukulele. In the evening there was hula dancing and live music at the bars. The hotel was situated on the beach, surrounded by several similar hotels, and just off the main street that runs through Waikiki. Visitors who wished to leave the pools and beach area had only a short walk to find additional shopping and nightlife. The hotel was a part of a large international chain of hotels and attracted most of its clientele from the United States, Japan, and Australia. I was able to chat with visitors, in my roles both as a barista and as a tourist on the streets and beaches of Waikiki. The coffee shop where I worked was directly adjacent to the pool and outdoor bar area of the resort, itself overlooking the ocean. Customers stopped by for drinks, food, and often, advice on Waikiki. Working in this environment offered opportunities for informal talks with vacationers over the course of their trip and with other staff members employed by the resort who shared observations and insights gathered over their long-term employment in the tourism industry.

Since I had the privilege of around-the-clock immersion in my study site, opportunities for data collection came from additional sources. I lived in several accommodations over the four-month period I was in Hawaii, including budget hotels, hostels, and vacation rentals. This proved a valuable source of information on tourist accommodations offered in Waikiki and the people that frequent them, beyond the hotel where I worked. In addition to strangers I approached on beaches and in public areas, several valuable interview opportunities and numerous informal yet informative conversations came from friendly fellow hotel inhabitants eager to share the details of their trip. In further attempts to gain access to the widest variety of tourist experiences while limiting my expenses, I volunteered at a popular tourist attraction in Waikiki, participated in free or low-cost tourist activities, and attended free cultural events, such as hula performances, lei-making classes, and the frequent festivals and parades.

Relaxation, Leisure, and Identity Shifts

For vacationers seeking to leave behind demands and responsibilities, a trip to the beach is a break from the obligations of everyday life, eliminating much of the activity prevalent in their day-to-day experience. They are breaking with the idea of a utilitarian use of leisure time but not with the connection between work and leisure. Instead, this free time is a *reward* for the hard work they have already done. Maria describes her vacation in Waikiki: "Nothing. No responsibilities. Like a baby. Just eat, sleep, and do nothing." She continues, "I just decided to come over and be lazy. That's all it was about, this vacation. I work very hard during the year. So this year I said I'm not going to go anywhere, I'm not going to take any tour. I'm just going to do whatever I feel like I want to get up and do. That's it." Sandra, a busy working mother, observes:

> With kids I'm just so overwhelmed, and there's always constant demands. There's just constant demands. I'm a psychologist, so there's constant demands to be on and helping people. And when I'm not helping people, I'm dealing with my kids. You know, everybody's just always needing me and needing me [*laughs*]. I sound a little ridiculous, but the ability to just sit and do nothing is

awesome. . . . And I am a person who likes to be on the go. . . . I don't like to sit. I always have my kids doing something or going some-where. But for some reason, on vacation I am like the complete opposite. I'm, like, sit. Let's just sit and read a book.

This time is not being used for work, but it is still understood in the con-text of labor.

These respondents enjoy their rest, but they justify it as their due for the hard work they do with their families and in their careers. In a society that prioritizes work, self-indulgent leisure time can still be permissible. Fran-cine, a real estate agent nearing retirement, succinctly summarizes this view when she explains how she views her annual trip to Waikiki: "To me, this is my jewel for working so hard all my life. It's my jewel." Business had been bad for her the prior year, and she was tempted not to travel in order to save money, but as she approaches retirement, she sees the trip as something she has earned. "I almost didn't come this year, . . . with real estate being so hard as it was. [But] I said no, I'm just gonna go. It'll get paid some way."

Rick, a single man who came to Waikiki to relax for a week, has similar priorities. He has the added benefit of not having children or other family members to remain attentive to while away. His disconnection is even more complete without this restraint. He describes his trip: "No responsi-bility. Just have fun, you know? Forget your home life. Just get away. Ex-cept for myself; that's the only thing I won't get away from."

Leisure time on vacation serves a crucial role in identity shifts by of-fering actors a low-pressure environment in which to try out new roles and identities. It is a bounded period of time during which people may explore or try out new or submerged facets of self that may otherwise be considered risky, frivolous, undesirable, or out of character. Because it is nonserious, in contrast with everyday requirements, leisure time is a pe-riod to try out new roles or play with existing ones.[5] Separated from the demands of everyday life, the pressures and consequences of such a trial performance are reduced. In this situation a person can be a blank slate to an audience that knows nothing about him or her and who probably will not be seen again. Or if traveling with friends and family, a person may be granted some leniency in his or her temporary behavior or even encour-aged to act out a bit, since it is expected to be a time of reversals or excess.

Most leisure is not experienced among strangers but among friends or family. Shared leisure activities can be quite significant for these relation-ships. Family roles are often worked out in these leisure contexts in ways that can come to define them.[6] There are, then, two audiences to consider when thinking of leisure as testing competencies or trying out an identity: the audience that does not know the person and the audience that does. The first can be viewed as a blank slate, a group that does not know the actor and will not in the future, so that any behaviors will not have lasting significance or associations with self, unless they are later chosen to be integrated into the more stable ongoing self. There is more at stake with the group that knows the actor. Leisure identities will not necessarily be forgotten and may instead form an important part of an ongoing identity.

Long-term identities are maintained by an ability to withdraw from and reenter relations with others. With any social activity there is a degree of self-disguise or performance to meet expectations and conventions, which necessarily means alterations to the self. Over the long term in most social situations, people keep up a guise to present themselves in an acceptable way to others. For the most part, in their roles, people behave as they are expected to and not always as they wish. Conforming to well-defined roles and submitting to norms are forms of social control that channel behavior and suppress personal autonomy. Temporary breaks from this public life, then, are a means of reaffirming the private self or prioritizing interests and needs without this sometimes-necessary deception or alteration for an audience.[7] Moments of retreat offer "pockets" or "threads" of autonomy in a life that is often only episodically self-directed.[8] People can temporarily behave through choice rather than obligation and can highlight their personal style.[9] As Erving Goffman puts it, "Our status is backed by the solid buildings of the world, while our sense of personal identity often resides in the cracks."[10]

Vacations can be understood as excursions from the solid roles and responsibilities that shape day-to-day behavior. They are diversions into these cracks. They are both literally and metaphorically an escape. Stanley Cohen and Laurie Taylor conceptualize the reality of everyday life as an open prison where people voluntarily conform to the constraints placed on them. Day-to-day experience can be boring, demanding, unpleasant, or just repetitive. Without some release from the pressures and strains of daily existence, the controlling aspects of this routine can become difficult to bear, and people will be more inclined to drop out entirely. Vacations, then, are an escape route from the limitations of everyday reality, an "archetypal free area" in which people can temporarily get away from the constraints of routinized existence.[11] Other escape routes, such as doing drugs, gambling, or joining a commune, can offer a similar sense of relief.

Vacations and similar escapes exist as permissible breaks because they are not permanent. They help maintain order by giving people a temporary release from which they will voluntarily return. They are allowable because they are built on the premise of a shared future based in the knowledge that even though the individual withdraws today, he or she will return and contribute in the future.[12] Lasting escape is not possible, and usually not desirable, because individuals inevitably reassume their positions in their everyday lives. By providing brief, periodic remissions, when people do not need to conform and can act more like "themselves," vacations and similar breaks, like weekends, holidays, evenings out, or even going to sleep each night, make life more bearable. On an even smaller scale, coffee, lunch, and bathroom breaks perform the same function.[13] Such breaks are a reliable escape valve for people to let off pressure. They release tension.

Breaks and remissions can be considered as social control in them-selves, because they ensure that people will return and submit to the stric-tures of society. Just as the early industrialists learned when they began granting vacation time to their employees, giving voluntary time off al-lows people to rest, relax, and return for more. French sociologist Jean Viard suggests that travel and vacations are akin to soldiers' leave granted to prevent desertion.[14]

Francine reflects on the freedoms of vacation when she compares her life in her hometown of Meyers,[15] California, to her time off in Waikiki. She highlights how people can experience a sense of leaving their every-day life and travel to a different realm altogether where they can have a more self-directed experience: "Meyers is life, and this is living [*laughs*]. Two different worlds." She says that on vacation she is

> more relaxed. My mind isn't going so fast all the time [*makes a whirring noise and hand gesture*]. You have time to just kind of not think. I sell real estate for a living. I used to sell real estate for a living, right? Three years ago. But now, right now, with the real estate market in California—but it's less, um, mind stressing be-ing here with the water and the weather.

Celeste responds in a similar way when talking about her "retreat" in Waikiki. She does not like her hometown in California and often experi-ences depression, but she stays to be near her grandchildren and for her husband's work. In contrast, at the beach

> I am more relaxed. I'm more open to people. I'm not so critical of everything that goes on in daily life. . . . Nothing bad has happened in my life, I'm not deprived of anything, and yet when I'm in Cali-

fornia, away from the ocean—and I will tell you maybe why this happens to me. When I'm here, it's just like everything is nice. Nothing bothers me. I'm just totally relaxed at the beach. I was feeling [at home] that something was holding me down, I'm not doing what I'm enjoying. I was there not because I wanted to [be], but I was somewhat—quote, unquote—forced in[to] a situation because [of] my husband's work. I had no choice. And [here at the beach] is where I feel relaxed, happy, and totally content.

Both women experience a sense of personal contentment and relaxation derived from being away from the stressors of their everyday lives and commitments, over which they have little control. At home they often face difficult decisions and must take actions motivated not by choice but by obligation to others. Greg similarly describes how he loosens up a little on vacation in Waikiki, presenting a more playful self that he hides when at home in his small town in Colorado where "everyone knows me, or they know who you are," and he feels more circumscribed in his behavior:

Back home everybody knows everybody, so you do something, and people tend to remember it, but here you can do stuff and nobody cares. Like, I'll sing in stores when a song comes on. I'll start singing and dancing or something just for fun. Mostly just to embarrass my wife [*laughs*]. I'm like, "Oh, I love this song!" and then I'll break out and start dancing.

At home, the close ties of a small town define and limit how he feels he must behave. His friends, relatives, and acquaintances are an ever-present monitor on his actions. The contrasting environment of the beach, with its anonymity provided by strangers in a temporary environment, larger population, and general expectation of frivolous behavior from vacationing guests, invites a playful aspect of self that he feels he cannot normally express in his hometown for fear of social repercussions. This playfulness itself, or the ability to play *at* the limitations of daily life, is a key component of the temporary freedom of vacations.

Playful Identity Shifts

Building on the ideas of Arnold Van Gennep, who introduced the concept, Victor Turner contends that a rite of passage during the life course is a three-stage process of separation from everyday life, a period of liminality when things are in flux and rules become inverted or flexible, and reintegration back into the everyday.[16] In the liminal period the structured aspects of social life dissolve and individuals can entertain playful contradictions to their usual experience. With the removal of everyday social structures liminality becomes "a realm of pure possibility where novel configurations and relations may arise."[17] In the liminal state sense of identity can also scatter a bit, or at least become more flexible in concert with the shift to the less structured environment, becoming more open to new possibilities and arrangements of self. Liminality eases the transition to a permanent life-course change, which often alters a person's self.

Someone enters a liminal period when making a life transformation. Vacations, and other breaks for release or relaxation, are better described as "liminoid." These are distinguished from purely liminal periods by not being dependent on ritual and transformation, but they share the characteristics of being a temporary span during which social structure is relaxed and people may enjoy novel arrangements of the self. In leisure contexts the playful, or "ludic," aspects of rites of passage are for enjoyment.[18] This is evidenced in the vacation experience for many. Adults such as Greg, who likes to dance around and embarrass his wife, may break with age-based norms and engage in playful behavior in public areas.

In this respect many of the identity shifts done during leisure have a playful aspect, "playful" in the sense of trying out new roles, which may or may not be serious, in a low-consequence setting. Sociologists have long recognized that during play children try out roles and imagine different ways of being in an artificial interactional context with reduced real-life consequence.[19] Johan Huizinga characterized play as a voluntary act of freedom achieved by temporarily exiting real life and entering a realm designated as being "only for fun."[20] Play is an interlude in day-to-day responsibility that is a necessary complement to what is serious. The study of leisure identities shows that the interactive, socially situated identity shifts of play need not end with childhood. Through play individuals have the opportunity to "act otherwise," which through repetition and experience becomes the basis for "thinking otherwise." Individuals use their imaginations to devise alternative scenes and identities. "Through play our fancied selves become material."[21]

Play in adults can be understood as a kind of anticipatory socialization in which a person tries on the roles that he or she hopes to enact in the future or would like to enact in the present. These roles may later be integrated into self and identity or be left behind, just as they may be serious or they may be frivolous. Through playful adult activity like adventure, risk-taking, or hobbies, adults create personal frames through which certain identities are constructed and molded.[22] Thus, the way sociologists traditionally think about even play follows a utilitarian logic. Going back to George Herbert Mead, play is something children engage in to learn the roles and behaviors of adults. It has a purpose and a benefit for the development of the self, rather than being something fun that is engaged in for its own sake. Even among children, play is conceptualized as utilitarian.

These liminoid periods, then, contrast with everyday life. They occur within ongoing existence. To set them apart from everyday experience, moments of play must be defined as such by the people participating, so that they are not confused with serious behavior. People indicate to others when they are playing, using "metamessages" to communicate to others about what is taking place in an interaction. Gregory Bateson describes the playful biting and fighting of monkeys at a zoo as laden with metamessages that communicated to all involved that "this is play."[23] It was understood by both the participants and the observers that the tussling should not be interpreted as a sign of aggression. The framing of "this is play" situates the otherwise out-of-character behavior in a context of nonserious action, and people may act in a manner they otherwise would not without fear of social sanction, within certain limits. Wearing certain clothes and engaging in particular behavior are not just ways of taking on a role; they are also social cues or markers that indicate to others and to oneself that play is taking place. They communicate that what is being done at the time is not necessarily everyday behavior, and not reflective of one's everyday self, but that it is vacation behavior and should be recognized as such by others. These metamessages are sent with the implication that the performance should not be interpreted by everyday or real-world standards. Rather, the indulgent, risky, lazy, or comical presentation is all just a part of being on vacation.

When viewed later these metamessages have the further effect of communicating "that *was* play." Because they are done within the closed frame of the vacation, actions or behaviors are not meant to be interpreted as a part of an individual's everyday self. Rather, they are an element of the fantastical period. To those viewing a photograph or video of the event, metamessages of dress and comportment communicate contextual cues about what was happening in the past. This helps draw a symbolic boundary around the frame by communicating that whatever happened on vacation does not need to reflect everyday life and does not necessarily continue into it. Frames assure us that particular behaviors and attitudes remain in a bounded space and time and will not travel outside the bounds.

To navigate these breaks a good deal of work on presentation of self is necessary, involving the combined efforts of both the individual and those observing him or her. Georg Simmel introduced the concept of sociability to describe occasions during which adults create, with the support of other people, alternative realms based in playfulness within everyday experience.[24] Interactions defined by sociability draw their basic form from everyday life but are understood by all involved to be characterized by playful artifice. People may appear as stylized versions of themselves as they adopt particular roles for the playful interaction. They interact as if they are in a certain social reality. They participate in a shared pretense. Sociability is achieved when individuals come together in an atmosphere of fun and affection that allows them to interact as equals without interference of the material concerns that normally guide their interests.[25] This is most clear with Simmel's example of a dinner party or ball, in which the nineteenth-century elites of his social world interacted wearing a mask or persona of cordial amiability. At their parties they created a temporary social reality in which they could be flirtatious, mischievous, or nonserious in a way they could not in their strictly delimited everyday life defined by more practical pursuits. The outcome is an ostensibly friendly, equable atmosphere but at the cost of an artificial or superficial world removed from the realities and inequalities driving daily relations.

A more contemporary example than the nineteenth-century ball is a Hawaiian luau where tourists gather together to imitate a laid-back, festive island lifestyle. For the evening they enter a temporarily playful realm where they behave as if they are at a Polynesian family party. They gather together and socialize, laugh and dance, and play at a tame sexuality, with kissing and hula dancing. The more bold, or more interested in engagement perhaps, wear fake grass skirts and coconut bras and attempt a hula dance. Hawaiian luaus are orchestrated to encourage feelings of *ohana* (family) with other tourists and resort staff whom they might otherwise overlook and *aloha* (welcome) among strangers and visitors. Visitors to the island from all social strata gather at the resort luau in their vacation garb and play at being sociable.

A similar phenomenon can be found on the beach, where the egalitarian nature of a space available to all and defined with the purpose of leisure and relaxation allows people to share a social space where they can act as if they are companionable equals. Stylized roles are adopted as people adorn themselves with beach wear; claim and festoon a space for themselves with umbrellas, towels, and chairs; and set about enjoying their environment. Just as at a ball, while the ends are lighthearted, a good deal of self-conscious work goes into preparing and presenting one-self for the public display of having fun at the beach: tanning and strategic hair removal, building muscles or slimming, and filling beach bags with towels, books, toys, and games. The beach becomes a very public display of the personal done in a playful manner.[26] This is on show in Waikiki and on any beach, as people play in the ocean, lie in the sun, pose for pictures, and negotiate the shared territory that is at once decidedly public and strikingly personal.

Just because something is playful does not mean that it is not taken seriously. Chess and sports are play, but they are not always lighthearted; a golfer is very serious about improving his or her swing, and an oenophile is serious about learning the wines on a vineyard tour. Here the line between pretending and acting out identity is more complex than adapting a playful persona. These people are not pretending, but they are participating in identity-directed play nonetheless. These moments can be a time when people both pretend to be something they are not and delve into something that forms a core of self.

Play allows using imagination to formulate other social scenarios and locations that might not normally be encountered. It therefore offers the ability to experiment with being someone else or being more of something valued. It introduces agency into the formation of a sense of self. The free-dom of play offers people some flexibility in negotiating the mundane norms directing their actions. In the room that is created when the ordi-nary course of events is suspended, one set of active identities can be put aside and a set of dormant ones brought forth. A play world can be very much a part of the real world. As a result, vacationers enter a cognitive realm where they can be more open to playful forms of activity such as eating and drinking, alcohol and drugs, sex, "partying," and danger.[27] Owen, for example, speculates on his plans for his night out in Waikiki: "I think tonight I will get as drunk as I did last night. Drink as much as I can get into my body and then probably call 911." He flirts with both overin-dulgence and risk in hoping to drink enough to potentially put himself in the hospital. He notes the bounded nature of his play, riffing off the popu-lar Las Vegas tourism slogan, saying, "What happens in Hawaii, stays in Hawaii. It's an island; whatever happens here doesn't go anywhere."

Playful indulgence and identity shifts, then, can be expressed in two ways: by doing things very differently from how everyday identities and preferences are done, as Owen does, having traveled specifically to party in a spatially and temporally bounded place. Alternatively, people can do preferred things more, like Rick, who is a culinary enthusiast and appreciates the foodie culture of Hawaii: "I eat a lot more. Lots of good food around here. At least six times a day I eat here." Similarly, Celeste considers herself an "ocean person" and spends the mornings sitting on the beach. In the afternoons she swims, one of her favorite activities and much more inviting here than sitting by a swimming pool in chilly Northern California. She takes advantage of the climate when she gets to Hawaii. Similar are Leslie and her husband, two snowbirds and Christians who come to Waikiki every year to escape the cold winters in Pennsylvania. They establish a routine for each day of their three-week trip, coming to the pool from ten in the morning to four in the afternoon, bringing with them a six pack of beer and a series of religious-themed pulp novels to read. Their skin, tanned a deep brown, testifies to the amount of time they spend in the sun each day, relaxing, drinking, and reading.

Risk is another form of behavior in which vacationers not only play with the structures that limit their everyday experience but also push at the boundaries of what they may and may not do. Everyday life is arranged to be safe and stable. Routines, while creating monotony, also establish an expected and ordered course of events. Risk combines thrill, novelty, and danger to play with these reliable routines.[28] Risk probes the limitations that one normally lives with and tests one's character. It is a way of taking chances to break out of routine but also to prove what one is capable of in an environment where the stakes are less consequential than in everyday life.

Through risk and adventure people make statements about identity. When performed correctly it demonstrates a "strong character." This means that one must display courage, integrity, composure, and "gameness" in the face of the risk.[29] Hawaii offers an array of leisure activities freighted with risk: skydiving, cliff diving, windsurfing, bungee jumping, parasailing, jet skiing, scuba diving, cage diving with sharks, and hiking around active volcanoes. These activities range from real risk, as in encountering a shark while surfing or swimming and unprotected, to simulated risk, as in diving with sharks from the protection of a steel cage. With both forms one can establish oneself as an exciting, daring, or free person. Especially when risk is moderated or simulated, one's mettle can be tested in a relatively safe environment. In other situations, people may be willing to take on more risk than they otherwise might at home. Joanne describes a day riding mopeds around the island of Oahu with her husband during which they embrace risk for the introduction of thrill: "We wouldn't do that at home. That was different, that was fun. Dangerous as hell, but fun [*laughs*]. No helmet, don't need a helmet. . . . But now my husband says he's gonna get one when we get home."

Another type of risk involves the payoff of immediate reward or loss. This contrasts with the slow-moving patterns that build the structure of everyday life. Short-term elements of day-to-day experience tend to be more mundane and usually the outcomes can be anticipated. If risks are taken, they are usually not terribly consequential. Real risks are undertaken in everyday life, but these usually do not result in the fleeting experience of thrill. The risks of everyday life tend to play out over years, or even the life course, such as choosing one job over another, choosing whom to marry, or moving to a new state. Each of these decisions involves some element of the unknown and therefore is a gamble. In contrast, the thrill from risks taken during play usually is awarded instantaneously.[30] Betting and gambling of all sorts, including cards, slots, horses, and dice, disrupt the monotony of expected outcomes usually encountered in daily experience and distill the thrills and challenges that risk provides into limited, palpable moments easily consumed. The high probability of losing makes these short-term risks an irresponsible choice for everyday life, but they can add texture and excitement to vacations where this form of indulgence can be made temporarily allowable.

Romance is another aspect of the indulgent playful identity shifts that take place during vacations. Romance and sex are often an expectation of certain vacations. There is a well-defined cultural script for meeting and romancing a stranger on holiday and then moving on.[31] It is a culturally sanctioned opportunity for a fling, in which one can reasonably expect that the other party feels the same way. While this is a fairly standard holiday trope, it is emphasized in a beach vacation, with its assumptions of relaxed mores or enhanced sensuality. Stories and articles throughout the vacation literature demonstrate this desire with titles like "Love on the Beach," "How to Change a Crush into a Love Story," and "Your Summer Flings: Whom to Seduce? Whom to Avoid like the Plague?"[32] In the liminoid area of the beach more conservative sexual ideologies are often eschewed as people engage in promiscuous behavior, flirtations, or explicit conversations or jokes and dress more provocatively to evoke an ambience of sexual freedom that is not present in everyday life.[33]

The constructed romantic environment of the Hawaiian Islands—hospitable, accessible, beautiful, exotic, and natural[34]—makes them a popular spot for honeymoons, destination weddings, and romantic getaways. Waikiki and similar beach areas are environments that are both romanticized and sexualized for two different audiences. This is exemplified in the phenomena of sex tourism and its female equivalent, termed "romance tourism," in which people can rely on the inversions of vacations to provide a realm in which sexual access is available in a way that "would be highly improbable at home."[35] Men (usually but not exclusively) can travel to a new location and ensure sexual access by paying for it. The prevalence of prostitution, strip clubs, massage parlors, and highly sexualized hula dancers in Waikiki demonstrates the sexualization of the island vacation.

This inclination for indulgence, risk, and openness to sex is concretized in the offerings of many vacation spots. In Las Vegas, where people go specifically to experience excess, indulgence and risk are an institutionalized part of the trip. The all-you-can-eat buffet is a standard and expected offering of all the major hotels and institutionalizes overindulgence. It draws from and delivers on expectation of excess. The overt sexualization of space, including strip clubs and legalized prostitution, further concretizes the expected indulgences of the vacation, just as risk also is institutionalized in the legalization of gambling. It is excessive, but excess is the point of the experience that people seek out when traveling to such a destination.

Expectations, Framing, and Identity

Vacations are subject to a great deal of idealizing and fantasy. Much of this comes from the cultural context that defines their value to us as brief moments of freedom. They are freighted with cognitive weight that they be good. Especially for a vacation that involves a high level of investment of money and time, expectations are often high. The reality for many, though, is that the vacation will not match the ideal. The hotel may not be as nice as expected, the risky gamble may result in the loss of money, the short-lived romance may not materialize. The weather may be terrible, the kids might not behave, you might get in a fight with your partner. The ideal can sit in sharp contrast with the actual experience. Most tourists realize that the fantasies, scripts, and stereotypes of their vacation will not come entirely true. One consolation is that they can project themselves into the fantasy and imagine it to be so before and after the fact, even if not entirely at the time. Fantasy is an important part of the experience.

Framing is important for understanding meanings and the fantasies and expectations that develop around them. Frames have the capacity to transform the meanings of a given situation or action because they define situations, acts, or objects as a game, a fantasy, or a joke.[36] For example, the frame of a boxing match defines a brutal fight as a game. The actual contents of a vacation—the people, the environment, the activities—may be humdrum, but the frame helps define them as exceptional. Erving Goffman describes a frame as a definition of a situation that is organized by specific principles that direct the events and the subjective participation of people in it.[37] It is a mental filter that guides how people understand and perceive the situation they are in. Frames help individuals "locate, perceive, identify, and label" events in a given setting.[38] They focus people's attention and help them understand what is going on given a shared set of preconceived definitions. This gives these events meaning, helps organize them cognitively, and guides people's actions. Other people are crucial, then, in creating the frames that identify what is going on in a given situation.

Frames shape what people think they are doing when they interact with each other. They assist people in understanding what is going on in an interaction with another person, whether the person is joking, playing, or arguing. Frames allow individuals to develop "structures of expectation."[39] Also called schemas, these are the expectations that are associated with situations, people, and objects. These structures of expectation similarly influence our thoughts and perceptions.[40] They guide what we see and what we expect from a given person, place, or experience.

The identity-enabling environments of theme parks, hotels, and resorts draw heavily on structures of expectation to deliver to people what they are looking for when they go away somewhere. This is made possible by the people who work in and create the environment. One's ability to successfully make identity shifts is assisted by others who make a person feel a particular way in a particular environment. Staff members are complicit in the impression-management work of vacationers by ensuring that a given place lives up to the expectations visitors come in with. They help create the frames that shape expectations.

Staff members balance between constructing a shared experience while doing a job and managing their own responses to what is going on. This extends beyond hotel and resort staff to anyone employed in the tourist industry. In river rafting, for example, guides must both construct a sense of danger and excitement and protect their passengers from the real risk of rapids.[41] Guides make the experience feel exciting during times that it may not be while preventing serious harm or too much alarm at other times. Exotic dancers, a popular off-resort pastime in Waikiki and other destinations, must be "charming and sexy" and pleasant with customers, suggesting they enjoy the attention both on- and offstage, while hiding their negative feelings about the interaction from customers.[42] At SeaWorld, nature is constructed as a spectacle that includes plants and animals but excludes the unpleasantness of dirt, sickness, and death of animals. Staff balance friendliness with efficiency in delivering an interactive yet safe experience with nature to the crowds, hiding the unpleasant and delivering a good spectacle.[43]

The believability of the group doing the framing is essential. Both parties, visitors and staff, must project a sense of immersion in and commitment to the role for the framing to be truly successful.[44] One particularly enthusiastic driver of a novelty trolley that takes tourists through Honolulu, for example, jokes with customers, sings songs, plays loud music and dances to it, and tells stories about the area. Sometimes he switches into an exaggerated Hawaiian accent and uses pidgin words to color his speech. Toward the end of his ride, he leans over to a passenger near him in the front who has been looking bored throughout the trip and says conspiratorially that he is usually not anything like this when he is not working, "You have to act the part, you know?" This aside itself seems part of the act as he tries to build some camaraderie with someone who is not interested in his performance.

An event or site that is new for the visitors, and may even be a peak experience, is one repeated over months or even years, sometimes multiple times a day, for staff. Yet to be effective staff must act as if what they are doing is just as interesting to them as to their visitors, who are likely doing it for the first time. While it may be the fourth trip past the Waikiki zoo that day for the trolley driver, seeing the giraffes stick their heads above the fence is new for the passengers, and so staff must maintain the enthusiasm level of both themselves and the tourists for the experience to be optimal for the tourists. Making jokes, playing games, and flirting with passengers are tactics to ease the monotony for staff. A half-hearted performance or one marked by evident role distancing will not create the frame for the passengers.

Vacation institutions like resorts and hotels seek to create for visitors the experience of being in a place and the feeling that they *belong* in that place. Vacationers must feel at all times that they are welcome, that they are visiting someone else's world and are invited into it. Staff members learn that they must act in a way that affirms the visitor's self-image as a welcomed guest in a particular location.[45] About her time in Hawaii, Cindy echoes the sentiments of many visitors: "I feel like I live here. Everyone's so friendly and welcoming." The importance of what is colloquially called the "aloha spirit" is frequently echoed in recruitment ads and training sessions where employees are reminded of the importance of making visitors feel welcome. Above all, the tourism industry does not want vacationers to feel out of place or awkward. They do not want them to have an experience in which they feel their identity shift is incompatible with their environment or that it is not welcomed.

This includes the challenges to self-identity that occur in slips, when people are not sure how to interact or act in a way that is not appropriate for a situation. Culture shock occurs when people move from one community to another and the ease of one's cultural competence is removed.[46] Being away from home and put in a new environment makes many feel insecure or just eliminates a general proficiency that comes from awareness of one's surroundings. When traveling, vacationers constantly find themselves in situations where they do not know the expected way to act. They do something wrong, show up at the wrong time, or say the wrong thing. Their ease of general cultural competence, which they take for granted at home, disappears; their cultural tool kit does not match the new environment.

Because travel itself is a learned skill, interactional competence to handle new environments with confidence and grace can be developed. Some insulate themselves from moments of difficulty by staying in resorts or hotels that take care of things for them. When on vacation, everyone to some extent relies on others to provide for them the reassurance and ease of interaction that they normally enjoy in their everyday environment. Visitors depend on staff members who provide comfort, security, assurance, and a smooth and pleasurable experience. The vacationers I spoke with worried about any number of details usually taken for granted at home. They needed help with basic necessities like where to find a bank, grocery store, or pharmacy; how to use the currency; how to use the bus system; how to find their way from one place to another; and how to order a meal. They worried about physical and sensual differences, what a new food would taste like, if something would make them sick, or if something was clean enough. They worried about their security, whether they would be recognized as visitors and taken advantage of during a transaction, would be targeted for a theft, or would get lost on their own and not be able to find their way back. They worried about wasting their limited time and money, whether a restaurant would be any good, if a guided tour would be worth the price, or if an anticipated activity would be fun or even safe. While working in the relatively public space of the resort lobby coffee shop, I saw people constantly asking for help to meet these basic existential concerns.

For some this uncertainty is a reason not to travel to new places but to stick with familiar destinations and environments. Others rely on staff, a concierge, a friendly waiter, or a tourist information bureau to provide advice on what to do and how. Like doormen, secretaries, and butlers, staff at hotels and resorts provide some security in the form of protection from uncertainty.[47] They are an interface between the individual and the outside world. At a hotel or resort, rather than keeping the world out, as a doorman or secretary might do, they assist a person in going into the world. They facilitate a person's experience in a new place and make it easier to interact when basic knowledge or cultural competence is missing. They guide people's behavior and eliminate uncertainty by making unfamiliar things easier and clearer. They do their best to make the reality that vacationers encounter meet the fantasy they anticipated.

Successfully framing a situation in this way for someone else requires ensuring a belief in intersubjectivity on the part of the other party. Unless given reason to think otherwise, people will operate under the assumption that everyone in an interaction is approaching it from the same standpoint. In this way, they are able to share an experience despite their own subjective understandings and "inner life," because they take for granted that others are experiencing things in the same way.[48] This expected intersubjectivity is what helps form the social and mental bonds that allow people to share experiences and perspectives.[49]

In the case of a resort or other leisure space where two groups approach the situation from different standpoints, one of leisure and the other of work, vacationers are not sharing the same experience with everyone in their environment, but they must be made to think they are with at least some. Key staff members present themselves in a way that reflects the free environment and encourages a sense of intersubjectivity with the guests. Bartenders, pool attendants, activity leaders, tour guides, and cruise directors, for example, present themselves in such a way to suggest an intersubjective experience of play, relaxation, or discovery. Pool attendants who serve drinks wearing bathing suits, bartenders who chat with customers and accept offered drinks (or appear to), and cruise directors who "stop working" to join in a game do so to suggest a shared experience of leisure with guests and reduce the perception of a work-play boundary between them.

At the same time, offering care is crucial to creating a frame in which visitors feel secure, and other employees must project an image of responsibility. Such staff members present themselves in a way that suggests professionalism and competence and reassures the customer. While a cruise director may be having fun, the captain of the ship will not be seen out of uniform. Wait staff at a poolside bar may wear floral bathing suits and shorts, but the lifeguard will still wear a red bathing suit.

The captain, lifeguard, and others are staff members for whom inter-subjectivity is not an intended goal on the part of management. Management do not want vacationers identifying with the people doing such work as cleaning the rooms and preparing meals because they are engaged in quotidian labor. A bellhop, valet, or housekeeper will usually wear a formal uniform, effectively removing individuality and denoting position. On-site labor is portrayed in a controlled manner because it is not necessarily something people want to be reminded of in their leisure time.

The people in the middle of this labor status hierarchy, the ones visitors interact with the most on a perceived social basis, are with whom vacationers are meant to identify. Presentation reflects this. Selection and preparation go beyond dress and mannerisms and into the racial and ethnic makeup of the people selected to do particular jobs around the resort. Staff who have the most contact with visitors and work in areas with the expectation of interaction, such as check-in staff, pool area attendants, class instructors, and management, clearly reproduce symbolic boundaries through their race, ethnicity, class, gender, age, education, language skills, and nationality.[50] People behind the front desk and anyone involved in activities representing Hawaiian culture such as hula and ukulele instructors are usually Polynesian. On the other hand, pool staff, who serve drinks and snacks and also chat with visitors and help them relax, tend to reflect the ethnic and class characteristics of the majority of customers and so are usually middle class and white. They are usually also visitors themselves, working a casual and temporary job for fun. When chatting, joking, or ordering from them, visitors can feel they are interacting with someone like themselves: on a break and having fun in the islands.

Because of the around-the-clock nature of the hotel or resort, there is a high degree of interaction between the two groups, even though the experience involves two very different standpoints. One group is essentially living for a short time in the work space of another group. At the coffee shop, staff see visitors in intimate situations first thing in the morning when they got their coffee, later wearing nothing but their bathing suits when returning from the pool, and stopping by for a pick-me-up while getting drunk in the evening. Staff see most of them at least once a day as they get their regular morning coffee. Tour guides have even more interaction, spending hours, even days or weeks, depending on the type of tour, with the same group of people. They share the close quarters of a tour bus and, if it is a multiday trip, the same hotel at night. Cleaning staff may enter rooms and have access to the visitors' space, along with their belongings. Concierges chat about evening plans and personal interests, solving problems that come along and need attention. Pool attendants get to know familiar faces of people lying by the water every day, and surf, tennis, and golf instructors have a good deal of physical contact with strangers trying to learn the sport.

Distinctions that are made between people, groups, and things create the boundaries that separate people both physically and symbolically. Despite the lack of physical distance and the high level of interaction, a large degree of social distance still separates the two groups, vacationers and staff. The experience of the person on vacation is one of abandon or at least enjoyment. Although they are within a bounded space and time in which they might leave behind the restraints that structure their everyday lives, employees at these sites also operate within a highly controlled environment where their actions are regulated in pursuit of offering this vacation ideal to others. There is an essential difference in experience when someone is paying to be there compared with someone who is being paid. That employees are at work ensures that they must submit to external regulations on their behavior, countenance, and presentation, which paying visitors do not have to.

The social distance between the two groups is not experienced in a symmetrical way. In one sense visitors have considerable power because they are customers and they bring revenue. In another, staff have power because visitors are so reliant on them for their short-term well-being. The reliance on strangers to provide cultural competence creates an asymmetrical relationship of dependency between vacationers and staff. A good relationship with a staff member can result in extra perks, like a room with a better view, a reservation at a popular restaurant, or a drink on the house.

Thus, while vacationers know very little about the personal lives of staff, employees of a hotel are often privy to a great deal of information, as well as physical access to visitors' bodies and belongings. The travel agent or front desk person often has a great deal of information on the clients' personal preferences, possible guests and co-travelers, and even financial limitations. The masseuse is given unusually high levels of physical access to visitors' bodies in a way that cannot be returned. Similarly, surf, tennis, and golf instructors have a good deal of physical contact while guiding strangers trying to learn a new sport. At the same time, bellhops, valet drivers, and housekeeping services are given close access to guests' belongings. There is an illusion of privacy in these situations that is built on a level of unspoken trust—trust that these people are employees doing jobs and that they will implicitly respect boundaries of privacy.

The overlap of one group's playful space with another's serious work space is illustrated by the asymmetrical experiences of freedom and control in the same environment. The two groups have very different experience of autonomy and constraint in the same place. The differences in dress and comportment between the customers and the staff at the coffee shop in Waikiki demonstrate this. Because the shop was located next to a pool and adjacent to the beach, customers often came to the counter to buy drinks and food wearing nothing but revealing bathing suits. Employees often remarked on the discomfort or unease they felt while serving scantily clad customers. For vacationers, not covering up and dressing as they pleased while ordering coffee was an expression of their relative freedom on vacation. For employees, even the frame of the resort and tropical beach was not enough to allay their discomfort at serving partially dressed strangers in their work space. In contrast with visitors' relatively free dress, staff had a strict dress code. At the coffee shop, black T-shirts, pants that covered the knee, close-toed shoes, and an apron with a name tag had to be worn at all times while working. Hair had to be pulled back, and adornments such as tattoos or piercings had to be concealed or removed, striking a sharp and intended difference between people at work in a particular type of service job and people at play.

Physical boundaries are drawn as well to keep associations of work and play separate for each group. Employees are limited as to where and when they can go to certain areas of the resort ground, whereas other areas are off limits to guests. Instead of entering through the front of the building, employees are required to enter through a separate employee entrance at the back of the building, near the loading dock and trash collection. Continuing his metaphor of people as social actors inhabiting roles, Erving Goffman describes those places where a role is enacted and where it may be put aside as front stage and backstage, respectively.[51] At the resort, these backstage areas include a network of hallways and elevators that employees use to move about the hotel and so appear at the proper place on the front stage of the hotel grounds, unseen by customers and their appearance out of place minimized. Staff are seen on the floor only in places that correspond with their work assignments. In addition to limiting the visibility of staff, this also ensures that reminders of work, like laundry, dry cleaning, trash removal, and hotel maintenance, are hidden from customers and carried out in places they do not go.

While the decoration of front stage areas reflects the novelty of the destination, backstage areas are stripped of all such cues. The simulacra, motifs, and cultural objects that decorate the halls and lobbies are absent in all backstage areas, which are defined primarily by cinderblock walls, few or no windows, and beige paint. Material cues for identity are related to proper employee roles, like motivational posters, slogans about team work and customer service painted on the walls, and codes of conduct. Décor in these areas is directed toward how to behave and what rules to follow as an employee.

Visitors have different ways of negotiating these social boundaries. Many act as they would at home with service staff. Others try to ignore boundaries and act as if boundaries do not exist by not acknowledging them. The result of this, however, is often to reinforce them. For the employee, since this is part of the job, the interaction usually does not include the option of not participating. Visitors may wish to learn more about local residents or include them in their vacation, but this often is done in a way that reduces them to an element of the total experience of being in a place.

In a post on the now-defunct travel blogging site TravelPod, a woman at a Hawaiian resort illustrates this: "One of my steadfast travel rules is to never, ever, ever miss the opportunity to chat with a local. So the minute my porter at the [resort] loaded my bags onto his cart, I followed him and started yakking." Although she interacts with the porter in a friendly way, that does not change her expectation that he will carry her bags for her, ensuring an asymmetrical exchange. By pretending they are approaching the interaction from the same position, the woman ignores the man's standpoint and that he is compelled to participate in the conversation by the nature of his work. He does not have, and was not given, the option to bow out.

Because of the high degree of overlap in time and space between the two groups and the imperative for employees to be friendly, some vacationers do not seem to realize that a boundary exists. Such vacationers often see staff as potential buddies or sources of information without sensing the artificiality behind the interaction. While employees may, or may not, have been genuinely friendly, the motivation for their behavior is grounded in the requirements of their job. Because of the enforced presentation and the intentional selection of staff for certain roles with which visitors can identify, sometimes vacationers have trouble recognizing the social boundaries between employee and customer that exist in any other commercial setting.

At the resort coffee shop, where comportment was relaxed and staff were encouraged to socialize with customers, employees were occasionally approached by guests who wished to spend time with them, such as go snorkeling or get a drink, not realizing that the relationship was more transactional than social for the employee. Tess, the manager of the coffee shop and who was friendly with customers, admitted she had been approached many times to do things outside of work, during what would be her leisure time. She was not interested, because it would have been an extension of work. Her response, "I work all the time," was close to true given the long hours she put in but rarely convinced persistent customers who did not believe the life of a resort employee was not as leisurely as their vacation. When she was recognized by customers outside work and around town, they had a similar reaction, asking questions and sometimes looking for company, not realizing that her role as staff member, and therefore tourist support system, ended when she left the hotel. Their perception of her as someone put in place to support their identity shift did not acknowledge the boundaries of her work space.

This dynamic was highlighted when hotel guests expected staff members to break rules for them or look the other way—for example, when they wanted to do something that was not allowed by hotel regulation or was subject to legal restrictions beyond the control of the hotel. Alcoholic drinks were not allowed outside the bar and pool area, and this was clearly posted throughout. By assuming familiarity with staff, customers often expected that they could sidestep rules and regulations and that friendly staff members would allow them to break the rules. Because, for the most part, the idea of rules had been stripped or hidden from these places for visitors and because staff were instructed to act as if friends, some misunderstanding was inevitable. In a typical instance, a woman sits at the bar with two male companions, near a sign that clearly states, "No alcohol outside the bar area." She has been joking with the bartender, who laughs at her jokes, although his smile seems a little too large and his laugh a little too loud to be completely genuine. Her friends decide to leave, and she grabs the full drink she has just ordered to take with her out into the lobby, passing by the sign and ignoring it. The bartender stops her as she leaves and tells her she cannot take it with her. She looks surprised and refuses, replying, "Oh, are you sure?" and smiles at him conspiratorially and flirtatiously. He takes the drink from her and tells her he will hold it for her at the bar for when she comes back. She gives a surprised frown in response but complies.

Bartenders in particular must be friendly and relate to customers, creating a fun atmosphere for them, and at the same time be ready to enforce rules with these same guests, who may not want to follow the rules. In this case the customer mistook the bartender's friendly conversation and attention as a sign that he shared her standpoint of the resort being a place where rules become flexible. This changed for her when he abruptly, but politely, switched to enforcing the rules of the bar. For these visitors, in their tendency to see employees as props in their transitory identity shift, something that is aided by the work of the vacation industry institutions, inappropriate behavior can result, without an understanding of wrongdoing.

Some people seek a vacation that offers rest, relaxation, and release. They use playful behavior to express identity facets that they could not at home. Their behavior introduces opportunities for playful agency into their self-identity. Adults engage in playful activities like adventure, risk-taking, and romance to try on and act out new or desirable roles. Not everyone approaches vacations as the beachgoers in this chapter did, though. While some trips are an opportunity to rest and relax, others are more utilitarian, used to learn, or develop the self, or actively engage with something new. Chapter 2 looks at this complement to relaxed vacationers, ones who seek edification and challenge in their temporary reorganization of self.

2

Tourism and Travel

Enrichment and Edification

R andal arrives in China enthusiastic and ready to go explore the new city where he will be spending the next three weeks. As a Chinese studies major he is eager to see firsthand what he has been learning about and expand his knowledge of the country. He has been studying Mandarin Chinese for months and carries a pocket translator to help him speak with the locals. Randal intends to fit in and explore as much as he can during his trip. He plans to climb the Great Wall and go to the Shaolin Temple to practice Kung Fu with the monks. He wants to go to the Chengdu panda preserve and pet a panda.

While this is his first trip to China, it is not his first trip abroad. He has traveled to many European countries. Randal does not consider himself a "tourist." He frowns at the term, knowing he is something different. Tourists are the people on the tour buses. The ones who follow tour guides and wear matching shirts so they do not split up and get lost. Randal knows himself to be more savvy than that and much more experienced with getting around the world. His background knowledge of China also differentiates him from the others. On a trip to a museum he does everything he can to leave behind his tour group and make the excursion his own. He tries to ask the guide questions in Mandarin. He disappears for half an hour and is spotted chatting with a group of young Chinese women working as docents at the museum. He skips the group meal at a nearby restaurant that offers an English version of the menu and buys some dumplings and kabob from a street vendor.

Tourism reflects Americans' complicated relationship with leisure and time off. It is a desirable use of vacation time because people can use their time to learn, explore, and interact with something different from that of their everyday life. People travel to see new things and have experiences that they cannot at home. It offers the opportunity to acquire cultural capital through travel and experience with the world and to develop the self through exploration and edification. This approach builds on the history of vacationing as an opportunity for personal enrichment. Under the Puritan ethic of self-improvement, vacationing was considered a productive endeavor. Approaching vacations through this utilitarian philosophy ensures that some individuals will use their time off to achieve some end. In this regard vacations can hardly be thought of as empty time. Many feel they must use their vacation time to be as active as possible, learning about a new place, experiencing a new environment, or achieving a goal. The recent popularity of such vacation activities as volunteer tourism, ecotourism, and the more traditional cultural or educational tour reflects the tension between leisure and industriousness that exists in American culture. These kinds of experiences have many levels of cost and accessibility: Disney World's Epcot Center, Road Scholar, Eurail, Outward Bound, alternative spring breaks, and all varieties of packaged and educational tours. During each, people can learn something, help someone, or gain a new skill and return with the bragging rights. These forms of "serious leisure" offer opportunities for identity enhancement and self-fulfillment.[1]

Marcia, a frequent international traveler, says, "A vacation, for me, is usually travel to different places. I'm not a person, nor is [my husband], who likes to just sit on a beach. I like to be active. I like to learn something. See new things. Meet new people." Jim corroborates this view: "If I'm on vacation, the thing for me is that I get to experience other things in life. Not necessarily just become lazy and sit on a beach or just waste away. When I go out, I get to learn about different things." Marcia, Jim, and people like them who make these claims do not want a wasted or unproductive trip and contrast themselves with those who prefer to relax on the beach. The self-making aspect of this work is demonstrated in what they say. Beyond explaining how they define vacations, they are commenting on how they define themselves. In describing someone else's experience as shallow or meaningless, they are staking a claim for themselves as having higher ambitions, of being more genuine, knowledgeable, or able.

The tourists discussed in this chapter are therefore engaged in a particular form of identity work in which they are building a facet of personal identity tied to travel itself. The added value of such trips lies in the idea that people do not just expand their experiences and learn new things but accrue cultural and social capital in the process. The capital acquired through long-distance tourism, cultural tours, or altruistic tourism makes the activities a desirable use of time off for travelers looking to situate their vacations within a frame of worldly experience, sophistication, or philanthropy.[2] Such destinations and activities are useful to those searching for a means to establish and maintain social differentiation. They are moving beyond a form of travel that is for sheer relaxation and instead offers opportunities to learn. It helps them develop and present a self that is adventurous, broad-minded, discerning, independent, intrepid, and experienced.[3]

Entwined with this accumulation of capital is the experience of authenticity. For some vacationers an objective of travel and tourism is a search for "authenticity."[4] These tourists travel to experience a culture, to see local life as it really is. Having an authentic experience is a way of drawing distinctions both back home and with other tourists at a destination.[5] It feeds into an identity facet central to the traveler of tourism that is more real, not superficial or commercial. Achieving it sets one apart. As tourism spreads around the globe, many vacationers find that the quest for an authentic experience becomes more difficult and methods and destinations have concomitantly expanded. Volunteer tourism and its kin are the latest in a progression of attempts by tourists to have an authentic experience in visiting a foreign culture.[6] Experiences that bring tourists into day-to-day contact with a people and place are considered to deliver authenticity, because this is not seen as a tourist performance but rather an encounter with someone else's everyday life. In this context tourists hope to not only observe but also interact with local groups beyond the regular tourist track.

A visit to China, for its distance, exoticism, and difficulty to navigate, adds to the cultural cachet that comes with long-distance travel. It has long been an object of curiosity for Westerners because of a history in which the country was largely inaccessible and mysterious. Dating back to Marco Polo, China and East Asia held a particular exoticism for Westerners. Little communication between the two regions left the country a mystery to be interpreted by few intermediaries. Marco Polo established traits about China that would be accepted and shape Western thought on the country for centuries, set forth in books such as the tellingly titled *The Book of Wonders*. The basics of this portrayal included refinement and luxury, a culture of exoticism, mysterious women, ingenuity, and invention. China was

reified as an unknown, mysterious world, but one that was potentially ad-
mirable and attractive. Sinophiles gradually emerged in the seventeenth
and eighteenth centuries, including Rousseau and Voltaire, who praised
China as a country of astute political and moral thinkers. For most of its
history, however, China remained remote and difficult to get to by the average Western traveler. For most, experiences with the country had to
come secondhand. Even by the twentieth century, representations of
China in the West were solely from Sinologists, missionaries, and diplo-
mats, who contrasted the country's developmental progress with the
West's, often unfavorably after China's turn to communism.[7]

This legacy can be seen in some vacationers' reasoning for coming to
China. Luke chose the destination because it is "as far removed from the
West as you can get. Not just because it's the East, but the culture's so different and the language is so different. The mind-set is different. If you
start to follow the language, you can see how people are thinking differently." For many of these tourists, China promises a contrast with their
everyday life culturally, linguistically, and even cognitively. Everything
about the country seems to be a tantalizing switch from their usual experience.

While this exoticism makes China an intriguing destination, it also
makes it intimidating for many visitors. This is especially true for those
with limited travel experience or those whose international travel has
been largely limited to North America or Europe. Linguistic and cultural
barriers present a strong challenge to tourists unacquainted with the
country. Not being able to speak or read the language, encountering foods
with unfamiliar ingredients prepared in unfamiliar styles, and dealing
with differing local norms can be significant changes for Western tourists.
Anna says, "The language barrier here I think is a lot harder than if we
went to a European country. You seem to be able to get by there, even if
you don't speak the language, maybe a little bit easier than here. I think
the customs are so different."

In addition to what can seem to be insurmountable cultural differences, another challenge to tourists wishing to see China is the size of the
country and the distances to be traveled. A visitor has to consider the
enormity of China, a country roughly the size of the United States. Anyone
who wishes to see much of the country in probably a once-in-a-lifetime
trip will need to do a significant amount of travel by airplane or overnight
train between far-apart cities. A multiweek trip to see the major sites includes much travel time just getting from place to place. It is similar to
visiting the United States in a week or two and seeing New York, Chicago,

and Los Angeles. Letting an organization take care of things, whether a tour group that leads travelers around the country and sees to the planning details or an educational organization like a study- or volunteer-abroad company, can help simplify such intimidating itineraries.

To investigate this type of vacationer, I spent the summer of 2008 with volunteer tourists in Xi'an, China. For the country, this summer was marked by two major events: the Beijing Olympic Games and a violent earthquake that devastated a city in the nearby province of Szechuan. The earthquake left some travelers wary for their safety, especially those who had been in the country at the time and had felt it five hundred miles away in Xi'an. At the same time, the excitement of the Olympics overshadowed much of this concern. Several combined their volunteer time with a trip to Beijing to see the games. I signed up with an organization I pseudonymously call Volunteer Tourists International (VTI) that provides brief volunteer-oriented vacations around the world. The Xi'an location was a popular site for people interested in learning a bit more about China from a safe base. I specifically chose VTI because it offers trips as short as one week, although many international volunteer tourists travel for longer periods, and thereby attracts a crowd specifically looking to integrate short-term volunteering into their long-distance vacation.

The city of Xi'an itself is a popular destination for both international and domestic Chinese tourists. It holds a significant place in Chinese history as the location of the Qin dynasty in the third century BC. The city draws large numbers of tourists because it is the location of the Terra-Cotta Army, a standard stop on any cross-China tour itinerary. Named a United Nations World Heritage site, the eight thousand life-size terra-cotta figures guard the mausoleum of Emperor Qin Shi Huang and remained underground until they were uncovered by a farmer in 1974.[8] The city is also significant as the starting point of the Silk Road. It has a sizable Muslim population known for their historic district in downtown Xi'an called the Muslim Quarter, which includes a large tourist market popular for souvenir shopping.

These volunteer tourists were looking for something more than the typical tourist experience, and VTI offered a trip that combined sightseeing with a sense of living in a place. The goal was to offer an authentic Chinese experience but with a cushion of security provided by the dedicated local Chinese staff and comfortable accommodations. The vacationers lived in shared apartments in the center of the city and, after two to four hours of volunteering each day, visited museums and temples, shopped at the markets in the Muslim Quarter, and explored. At night they went out to bars and clubs. They spent the majority of their time in the company of their group of fellow tourists, eating meals, going to volunteer, and touring the city. VTI also organized activities such as trips to see the Terra-Cotta Army, hiking in the countryside, basic language lessons, and cultural activities. Other events, like short trips to other cities and sites around the country, were independently organized by small groups of the tourists with help from program staff, if they had the time and the inclination to leave Xi'an on their own. A new group of ten to twenty tourists would arrive every two weeks, creating a constant turnover but also group cohesion among those who arrived together.

I lived in the apartments with the vacationers and participated in volunteering, shopping, weekend excursions, meals, and frequent trips to bars and cafés in the evenings. Because of the high degree of group interaction, I was able to build a strong rapport with the travelers, despite their short stay. I gained details in formal interviews and casual conversations on how they had prepared for their trip, what their expectations had been, and what they thought about the country. I observed how they spent their days, what they did in the evenings, the company they kept, and their activities. What emerged was a picture of a group of tourists engaging in identity work that drew on adventure, curiosity, altruism, and sometimes, professional growth.

Identity Shifts in Long-Haul Travel

The academic literature on tourism and vacations has long identified travel and time off as an opportunity to play with or alter identity. Tourists are understood as being able to forge a sense of identity through interaction with an exotic other, through a period of separation with the familiar, or through the challenges and opportunities of being in a new place.[9] This identity work during tourist travel fits into a personal narrative of self and biography. By situating themselves in spaces that contrast with their everyday experience, individuals create identity claims that communicate components of a malleable, multifaceted self.[10] These claims can last beyond the trip and help shape an ongoing identity facet of "traveler."

In China identity shifts were manifested in three key ways: those traveling to the country because of the personal meanings it held for them, those participating in long-haul travel to develop a self-image as adventurous and cultured, and those seeking to express altruistic aspects of self through travel and volunteerism. These reasons were not mutually exclusive. For most people, their identity shift during a long-distance volunteer vacation combined some elements of each of these facets at different levels of significance.

For some, traveling specifically to China was a long-held personal goal. The explanations they gave for their travel derived directly from some prominent facet of self that was prioritized for the trip and moved to the forefront. Kelly, for example, is a Chinese American in her midtwenties who wished to travel to China, she says, to "learn more about my culture and my history." She wanted to see where her extended family came from, enjoy the food that she grew up eating with her parents, and attempt to practice some of her rudimentary language skills. She explains, "I feel like I'm pretty Chinese when I'm at home; like, I feel like I'm pretty close to my heritage. But coming here, I realize that's, like, not even half the stuff."

Linda also chose to come to China for personal reasons. She is a college professor who teaches Asian studies and studies Asian cultures in her free time. For her, the trip was an opportunity to gather information, photographs, and stories to supplement her lectures, as well as to do some casual research on the culture she loves. Her current trip is one in a series of visits to China and East Asia. "I teach Asian studies, so it is sort of a working vacation, a little bit. I've always been interested in China. I've spent extensive time in other parts of Asia, like India and Malaysia and Hong Kong, so this was sort of the balance for that." Her professional identity was in the forefront for much of the trip. This facet of self was highly integrated into her leisure interests. She could not put work away entirely and spent a lot of time thinking about how she could improve her lectures, taking photographs, and visiting museums to gather information. In addition to work she also managed to integrate additional aspects of self into her travels in a way that had personal resonance. On an earlier trip, for example, she completed a tour of Jewish communities in China:

> It was your basic China tour with a Jewish theme. So it was your Forbidden City, Great Wall, all that kind of stuff. On the other hand, it was a little bit different in that we did things that a lot of people don't get the opportunity to do. We went to [synagogue] services in Beijing. We went to services in Shanghai. We ate at kosher restaurants. Things that people say: "Oh, I didn't know there were kosher restaurants."

By personalizing her trip she was able to have an experience few shared and one that was meaningful to her. Her religious identity was foregrounded in addition to her professional interests in Asian culture.

Marcia is a seasoned traveler who, while not Chinese, has personal and familial ties to the country. Her sister-in-law is Chinese, and her brother is a diplomat who spent time in Beijing and Shanghai. She had visited China several times over the last thirty years and watched as it developed. "I'm very interested in China myself because of my family's involvement. And it's a big force in the world, so I find China very fascinating. I was here first in 1983, and then I've been back many times, so I love seeing the transition." For her, this trip was the most recent in a series over her lifetime during which she observed political and cultural changes firsthand, which she carefully documented in detailed travel files.

To participate in travel in this manner is to have a strong link to a destination, usually dependent on a particular set of skills and tastes that need to be developed before leaving for the trip. The experiences of this type of tourism require an appreciation or search for art, food, music, or architecture that is already known to the traveler. The acquisition of certain types of specialized knowledge, like a foreign language or information on the history of a region or country, is meaningful, as is the development of particular social skills, like how to talk with the locals or how to follow local norms.[11] These activities require a relatively high investment of personal resources that must occur before taking the trip. Because of its greater degree of involvement—physical, intellectual, and financial—this identity shift is different from forms of tourism that are socially, financially, or geographically more accessible or from forms of tourism that are for the sake of seeing the world. It is an expression of self that is linked to the destination.

The destination itself is not always central to the experience. Instead, what is important is the act of travel itself. Travel is not just a means of understanding the world; it is also a means of self-fashioning through a worldly performance.[12] For travelers of this sort, China is one destination of many when seeing the world. It involves the demonstration of a self that is open-minded, adventurous, and adaptable. In these circumstances, one will eat new foods, try new things, and go new places. There may be hardship involved, but it will be surmounted and then shared later with friends. The destination for these travelers is often interchangeable with other locations that meet the right criteria of distance, exoticism, and adventure. To several of my respondents, China was just one of several long-distance opportunities they considered. Anna explains:

> [My husband] actually chose China. I didn't really care. I just wanted to go somewhere that we've never been before and some-

where that I thought that maybe traveling on our own would be difficult. And so I wanted to go to either Thailand or China or India, because I felt like that was very unfamiliar to us. And he picked China, just kind of randomly; he said, "That one looks good."

Steve says, "I chose China because I've never traveled abroad before, and I figured, 'Well, let's make up for lost time.' And so I wanted to go to a country that isn't exactly a common destination like somewhere in Western Europe or Canada or Mexico might be." Because Steve has traveled so little, he chose to start big. And he wanted to go to a place that would immediately differentiate him from his peers. A place that was unusual and a little out of the way. He is also on one side of the divide between people who travel to do this type of identity shift: those who already travel a lot and are reinforcing a sense of self through the act and those trying to develop a new facet. For many of the people undertaking long-haul tourism, travel itself was already an important part of their self-identity. Long distances and, especially, unusual locations attract experienced tourists for whom "traveler" is a role with which they are quite familiar. Taking such a trip is a manifestation of this facet of self. Many of the participants had grown up in families in which international travel was not unusual. Connie expresses pride in her daughter for her poise while abroad, acquired from previous international trips:

Traveling with my daughter has been amazing. She's very mature. She's very well traveled. She's gone on trips with her school. She went to Ireland two years ago. She went to France this year over spring break. This is school trips, staying in super-dumpy hotels. And she's gone to camp every year for eight years, for a month. So she's very outgoing.

A set of skills and preferences accrue from travel that translate into social capital, which vacationers draw on as they go through their trip. They know how to navigate cities, how to pack, what kind of equipment they should come with, and how to handle difficult situations. They also travel with idiosyncratic preferences for how to do their trip that they developed through experience, most of which meant eschewing traditional tourist activities and signifiers. Marissa, for example, loves to travel and has a little Chinese-language skill. She insists on taking public transportation instead of the safer cabs usually preferred by tourists. Rodney refuses to participate in group tours, going off on his own and speaking with locals whenever he can.

International travel can be intimidating, not least because of experiences that challenge one's poise or confidence in an interaction. Such occasions, while frustrating, were an opportunity for experienced tourists to further develop their traveler identity and show off their acumen. Attempting interactions with locals, navigating the public transportation system, eating food of unknown origin from street vendors, exploring dangerous parts of the city, and generally trying to go beyond the typical tourist experience of observing the culture from a distance moderated by the tourism industry was a manifestation of this identity work. It demonstrated the facility for foreign travel that had been developed over time or that was aspirational and being developed.

The desire to develop an adventurous sense of self was demonstrated one night in a trip to a Korean restaurant in a neighborhood of Xi'an. Rodney, who has some skill in reading Mandarin, observes that the menu has a section of dishes using dog meat. Eating dog had often been a joke among the visitors on the basis of the stereotype of Asian cultures eating it, but the actual opportunity to do so rarely came up in the tourist-oriented restaurants they visited. Someone says he will try the dog, and excitement quickly spreads around the table as more people agree. Even those who were initially reluctant and responded negatively to eating it soon agree that they too will try it. A dish is ordered and brought to the table and spread among fifteen people, leaving a bite or two of dog meat for each. Everyone at the table, except one, eats the meat. They eat it quickly, remarking it tastes like beef. Once the excitement dies down, however, a few express sadness and some regret, because they were thinking of their pets back home. Nonetheless, they had been able to put their adventurousness to the test and on display for their fellow travelers and for people at home who would see the pictures they took.

Others who were less experienced with travel but were seeking to build such a sense of identity struggled more and demonstrated the degree to which travel aptitude is learned through experience. Food was a primary obstacle. Encountering unknown flavors and often unidentifiable ingredients could be unsettling. Not everyone was interested in eating dog or the numerous other new and sometimes unknown foods they encountered at almost every meal. During moments when they were not influenced by the excitement of the group, they could be quite timid about what they were willing to consume. Many turned to eating Western food whenever they could find it.

Others grew uncomfortable with their obvious foreignness. A downside of this rearrangement of identity was that some identity facets such as race, nationality, or ethnicity were involuntarily foregrounded in a way they had not anticipated and did not welcome. The white and African American tourists were clearly not Asian and not local and attracted attention in a way that they were not accustomed to at home. Mona, a blonde, white American woman describes her discomfort at the attention she feels she receives when walking around the city. She acknowledges that she wears her flip-flops out on the street, which violates a cultural norm and may attract some attention, but she feels that the real problem is deeper than that:

> I feel very much under a microscope, and I don't know if it's the fact of the needle-in-a-haystack American walking down the road, I don't know if it's the blonde hair, I don't know what. And I'm not—again, I'm being very arrogant . . . wearing my flip-flop slippers outside. People are probably like, "Oh my god, look at her." I'm not necessarily trying my hardest to fit [in] in that way, but I feel like I can't do anything with anonymity here, and that's stressful. That's stressful. And I don't like to be stressed out. . . . For being as boisterous as I seem, I don't like to be focused on, you know? I like to kind of blend in, and that I miss. I miss the blending-in part, because this is weird. This is—this is odd. But people told me to anticipate that, so I knew that coming in. But I just—I really feel like people are constantly looking at you, and I don't like that. I don't like that.

Zeke, a black college student, also experienced this when he encountered the stereotypes and curiosity of Chinese people who had almost no experience in real life, outside of the media, with African Americans. He chose to think of this challenge as an opportunity:

> They stereotyped the shit out of me when I got here, but I mean, because I'm half black, apparently they think I'm great at basketball and I'm a hip-hop sensation. I want to tell them I'm not any of those things. I'm a normal kid, normal American. Not every black person in America does this or that or everything else. I think that's the thing I'm always going to remember, is the people that stereotyped me and [that] I helped to show them that it's not like that.

For Kelly, as an Asian American, her Americanness was apparently very obvious to local Chinese and attracted additional attention in a way that unsettled her. She traveled from a place at home where she was one of few Asian Americans to a location where she was surrounded by people who shared her ethnic heritage. Instead of her Asianness being a prominent identity facet, her Americanness suddenly was. Observing Chinese could tell she was American by the way she dressed and spoke and would respond to her differently, sometimes even challenging her on her language skills. She feels very judged that she does not speak Mandarin well enough, a problem that she did not encounter back home in Massachusetts. "I hate not being able to speak Chinese, and it's kind of embarrassing when people ask you if you can and you can't."

A third key aspect of identity at play for these tourists was that of altruism. Although volunteering was not the focus of the vacation, it was also not irrelevant, and it was a key appeal of the trip for many who had a sense of self that valued altruism. Using their vacation time to volunteer allowed them to highlight this sense of self in a way that combined their personal interests of volunteerism and travel. Roger comments on his motivation to teach English on vacation: "I've done a significant amount of tutoring to fifth graders back home in English and math—American fifth graders in English and math. And I was interested in teaching, and I was interested in coming to see China." Ostensibly, this was an opportunity to integrate a philanthropic predisposition often employed at home, but when mixed with the sociocultural benefits of travel it offered additional instrumental advantages in shaping how Roger saw himself and how he wanted to be seen. The cultural capital benefits of volunteerism were not lost on many participants. Mona, the stay-at-home mother who felt out of place, comments:

> I chose to volunteer because I come from a very philanthropic-minded family, and I have always volunteered in some capacity. This is the most global in perspective I have ever done. I am a member of the typical things, the Junior League, I serve on the board of my children's school, I'm a Brownie leader. I do all those typical fund-raising mechanisms for causes that everybody does.

Mona lists the usual volunteer activities of an upper-middle-class mom "that everybody does." Volunteering in China, on the other hand, is not something in which everyone in her community can participate. By doing so she is indulging her philanthropic side but in a way that sets her apart from the other involved moms. Helping earthquake victims in China comes with an additional cultural cachet beyond fund-raising for the local PTA. She continues:

> The day that the earthquake happened in China, I was on my computer and seeing all these images of people with backpacks on and everything, and I was just struck by it, and I thought, "My goodness, well, why don't I go volunteer in China in some capacity?" And I decided to come, and in the course of three weeks, I pulled the whole trip together, and I kind of told my family, "Hey, I'm going to China for a month. Love it!"

The instrumental aspect of volunteering was exploited in other ways as well. Connie brought her daughter with her on the trip for two purposes. She saw it as a way that could instill the value of volunteering and get her involved in the world, but it was also a chance to show her daughter a different side of her. The trip was an opportunity to demonstrate to her daughter a picture of her broader self, beyond the familiar identity of mom. By their volunteering together during their vacation, she is spending more time with her daughter but also modeling a way she would like her daughter to behave in the world and introducing a more complex version of her identity to her teenage daughter:

> I wanted to do the volunteer thing with her. We definitely said we'd come on this trip because of the volunteer component, and I wanted her to do that and to do it with me and to see that I'm more than just a mom. I'm a person who works. And that it's good to give back. And she just jumped right into it.

Rather than a platform to background her maternal identity, as Mona used it at times, Connie used the trip to add nuance and flesh out a picture of her for her daughter beyond the mom that her daughter saw every day at home.

Others were blunt about the instrumental advantages of combining volunteering and vacationing. According to Jeff, "I always do volunteer work to put on my résumé for law school. So you take volunteering and traveling, and you get VTI. So it's a great way to vacation." Luke similarly comments, "It's sort of a vacation that you can get something out of. . . . Vacation with benefits." For many of the college-age students in this study, volunteering on vacation was an investment of social capital that had been instilled in them from an early age. They had been taught that giving back was an important virtue and, in this case, one that could be listed on their résumé. The result was a combination of education, privilege, and family socialization that gave these young people the know-how to tap into the symbolic value of travel and apply it to reap benefits from peers, family, teachers, admissions committees, and future employers.

The identity work most were engaged in was some mix of these three factors, which were individually more or less meaningful. Some strongly identified with the volunteer role, while others deemphasized it. Others were very pleased to be in China, while for some it was just one possible destination among many. Usually the three would mix together and complement each other—for example, mixing the social capital benefits of long-distance travel with volunteering for Mona or combining a love of traveling the world with a visit to a country of personal significance for Marcia.

Finding Identity in Authenticity: The Artful Traveler

Travel for many of these individuals was itself an important part of their self-identity. By participating in this trip, they were foregrounding and building their identity of "traveler." Tourists are collectors of cultural capital. Either through their unusual experiences, their particular knowledge, the exotic destinations, the inaccessibility, or the activities they do at their destination they acquire and demonstrate credentials that are socially valued and confer prestige on them.[13] With a little experience they come to possess the attitudes, knowledge, preferences, and behaviors necessary to make this claim.[14] They think that international travel is important, especially to less popular destinations. They know how to go about getting to a foreign destination and what to do once they are there. They have strong opinions on how travel should be properly done once arriving: what to wear and not wear to signal one is a tourist (or not), when to take pictures and when not to, what to take pictures of, what one should eat and sample, and with whom one should socialize. They possess extensive equipment for travel, which can be quite expensive in itself: suitcases, cameras, clothes, books, and electronic guides.

This is reflected in Marcia's experience. She is a frequent international traveler who has been to many countries outside Europe, including China in the past. She explains how her perceptions changed over time and with increased practice:

> I mean, I remember how jarring it was when I first came to China. How exotic. But I guess because I've been here enough, . . . it's not

that unusual. And some of it's also my personality. I mean, I'm just independent, and I'm not intimidated at all by the traffic and crossing the streets, and dealing with the dirt, you know, in the streets doesn't bother me and that sort of thing. I'm just resilient and independent, and I guess that has something to do with it.

Travel competence is learned. The savvy that Marcia describes is accumulated through repeated trips. She can link her confidence and ease in Xi'an to personal characteristics like being independent and resilient, but she has gained this know-how through years of experience. Marcia has developed an identity that has grown out of her competence with travel. She thinks of herself as a skilled traveler, and this now influences the trips she takes and how she interacts with an environment once she arrives. Just like Connie's, her perceptions of the familiar and the exotic are shaped by these accumulated experiences.

Critically, skilled travelers have confidence in their knowledge that they can define what proper travel is. By traveling to a location that is not yet widely known and by participating in an activity like volunteer tourism, they manipulate the code of what real travel is and help redefine what is legitimate enough to fit this label and what is not. While volunteering is on its face altruistic, it is also an assertion of particular preferences and attitudes of high-skill travelers about what travel and tourism should be. It requires a fairly significant investment of time and money and helps move tourism along its constant redefinition of what is "high" and "low" skill.

The key source these tourists draw from to establish these boundaries is authenticity. When looking for authenticity, people are looking for credible or sincere performances of everyday life.[15] With the growing ease of travel, the destinations available to the average tourist expand. Mass tourism, by definition, is socially, financially, and geographically accessible to large numbers of people. As the destinations available to middle-class tourists spread across the globe, people become more savvy and local cultures embrace the commercial possibilities. This changes what visitors find when they arrive, and the experience of authenticity becomes ever-more exclusive. Cultures being visited inevitably construct artificial sites, to give tourists what they are looking for and to give themselves a measure of distance from their observing visitors,[16] much like the Hawaiian resort luaus discussed in Chapter 1. This "staged authenticity" both gives tourists a sense of verisimilitude and keeps them from getting too close.[17] As local cultures become increasingly staged for outsiders, then, tourism itself destroys their authenticity for those who come to see them.[18]

Experienced travelers today recognize that a lot of what they see is artificial and question the credibility of the performance. There is much academic debate about whether authenticity is real or even possible, but I treat it here as the tourists see it. To the tourists doing the consuming, this debate is irrelevant, because authenticity is very much a possibility. They believe authentic experiences of culture exist, and they are intent on finding them. Finding or at least looking for authenticity is important in doing the traveler identity correctly. If it is not at least attempted, the perception of oneself as adventurous, intrepid, or open-minded can be undermined.

Popular success for a travel destination undermines the authentic value of the site because first it becomes too full of other tourists and then the commodification of the culture ensures superficial experiences. Insiders to a scene or culture lament when popular attention spoils their scene. Too many people in the know ruin the insider credibility.[19] Travelers seek out new and more "real" destinations that have not yet been touched by the corrupting forces of mass tourism. As a result, people constantly change what is considered good or real travel, moving into other places and activities that they believe will bring them closer to something they think of as real or unspoiled by fellow tourists. Thus, a place like China should be real, not full of Western tourists or Western infrastructure.

Many of the destinations now being sought are fairly cheap to visit, often situated as they are in the developing world, if one is truly willing to live like a local. Backpackers have long sought to differentiate themselves from other tourists by how much they interact with a culture. Staying in cheap hotels, taking buses, eating in local restaurants, and avoiding perceived tourist traps amount to budget travel that draws status distinctions based on experience and a kind of roughing it and a closeness to authenticity, or realness, of a place. The relatively low cost of travel in places like Asia and India has made them popular destinations for backpackers, who can get an intensive travel experience on a small budget.[20]

On the other end of the cost scale, upscale tourists now pay much to have a local experience. In the past, the more people spent, the more they would be removed from the everyday life of the place they visited. This has now changed. As one travel operator says, "I want to create trips that are not formulaic but cater to the sophisticated twenty-first-century traveler, those who have moved beyond materialism and conspicuous consumption. It's not about what category hotel you stay in; it's about the character of the hotel and the experience of the hotel."[21] Elite tourist-media outlets such as Conde Nast Traveler advocate for "real" travel, in contrast with the "false" experience of package tourism. Such a trip is still about conspicuous consumption, but it is just a form of consumption that allows a perception of something as being more real or achieving status through experiential rather than material means. In a way, these travelers are paying not to think of themselves as tourists.[22] They are paying for the privacy and exclusivity that sets them apart from the masses of tourists.

Context matters in considering whether tourists are seeking authenticity.[23] In a setting like Waikiki, authenticity is not the goal and is often overlooked entirely. Edification is not part of the experience. In fact a little kitsch is often appreciated. But, usually, in international travel the intended experience is different. These vacationers wish to get a taste of the real. Volunteer tourism, especially to exotic or very different cultures, is one context in which authenticity becomes paramount, and it has developed in response to this ever-evolving search for authenticity. These tourists want the authentic original, even if they know it has gotten harder to come by. They still seek the rural, the primitive, the pure, the unpolluted, and the childlike.[24]

Tourism has been likened to art. The artful performance of a journey follows established conventions and codes, including norms of preparation, modes of transportation, journey duration, itineraries, manner of dress and demeanor, formation of social relationships on the trip, what to look at and how to look at it, and how to end the experience.[25] There are many parallels between constructing authenticity in travel and constructing authenticity in art. Howard Becker created the concept of art worlds to describe the people creating art and also the knowledge, norms, and conventions that shape a particular field.[26] Being a savvy traveler is a performance of the self that denotes such competence and capital.

This search for authenticity, then, is a method of constructing and reconstructing boundaries within which to situate these identity claims. In a world of increasing accessibility, finding the authentic is the key to what real travelers do and what tourists cannot. When any art world exists, the boundaries of what is acceptable are defined by the people who create it and the elites who consume it, in a process that assimilates those who can properly participate and denies access to those who cannot.[27] "Real" travelers and the industry that has built up around them, including the media, make claims as to what can be considered a proper travel experience and what is just commercial or, even worse, superficial. The distinction between tourism and travel and the proper ways of performing the latter establishes a boundary around those who choose to derive a source of aesthetic and social identity from travel. Any time people identify with others, they are perceiving discontinuities between insiders and outsiders—those included in or excluded from a social cluster—respectively. Characteristics of that identity are created in relation to those on the outside. Boundaries based on these distinctions between "us" and "them" are the basis of a sense of identity.[28]

Many vacation choices are excluded from the world of travel because they are deemed not belonging to the aesthetic. Some experiences are assimilated into the high-art world of travel, while others are left out. As the experience becomes more democratized and the capability of the average traveler expands, what is allowed in continually shifts. A distinction such as the one made between the "nobility of art" and the "vulgarity of pure entertainment" is relevant when distinguishing between attitudes around niche tourism and mass tourism, just as there is a distinction made between true art and popular entertainment.[29]

Distinctions are necessary for creating identities. Distinguishing oneself as a real traveler, as separate from other tourists, is marked by the search for the elusive authentic experience. The perceived authenticity of the destination is important when doing identity work. These travelers are using this claimed authenticity of place and experience to establish an aesthetic and social identity.[30] The *New York Times*, whose travel section often features far-off locations, is one of the resources to which travelers can turn to determine the definition of what "real" travel is. The *New York Times* Frugal Traveler, Seth Kugel, ostensibly writing for the low-budget set, demonstrates the importance of being an authentic traveler, in contrast to being a tourist, as he asks his tour guide for the perfect aesthetic experience of a good meal in the Chinese city of Chongqing:

> It had to be cheap, have no English menu, perhaps in a run-down neighborhood and serve local dishes spiced for local tastes. "I know some places," she said. "But they are unsuitable for tourists." "Yes!" I shouted. "Perfect! Take me to the place most unsuitable for tourists." A few hours later we were sitting at a sidewalk table, drinking local Shancheng beer from bowls, our hands in plastic gloves as we used toothpicks to extract snails from their shells after digging them out from under an avalanche of Sichuan peppers.[31]

To Kugel, it is essential to move beyond the realm of tourism in Chongqing to have the right experience. The more "local" it is, the better. This is similarly evidenced by the line of guidebooks called *Not for Tourists*, which claim to give access to this local perspective.

In addition to their perceived lack of interest in authenticity, bias against tourists is also strong because of their behavior. The idea of looking like a tourist or acting like a tourist implies being rude, loud, and unsophisticated; an outsider. Prototypical tourists are perceived as

> lacking initiative and discrimination. They are unadventurous, unimaginative, insipid. For them, travel experience is akin to grazing—they mechanically consume whatever the tour operator feeds them. Their presence coarsens the quality of tourist sites. Mass tourism is often likened to a plague which destroys the beauty and serenity of civilization.[32]

For the self-proclaimed traveler, then, and others doing some sightseeing, a risk in taking up the role is being defined as belonging to this discredited group. Even though they are technically tourists themselves, they do not want to be considered so and fear being lumped with all the other tourists around them by association. Some role distancing is therefore necessary to differentiate and define themselves. Visitors actively draw distinctions to separate themselves from other tourists and define themselves as something more. While some tourists in China were eager to talk with other visitors, to share stories and talk about home, others avoided any such interactions, avoiding eye contact with Western strangers in the street, lagging behind in tour groups, or attempting to engage locals and tour guides in rudimentary Chinese conversation that excluded others who could not understand. They were using negative tie signs, or signals to others that they were not connected with the discredited group that is tourists.

Among those who felt a need to distance themselves, a frequent response when seeing tourists on the street or at bars was to make comments about them or act in ways that would be sure to stifle any potential interaction. A typical evening at a bar with my group illustrates this attitude. A Xi'an street near major tourist sites lined with bars and restaurants and colloquially called "bar street" is within walking distance of tourist accommodations. My group would usually go out here to drink in the evenings. On a pleasant Friday night when the weather is warm many of the outside tables at the bars lining the streets are filling up with both locals and foreign tourists. After we have been sitting for about twenty minutes a group of American-looking tourists walk down the street, looking around for a bar to stop and have a drink. They see us and start heading over to our table. "Oh no, foreigners," Xavier groans. "Don't make eye contact." We all look away as they come by, at each other or at our drinks, to avoid any signal that might invite a conversation. They end up being seated at a table near ours, and Kelly turns her chair so that her back is to them, cutting off any attempts at conversation they may try to make. Turning her back on the other group of American tourists was a distinct negative tie sign intended to show there was no connection between our group and theirs to anyone who might have been observing. It also discouraged any further attempts at contact by letting them know that the people at our table did not consider themselves compatriots of the other Western tourists. This need to distance themselves seemed to be characterized by a kind of possessiveness of the experience of being in that place, that it was for themselves alone. Other people similar to themselves, other tourists, were not welcome there or were seen almost as intruders on the experience.

Experiential Authenticity

As the potential for mass tourism reaches farther around the globe and expanding air travel makes distant destinations more accessible, the search for authenticity has moved away from seeing and visiting and into experiencing. Many are no longer satisfied with just observing or gazing as a means of witnessing the authentic. They instead seek a deeper participation in the culture. Part of this new search for authenticity is an attempt to have the experience for oneself of being local. Instead of just observing the sincere acts of others, one attempts to join the performance, to participate in the resident culture at a more intimate level than when visiting as a traditional tourist. Hands-on experiences that bring one into contact with a people and place are considered to deliver such authenticity. These are experiences in which people can interact with locals, learn about the culture, and even live in local neighborhoods.

Participants in the China volunteer program took part in activities meant to take them beyond the typical superficial tourist experience and into a firsthand interaction with the culture; they took painting, music, language, Chinese calligraphy, and acupuncture lessons; attended short lectures; took cooking classes; ate a meal with a Chinese family in their home; and visited nontypical tourist destinations like hospitals. They spent time with locals with whom they worked in their volunteer placements or met in the city. Volunteer tourism provides this opportunity because the purpose is to engage with the local population, to interact with people instead of just see them. It is an attempt to escape the bubble of home that surrounds the tourist experience. Jodie explains, "I've always wanted to do volunteering purely because I thought it would be a good way to get close to the people of the country as such, rather than sort of just being surrounded by people of your own country [while on tour]." Organized experiences that bring one into contact with a people and place are considered to deliver such authenticity in a secure setting. Volunteer tourism allows one not only to see a foreign city but also to interact with it and contribute to it. Participants do not talk with just a tour guide or hotel staff; they work each day with teachers at schools or orphanages or at helping professional adults learn English. They practice English with people, clean parks, or clear trails. As a result travel becomes a more embodied experience that moves beyond just the visual primacy of sightseeing. Linda says:

> I had been to China before as a tourist, and I just didn't think it was enough substance, for one thing. I wanted to spend some time in one place, but not necessarily by myself. So I thought this would be a good balance in terms of being able to spend some time on my own but not totally on my own. So volunteering, plus a benefit in particular because I wanted to do something while I was here, *not just walk around and look at things.* (Emphasis added)

Steve explains:

> I didn't really want to [come to China], really, as a tourist. I kinda wanted to engage in some sort of service project because *I thought that might be a little more*; it would help me to immerse in the culture more than walking around with a camera and just staying in a hotel. (Emphasis added)

One of the appeals of this volunteer-abroad program to its participants was that it was not located in Beijing or Shanghai but in Xi'an, a smaller Chinese city. Many volunteer- and study-abroad programs are located here. It is also a standard stop on the tourist itinerary because of its historical significance and its excellent museums. Its relative unfamiliarity for many Western travelers, however, makes it seem somehow more authentic, or more Chinese, than the increasingly international cities of Beijing and Shanghai. There is the sense that instead of visiting a city that has been altered by the presence of other Westerners, they are coming to a place where they can both view and interact with Chinese people going about their daily lives. It offered the perceived potential for a more off-the-beaten-track authentic experience. As Roger notes:

> I thought it would be an interesting chance to spend a significant amount of time in a city that was not Beijing, not Shanghai, not such an international city, where I felt like I could learn more about, I would have said, the real China, which doesn't really make any sense, because China is such a big and diverse place, as I have now found. But I definitely wanted to be in a place that didn't have quite the international influence that Beijing and Shanghai had and not quite the modern feel.

Zeke says:

> I felt like I didn't necessarily want to be in a large, commercialized city with a bunch of Westerners. I wanted to be in touch with different people. I feel like I got that here. I feel like since I've been here, I've been able to call up a lot of Chinese friends and hang out. So it's been a lot different. Plus, I feel like here it's a lot more cultural than it would be in Beijing or Shanghai or even Hong Kong, for that matter.

The size of the city and its less cosmopolitan nature than some of China's megacities make it "more cultural." Leslie shares the sentiment, describing the nearby city of Chongqing, which ended up being her favorite place in China: "I liked how rustic it was. It was very different. It was what I envisioned China as." This comment was partially in response to the reality she found when she arrived in Xi'an, which turned out to be much like any other large modern city in China or elsewhere. Many, when coming to China, and specifically the ancient city of Xi'an, were searching for a Chinese authenticity represented in antiquity, not realizing, or ignoring, that most Chinese cities in the present are megacities that have been built, torn down, and rebuilt over the last twenty years of government-led development. The medium-sized, by Chinese standards, city of Xi'an is home to roughly eight million people. Visitors were thus surprised and even expressed disappointment in Xi'an, describing it as "like any other urban, metropolitan city center," "busy, loud, and dirty." They do not want to travel to another continent to encounter an environment much like the home they left. This did not meet their idea of rustic, mysterious China. Jackie shares her response to the city:

I expected Xi'an to be a poorer town. I did read about it, but I sup-
pose I only read about the ancient side of it. I didn't realize that
there would be such modern parts and all that beautiful new building all around. The Pagoda and the Tang Paradise [an ancient-Chi-
nese theme park], you know, it's a really wealthy-looking area.
Quite spectacular. I didn't expect it to be like that.

The irony is that they are coming closer to achieving the real Chinese
experience they claim to be looking for when they are surrounded by large
apartment blocks, air pollution, and traffic, however much this clashes
with their romanticized idea of China.

At the same time, although authenticity was what they claimed they
were looking for, too much can be challenging in a culture that can feel
very different. At times Xi'an came to feel too unlike home, and the tourists began to look for escape routes back to the comfort of the familiar.
They wanted an experience that put them close to a different culture, but
they also wanted to be able to pull back when it got too overwhelming for
them or when they felt homesick. Even the most experienced travelers can
get frustrated at times. Roger, a New Yorker who chose Xi'an because he
wanted to visit a city that he claimed was less "international" and "modern," explains his growing frustration with the city toward the end of his
trip:

In Chinese cities there truly are people everywhere. It's quite
crowded, it smells bad, it's dirty, the air is disgusting, there's lots
of traffic. There's very little escape from that here in Xi'an, and in
a place like Shenzhen, I would guess it would be even worse. But in
a place like Beijing or Shanghai—and I haven't been to Beijing, so
I really shouldn't comment on it—in a place like Beijing or Shanghai, I feel like there are different places you can [go to] escape from
the chaos. And really it's a pretty chaotic place. There are places
you can escape from the chaos there.

What was originally the appeal of Xi'an became the challenge as he
came to feel confined and overwhelmed by the city that he believed lacked
the Western comforts available in larger cities. He wistfully compares
Xi'an to cities he believes can provide what he is looking for.

The vacationers devised strategies for dealing with their need to reconnect with home. The most popular were going to bars filled with other
Western tourists and eating fast food like pizza, chicken, or ice cream that

reminded them of the United States.[33] Toward the end of her trip, Kelly dealt with this feeling by visiting the bars located in hostels throughout Xi'an that targeted Americans and Europeans. There she could drink Heineken instead of Tsingtao, play pool, and listen to Western pop music. The easiest and most popular thing the tourists could do if they wanted to retreat from their unfamiliar environment and reconnect with home for a while was watch pirated DVDs of American television shows and movies that were available at the many markets and DVD stores around the city. After spending their days out exploring, they could return to their accommodations and envelop themselves in the familiarity of the United States by consuming episodes and sometimes entire series of American television shows.

Another reason vacationers would retreat was in response to the ongoing stress of engaging risk. Encountering the realness of a culture is a way of playing with risk while traveling. For some this risk is stimulating and a reason for travel, but for others it is enervating. Unlike the beach vacationers for whom risk was a delimited experience during their trip, such as going bungee jumping and then heading back to the hotel, for these vacationers the perception of risk was threaded throughout the experience. It was desirable as an essential part of the trip but also tiring.

Some of the associated risks—theft, getting lost, or getting sick—are real, and some are imagined. Other than the risk from germs, China is actually quite safe for foreign visitors, even though the perception was often different. Whether real or not, these threats are present in the mind of the traveler. Especially with participatory tourism, finding the balance between creating an experience that feels like one is really engaging with a location and remaining in a zone where one can feel safe is a delicate task. The task often fell to local staff, who had experience and expertise in creating the right balance between risk and comfort. The tourists often did not realize the amount of backstage work being done by VTI staff to ensure that they were comfortable and safe but still felt like the experience they were having was authentic and interesting. Much like the staff at a resort or hotel, the employees of VTI worked hard to construct an experience for their visitors that balanced safety and acceptable levels of risk.[34]

This challenge was often compounded by the real difference between what many said they wanted and what they were actually willing to put up with once they had been in the country for a while. Although they wanted to contribute, the challenging realities of Chinese life were not appropriate for all. Often participants expressed disappointment when they felt they were not getting the real experience of truly helping that they had signed up for. Schools that could accommodate the disruption of a short-term, unskilled English "teacher" tended to be wealthier schools. Other volunteers spent their time helping professionals such as doctors and museum guides practice their English. These short-term trips of less than four weeks are often composed of activities of this nature because they require less skill and no specific qualifications on the part of the volunteer.[35] As is the case with VTI, anyone could sign up and would be given an assignment. The result, however, was often tasks that did not satisfy those wishing to engage their altruistic sense of identity. Many felt this did not live up to the expectation of giving back. According to Xavier, "I expected the kindergarten to be less well off than it is. It's a fancy kindergarten. I mean, we're helping rich kids." Anna, who met with doctors from a local hospital to speak English a few hours a day, corroborates this: "Now, I feel kind of funny saying we're doing volunteer work, because I'm hardly doing volunteer work. So maybe now we tell people it's a cultural exchange kind of thing." Linda, who helped tour guides practice their scripted English-language tour at a local museum, agreed: "For the most part, I'm a little disappointed in the placement in terms of doing things. I haven't really done anything, I don't think. I've been toured, but I haven't actually done anything."

Many of the participants were not sensitive to the challenge VTI faced of finding short-term placements where participants could feel they were contributing but also would not be too upset by their circumstances or be placed in dangerous situations. Many, being from upper-middle-class American and European homes, were not ready for the harshness of poverty, even if just as an observer. They had to be in a place where they could feel comfortable participating within the limitations of what they had to offer. This went beyond their volunteer work. Their accommodations, the food they ate, and the places they visited were all orchestrated to strike a balance of authenticity and comforting familiarity, to challenge and stimulate but not overwhelm.

Staff had the added burden of fulfilling a role that placed them somewhere between knowledgeable local, a provider of support, and travel buddy. The tourists sometimes had trouble separating employees who were doing a job from people available to be friends during their vacation, putting employees in a predicament similar to that of staff members at a resort. While part of their job was in fact to be a temporary friend, they still wanted to go home at night and not out to a bar. These lines were further blurred given the high levels of dependency, amount of time spent together, and close quarters, because offices were located in the apartments where some visitors stayed. In addition to spending time together, this expected intimacy extended to a desire to get information from staff that the visitors might otherwise not feel comfortable soliciting from a stranger. Staff were expected to be representatives of that place in many ways that an average local person would not be in terms of their time, their friendship, their accessibility, and their knowledge.

In a way, the tourists were paying for access to locals through the staff in the same way they were paying for access to the country. The staff members themselves, and other members of the local community involved with the group, were seen as authentic connections to the local culture with whom people could speak and spend time more intimately than with those who work as a tour guide or in a hotel. This expectation is illustrated by Connie, who was frustrated that the local staff would not have more forthright conversations with her about Chinese politics. In a country where political differences could often be a delicate issue, she envisioned her experience as giving her access to a place where she could have candid discussions that she otherwise could not have had with a stranger:

> Jane and Marie[36] are very skittish about answering political questions. And they say don't ask those questions [of people outside VTI], but why can't we ask them of the staff? How can we learn what the people are really thinking if we don't ask those kinds of questions? I understand that we don't want to stir things up, but I'd like to know why they feel that way. You know what I mean? I wanted to get more education out of it. And I didn't want to rock the boat outside of VTI, but I thought we could have some really great discussions in house.

Since they are paying for access to authenticity, this view follows the logic that they feel they should be able to talk to staff as if they were not visitors. They should be able to interact with these locals in a way that disregards the boundaries of nationality that separate them from other locals on the street. The tourists were often very critical of what they knew of the Chinese government, especially its human rights abuses or environmental damage, and did not bother hiding their criticisms while in the presence of Chinese staff members. They also often openly made jokes such as not wanting to end up in a Chinese prison. This perspective acknowledges staff as staff but not as locals themselves being asked to discuss sensitive political topics with visitors of varying amenability and often undisguised condescension or outright hostility to staff members' viewpoints. Their role made it acceptable for the vacationers to feel they could be openly critical or mocking, in a way they would not be with other local residents. Once again, staff members were essential in supporting the identity shift while having to perform in a way that separated them from their own everyday life and being props in someone else's vacation experience.

Some people on a tourist vacation elect to use their time in a productive manner, to learn something about the world or to edify themselves in some way that they would not otherwise be able to if they stayed at home or did something more relaxing. In exchange for experiences that can be challenging, tiring, or come with embarrassment, uncertainty, and risk, they are developing a facet of self based in curiosity, adventure, and distinction from others. Both travel and education confer capital. Whether it is a family visit to Washington, D.C., or two weeks in Europe, or a trip to China, tourism involves seeing and learning something new. It allows one to infuse a leisure experience with intangible resources for the self and self-image that are taken home. While this chapter has focused on the experiences of volunteer tourists, it is also representative of the broader tourist experience. Through travel, people express and build on identities. When traveling, people want something authentic, but they also want the comforts of home. They differentiate themselves from other tourists on the basis of what they see as their own rich experience. They behave in particular learned ways that denote skills.

Niche tourism is growing in popularity and is particularly amenable to the development of individualized identity facets, because people may partake in specialized forms of tourism that comply with their interests. In these concentrated environments one can focus on a particular facet of identity for that short time. This extends beyond volunteer tourism into the multiple types of trips people take. An oenophile taking a tour of Napa Valley can sample wines, speak with the vintner, and interact with like-minded, knowledgeable visitors. The appeal of the experience, in addition to getting to enjoy some good wine, is to hone an area of knowledge linked with one's sense of self and share it with others. The desire to do something authentic that complements the self can be seen throughout the tourism industry. Package tours increasingly seek to include moments of experiential authenticity that aesthetically integrate people into their temporary environment. The opportunities for specialized travel are as diverse as people's inclinations.

These people travel to engage their interests. They go to new places to practice a hobby or develop a skill. But distance is not always necessary to indulge such an aspect of self. Other vacationers who lack the resources or the inclination for such travel make similar identity shifts in their everyday environment. Chapter 3 discusses these stay-at-home vacationers who use their time off to immerse themselves in hobbies, develop interests, or learn something new without leaving their neighborhood. Their experiences share many of the formal properties of peripatetic tourists, including indulging interests, exploring, and enjoying self-development without leaving home.

3

Staying Home

Familiarity and Proximity

On a hot day in August when the kids are out of school, Beth and her family take a trip to the county fair. Her husband, Bob, has taken a long weekend away from work. Bob's job keeps him busy, and it is difficult for him to get a full week off at this time of year, so the family takes a day here and there. They go on a Friday to avoid the weekend crowds. The kids eat ice cream, play on rides, and get silhouette cutouts of themselves to take home as souvenirs. The parents eat a lot too while they take lots of pictures as the kids play with the animals at the petting zoo and try out the carnival rides. Bob promised not to constantly look at his phone and check work email, and for the most part he has kept that promise.

Beth is a counselor who sets her own schedule and has a little more flexibility than Bob. She has taken some time off to spend with the kids between summer camp and the start of a new school year. All she needs to do is keep up with email and phone messages in case an emergency comes up. The kids have a couple of months' vacation before they must return to school, Beth has a couple of weeks, and her husband gets just the long weekend. By necessity they must stay close to home, so they look for nearby entertainment for everyone that interrupts their daily experience. The fair is about an hour from home, far enough that it feels like a journey, but not so far that the kids get impatient in the car. Admission is cheap, and the biggest cost is tickets for the rides and snacks. When they get home that night, the kids are tired out, everyone is full, and there is no buildup of laundry that must be addressed. Beth considers it a good day.

Part of the American mythology is that this is a mobile country. Taking to the open road and traveling where we like is considered a right and a marker of freedom. Generations of artists, musicians, filmmakers, writers, and advertisers have told us that hitting the road is an American ideal.[1] Over time the idea has developed that we are entitled to travel and that we should travel as we wish. Taking some time off and getting away, exploring the country or the world, is treated as an American privilege; something we all can and should do. This ability to travel is something that Americans take for granted, but it is not a privilege that has been made available to all. The Great Recession of 2008 brought forward the reality that American mobility is more of a myth that has been divided along class lines. Suddenly, in the face of economic distress, large numbers of people accustomed to assuming they would travel decided to cut back a little and spend their vacations at home. While freedom of mobility is something that the middle and upper classes took to be part of the American experience, the recession showed that travel is a privilege that has not been evenly distributed. If mobility is a "fundamental human right,"[2] it is one that has been denied to Americans who have not had the economic circumstances to fund it.

In the early twentieth century, staying home on vacation was not considered unusual for most people. The cost and effort of travel was prohibitive. But in the postwar years of economic prosperity and status competition, travel on vacation became thoroughly normalized for the average middle-class American. By the late twentieth century, to not go away during a vacation was to do nothing, suggesting that a person who has not gone somewhere has not had a vacation at all. Nelson Graburn, an anthropologist who pioneered the study of tourism in his field, explains this attitude: "People who stay home for vacation are often looked down upon or pitied, or made to feel left behind or possibly provincial, except for the aged and infirm, small children, and the poor."[3] He is not alone in this assessment. Cindy Aron, in her seminal history of vacations in the United States, does not consider vacations taken at home in her analysis, seeking instead to understand how "taking extended trips away from home became part of American life."[4]

As discussed in the previous chapters a very strong work ethic is a U.S. tradition, and it has extended into how we use our leisure time. Strong moral feelings are attached to work and play and, specifically, which should be done when and where and what is proper in certain times and places. Proximity is an important part of how people perceive what is appropriate. The closer things are to each other, the more people tend to see them as being similar. Distance helps define difference and vice versa.[5] Work is lumped with home, while leisure and relaxation are split from it. My interviewees, both the people who traveled and some of the people who stayed home, reflected this basic attitude on how and where we should spend our leisure time.

Everyday life is closely associated with work, which makes up the majority of day-to-day activities. Vacations, on the other hand, are voluntary, fun, and indulgent, and they are relatively rare. Therefore, they should be separate from the realms of daily experience, especially those closely associated with work. Life can be understood as alternating between two modes: long periods of serious work while staying at home punctuated with brief breaks of being away for leisure.[6] Not leaving home during this break is wasting time, considered a lost opportunity, and time that will be inevitably filled with reminders of work. Luke, who likes to travel far away on his vacations, explains this view: "The reason to take a holiday is to not be where you are already." The very purpose of a vacation is to get away from his everyday environment and see something new. He continues, "If I have time off while I'm at home, it's not really a holiday, a vacation; it's just sitting around your house doing nothing. So you kind of have to get away from your normal environment. You kind of have to try new things, like a different culture." For people like Luke, to not go away is to feel less than normal or not to be able to participate in contemporary life to a suitable degree. To not travel is like not having a car or a nice house. It is a status marker that is linked with health and well-being.[7]

This perspective ignores the long tradition of people who take vacations without leaving home. Excluding them in the academic literature on vacations and tourism overlooks an important part of the history and culture of vacationing in the United States. It also ignores a major reality of vacationing: it can be expensive and even burdensome and not everyone has the ability to pay for it or the inclination to deal with the hassles. Time off from work offers an extended period during which people can see to all the obligations of home life that they cannot when faced with the time famine of the workweek. The temptation to use this time to stay home and do repairs to the house or catch up with a backlog of chores can be stronger than the desire to get away from it all. While it may not seem ideal to stay home for leisure and do nothing, stay-homers fit well into the tradition of defining leisure in relation to work.

Among many, then, a normal vacation is a time away, but this is an assumption made by people who regularly go away somewhere. Those who usually do not travel on vacation do not always have a sense that distance is necessary, especially if their peers do the same.[8] Instead, people who stay home show that vacation is about an experiential change involving a contrast with whatever dominates everyday experience. This contrast is usually with the work obligations that make up their everyday lives. Just getting away from obligations is sufficient to create a vacation. Stay-homers share their definitions of vacation:

> Pretty simply not being here [at work]. Not working. Doesn't matter where it is, and it doesn't matter what I'm doing. If it were— and I haven't done anything like this—but if it were charity work or something like that, if I'm not here, or even if I'm here and it's not related to this, I would probably consider that vacation. (Alan)

> Not having work to do. It's a vacation if you don't have work to do, to me. So [work] means to me both work for pay and, because I'm a graduate student, [that] I'm still registered [*laughs*]. Not having that kind of work to do and also not having housework to do. Not having, like, cooking and cleaning to do. That would be a vacation. (Jamie)

> For me, it would predominantly be, because . . . I am a loner for the most part, although I invest a significant amount of time with my daughter—it's solitude. That would be a vacation. Being able to complete thoughts again, because work is so hectic. (Mark)

Stay-homers demonstrate that one of the most important aspects of a break, after removing work, is the interruption in the routines of everyday life. It is a cognitive transition reinforced by the shift in experiential patterns. The pressures of everyday routines are reduced to make the experience different in a way that is more significant than an evening or weekend break. Namely, the time is more flexible, less intense, and not as subject to the demands of others.[9]

Vacationing at home can be an active experience that replicates the creativity and self-creating properties experienced during travel. Integrating short trips and disrupted daily routines, like sleeping in or eating out, similarly introduces recreation into the experience. Staying home to do home repairs, painting, or improvements is creative work that draws on the individual's desires and skills to shape something new. In reality, "doing nothing" for stay-homers means being quite busy: going out to bars, visiting museums, trying new restaurants, making day trips to the beach, doing home repairs, attending concerts, seeing sites around one's hometown, indulging in marathons of television and videogames, taking trips to the pool, hiking, and camping in the backyard. Selena makes her vacation time at home feel special: "Leaving the apartment helps. Going into the city where's there's things to do, like seeing a show, or eating out somewhere in a different town. That makes it feel different. . . . And I like dancing too. I like going out salsa dancing. That's my fun thing." Pointedly leaving the house and doing things she associates with indulgence and fun help her make a mental transition, although not a physical one, and mirror the experiences of a vacation where one travels to someplace new.

I conducted my research in 2008 and 2009, the same time that a major recession, high unemployment, and high gas prices made saving and budgeting a priority for many Americans. People from all over the class structure realized that travel, even if just a road trip to visit family, was in fact a luxury they had taken for granted. During this time the concept of the stay-at-home vacation was reintroduced to the middle class and branded by the media as "staycations," a novelty to people who had grown accustomed to associating vacation time with travel. In recruiting my interviewees I drew from a sample of people from diverse socioeconomic backgrounds and day-to-day circumstances who stayed home for different reasons, although most related to finances. Some were working parents who felt the stress of travel made staying home worth it; others were graduate students whose work requirements made travel difficult. Others chose not to vacation for the increased financial security that saving their money instead of spending it on leisure would bring. A primary difference in this group was between those for whom traveling on vacation was normal and those for whom staying home was standard. The former group had to grapple with this new situation. The middle- and upper-middle-class vacationers discussed in this chapter were often confounded by their new experience of staying home. They struggled to make what should have been a relaxing experience into the kind of vacation they thought they should have. They lacked the cultural skill set for staying home. The latter group, on the other hand, did not grow up with the expectation of travel and so did not encounter the same cognitive dissonance that the others did. Staying home was less of a challenge for them.

These groups had similarities as well. Essentially, strong identity-based ties were keeping them in one place. Whether these ties were family, work, or finances, some identity facets simply would not or could not yield. For many, young children and demanding jobs were facets of self that could not be modified at that moment. Traveling to new places makes the work of rearranging facets of self easier to do. Thus, by staying in their everyday environments, mundane patterns of identity were omnipresent. All had to work harder to rearrange, reprioritize, and find pockets of freedom within routine.

Reasons for Staying Home

Although people offered their own reasons for why they chose to stay home, for most the root cause was financial. Mark exemplifies someone who stays home on vacation to save money and who grew up doing so. For him a staycation is not a novelty or something he temporarily has to do in response to a tough economy. It is what he knows. This personal history helps produce a clear yet complex motivation for staying home. His reasoning stems from saving money but is fed by a personal identity deeply rooted in his upbringing in the past and caring for his family in the present. This creates a mind-set about the experience different from some others, because it is not approached like a penalty or a second choice to some better option. It is just the way things are done:

> I grew up fairly poor. And I'm sure that my parents did what they had to do as parents; however, eating bologna and American cheese sandwiches is not my idea of food. And so from that experience being young, I'm constantly—I'm not insecure—but I'm constantly trying to improve and distill [ensure] my financial security. . . . I'm not provincial in any sense; I've traveled to twenty-seven countries. By the time I was twenty-five, I'd been in twenty-seven countries [with the military]. I like traveling. However, the higher priority is to ensure not only economic security now but for the future, not only for myself but for my daughter. It's a big priority.

For Mark, the vacation is strongly tied with maintaining a particular aspect of self, that of a prudent person who takes care of his family. His financial reasons relate to identity facets stemming from experiences with his childhood family and the responsibility he feels to his daughter. One way this manifests is in his approach to spending for vacations. He continues:

> I'm a very frugal and Spartan person, because I have very specific economic objectives that I know I have to accomplish, not only for

my security but for my daughter's security. Again, I grew up poor. That's not going to happen with my daughter. That's not to say I'm going to spoil her, but I'm not going to—she's going to understand—how can I say this—she's going to understand what it feels like to have economic security. And the reason why you have economic security, to accomplish that, one of the vehicles, is by staying home on vacation.

Mark has achieved a good level of financial security for himself in his adult life, but he continues to prioritize his family's well-being. He is not alone in this. Like many others who choose not to travel for financial reasons, he opts for restraint in the present to prepare for the future. Not traveling is part of his aspirational planning for his future self.

Erik, a graduate student, similarly trades present mobility for future security. Taking advantage of the opportunities available to foreign students in the American higher education system, he came to the United States from Madagascar to complete graduate training in the biomedical sciences. In one sense he represents astounding physical mobility, traveling from Africa to New Jersey. In another, his limited resources as a graduate student restrict his travel to the East Coast train line that conveys him to New York and Baltimore, where he visits friends. He can travel, but only along a delimited route and at the not insignificant expense of a train ticket. The trip on the local train into Manhattan alone costs close to twenty dollars, a large cost for someone on his tight budget. His time off from work, then, usually involves a day trip to the city to see friends, drink, and hear music. Other than that, his movements are limited to the small city in New Jersey where he has temporarily settled while he finishes his studies. He comments on his situation with resignation: "My sister is going to visit me here at least, so. But I'm grown up; even though it's not always fun, you learn to accept." Once he finishes his degree and secures employment he will presumably regain some of the mobility he has temporarily lost.

Several of my respondents were graduate students who limited their travel because of temporary financial constraints. Most of the students who curtailed their travel had grown up in the middle class and therefore usually traveled on vacation with their families. Not traveling was a temporary situation for them. They expected to travel later in life. Many of their explanations were built around imagining a future self who benefited from exercising self-control today. For them, staying home may be a temporary disappointment, but it is also an investment of their time and resources that will allow them to meet their goals. They believe they will be able to enjoy the privilege of travel at some point in the future. In the present, taking a vacation, even if just for a week or two, is a liability that would detract from their success. Whether their planning is for economic security or building a career, vacationing is seen as an impediment to that goal. For example, Jim imagines the travel he will be doing with his future family once he has received his doctorate and settled into his career:

> I'm not going to lie to you: When you're at lab at twelve o'clock at night and working, you kind of wish you weren't there. So it is annoying. I definitely wish I could see more. But I prioritize. I feel like if I put my time in now, I'll have more time later to do all these wonderful things. I don't really have much people to do it with now. So I figure I'll do it with my family when I get married. So I'm definitely going to do it. I just feel like this is more important for me to do. So I'm okay with putting in the extra time.

In a culture where work is often valued over leisure, this attitude is not limited to graduate students and certainly can structure decisions past school and into working life. Some people just cannot or do not want to stop working, often because they see the gains of hard work as preferable to any advantages accrued from pausing for leisure. The *New York Times* asked, compared with other countries, "Why don't Americans have longer vacations?"[10] The comments the article generated are telling about a work culture that values advancement over leisure. CMK in Honolulu says:

> The concept of leisure time off seems foreign. Time is the basic raw material that we all have to achieve [our goals] with, and I guess you could set some aside for leisure, but there's so much to see and so much to do. I have traveled for vacation but was frustrated with the poor use of vacation time. I can recreate and relax, take leisure time, when I die.

DOB in New Jersey explains:

> In my profession, if I took more than a week off at a time, I risked the voiced displeasure of management as well as having someone else take over my responsibilities while I was away—and hence step ahead of me in line for promotion. . . . And now, with technology accelerating the pace of everything, stepping away means let-

ting it all pass you by for a while. That is a frightening thought for many who think they will fall too far behind to catch up. It's incongruous with the culture of getting ahead.

This attitude is not shared by other countries where vacation is taken by employees and given by employers much more liberally. The United States does not legally require employers to offer paid time off. In the European Union, however, member countries must provide a minimum of four weeks or twenty days of paid vacation, and several European countries require even more. France mandates thirty days of paid leave, and Austria, Denmark, Finland, Norway, and Sweden guarantee twenty-five. The Netherlands, Sweden, Finland, and Norway go even further and require that employers guarantee vacations in continuous blocks.[11]

Ironically, in a culture where travel is seen as a status marker and staying home as a disadvantage, Americans are also expected to stay home and stay plugged in so as not to fall behind. At the same time that one is expected to travel to accrue social status, in the occupational status game, one also should not be away for too long, or at all.

One strategy for dealing with the short-term disappointments from this self-restraint and immobility is comparison with others who are not making the same sacrifices in working toward the future. Respondents often contrasted themselves with those who chose to travel, perceiving these others as wasting their money and time. This is similar to the tourists discussed in Chapter 2 who viewed their busy use of leisure time in a more favorable light than the use of those who chose to relax. Stay-homers often make a claim for themselves as being more ambitious, more hardworking, and critically, more *responsible* than people who choose to waste their personal resources of time and money on frivolous leisure. Alan explains that he usually stays home between Christmas and New Year's, when his university is quiet, "just because it's a good time to get work done. Depressingly so." But he feels it helps him gain an advantage: "Actually, sometimes it makes me feel better about myself because other people are out there, like, you know, they're wasting time, and I'm in here wasting less time." Mark also compares himself with others who took vacations but then made themselves vulnerable to the financial crisis:

Well, those fourteen million [unemployed] people, you know, they probably took their vacation, and they had their toys, their boats, and their water ski and all that stuff. And I don't have any of that, but I have, emphatically, financial security. Meaning these people that had their vacations, went to overseas or whatever, and they thought, well, they'll never get laid off or the American economy will never go bad. Well, that paradigm is not true. . . . So let's say, if I got laid off, I may not have memories of vacation and photos and postcards, but I can pay my mortgage. Versus these other people, who I have empathy for, but they have their great memories of their vacations that they went here, there, a hundred miles, a thousand miles, ten thousand miles. But they don't have the money to pay for their mortgage, and now they have a different kind of vacation.

Economic constraints are a primary reason for staying home but not necessarily the only one. Other reasons are not having traveling companions, poor health, taking care of others, or just preferring to stay home and avoid the hassles of travel. As Selena explains, "I don't like travel too much. I think it's a pain in the neck. Either you're stuck in traffic or it's expensive because you have to take a plane or train." Jim says he rarely goes away for his vacations and is happy to stay home. He has economic limitations on his travel, but he also does not feel particularly compelled to leave. He does not feel he is missing out by staying home:

All the fun that I've ever had in my life has been right here in this area, between here and New York. So I've never really had much of a reason to venture out. My theory about stuff is that usually everything you need in life is right in front of you. So for me, I like to drink. I like to have good company. I like nature. So if I go north I can just go hiking and disappear for a day. If I want to have fun with my friends, we go out to a pub and drink.

Jim's decision results from a combination of factors. It is the case that his limited budget minimizes his ability to travel, but there is more to his reluctance than this. He clearly does not buy into the explanation that leisure should be separated from home and that, to get away, one must travel and see new things. Alan does not want to travel if he has to go by himself. The presence of another person adds value to the experience that he cannot access while he is single:

I think a lot of experiences like that aren't really worth much unless you're sharing them with somebody. . . . If you can't share things with the people that are closest to you, especially things like that—I think [sharing] just adds tons and tons of value to it. Not that I wouldn't value going there by myself, but monetarily it almost wouldn't be worthwhile if I wasn't there with other people sharing it.

Alan's reasoning is not just sentimental. Because he does not have someone to share it with, he does not think it will be as good as it could be, and this makes the trip not worth the expense.

Each of these people has conducted a trip cost-benefit analysis, and travel always came up short. Whether they have other needs or demands, like taking care of their children, not missing work, or a fear that something will not be as good if experienced alone, they have all decided that the costs of a vacation away from home, in terms of time, money, and stress, are just not worth it. Their decision prioritizes a salient aspect of identity over whatever short-term shift they would make when taking a break for travel. Staying home offers longer-term gains that win out over what they perceive as the short-term benefits of getting away.

Learning Immobility

While some were accustomed to staying put, immobility during vacation time was something others had to learn. For those who view travel as a right, staying at home can be a big disappointment. It does not fulfill expectations of what a vacation should be. The middle- and upper-middle-class individuals I interviewed who were temporarily struck by the financial crisis and chose to cut back struggled more with staying put. Immobility challenged their self-identity of being a person with the means to travel. While travel is a skill that people learn and wield, the inverse is true as well. These people did not have the cultural skills for staying home. Some needed instructions and advice on how to turn their stay-home experience into something resembling their accustomed middle-class vacation. They wanted it to resemble the kinds of experiences they anticipated and desired, meaning time filled with travel, relaxation, or activity.

Beginning in 2008 the media and advertisers responded to this need by marketing the idea of the staycation. While stay-at-home vacations were intended to be about saving money and rejecting the consumerism of travel, the staycation was developed to profit from the concept of saving money. The idea was made palatable to middle-class consumers with a sense of privilege about the right to be mobile by catering to their economic anxieties and identity as financially stable middle-class Americans.

The staycation was promoted to help turn the home environment concep-
tually into somewhere new or somewhere else for people who were choosing not to travel for the first time. Much of this coverage revolved around
consumerist solutions for getting away while staying home.[12] Tourist
spots advertised themselves to locals instead of visitors as ideal destinations for exploring one's own city, and stores such as Walmart advertised
products that made homes fun, like barbecue grills, pool toys, patio furniture, backyard games, and inflatable outdoor movie screens. Walmart
even tried unsuccessfully to patent the term "staycation," which it used
prominently in advertising campaigns.[13]

While most of this attention was for marketing purposes, my respondents' self-reported activities displayed a need to re-create a real vacation
experience. For most, the staycation was an alternative to a trip they normally took, and they attempted to turn it into the event that their usual
trip away would have been. Those staying home for the first time reported
that their staycation ended up being expensive and stressful because they
tried to fill their time with the activities and travel they expected from a
vacation. Beth exclaims:

> I still spent a lot of money! Sesame Place was $200! For a family of
> four. They didn't give you a break for a kid. I couldn't believe that we
> were out so much and that we still spent so much money. You know,
> Point Pleasant—you go on those rides, they're expensive. The Kutz-
> town Festival—you buy a little thing, they get some food, they go
> on a ride, you pet an animal. Again, you spend over $100, so yeah.

The staycation Beth took in 2010 for the first time with her husband
and two small children she meant to be a fun experience for all involved.
While she did enjoy it for the flexibility it offered, she was frustrated with
the amount of money she kept spending to keep her family occupied. Her
family's usual trip to a lake probably would have cost less: "Our week away
at the mountains is probably cheaper. Because the hotel, the motel we stay
in, is so cheap, and you kind of just lay at the lake all day long." If she and
her family had not stayed home, she would not have had the compulsion
to fill their days with expensive activities and trips.

Jamie and her husband were similarly not pleased when they tried to
replicate the experience of travel by taking frequent day trips. In the end
this proved to be too stressful with young children, and they were happy
to alter the plan of their staycation halfway through the week and just be
at home:

Because there's a lot of driving. If you're doing a staycation, you have to drive. So that's not good for little kids either. So after three days, we were done. Like, we just wanted to be home and, like, not have any whining and crying and I want this and I want that. And you know, having to stop the car to nurse the baby. And anyway, that's what we wanted. So we did that for Monday, Tuesday, Wednesday, and then Thursday and Friday were going to be our beach days, and it rained. So we happily stayed home and relaxed from our vacation. [*Laughs*.]

Jamie's staycation was unsuccessful, and she was very unhappy with the experience, until she gave up trying to get the family to do things and they all just relaxed. Making it more difficult for her, she had planned to visit her extended family in Canada before opting to stay home. Unfortunately, she could not replicate the experience she had hoped to have in Canada. "I had it in my mind that we were on vacation, so that made [the staycation] doubly disappointing. Because it wasn't much; I really just wanted to get away, and there was no getting away. Not only did we not get away to Canada, but trying to simulate getting away was unsuccessful."

Jaclyn similarly struggled with the experience of immobility, which was new to her and quite severe. Financial distress introduced immobility to Jaclyn in both her vacations and everyday life. Originally from Hong Kong, she and her husband moved to Honolulu and opened their own import-export business. Their business was successful, and they were able to travel relatively freely, visiting family in Hong Kong and Canada. They also traveled frequently to Bali to get supplies for their business. Their work depended on tourism, and the unfortunate decrease in tourists because of the financial crisis forced them to close their business and take low-paying jobs. When they lost their business they also lost their mobility in a way that had real implications for their personal and professional relationships. Jaclyn and her husband now work as staff at souvenir stores in separate cities on Oahu selling the goods they used to import. They share one car. In the morning, after her husband drops her off in Waikiki, Jaclyn is relatively immobile until late in the evening when he picks her up. She kills time at a McDonald's before and after work. The loss of her personal mobility severely curtails her freedom because she must limit her days to going to work and waiting in inexpensive public places. The other consequence of the loss of their business is that their leisure and international travel has ceased. They no longer have the funds to see their parents and extended family in Hong Kong or even to leave the relatively circumscribed island of Oahu.

Jaclyn is eager to travel, but her husband refuses, telling her to watch the Travel Channel instead, saying it is just as good. Jaclyn disagrees, arguing that watching something on TV is not the same as seeing it in person. The Travel Channel does not satisfy the "compulsion to proximity"[14] that people experience. She still feels the need to visit relatives and friends and see desirable places and things herself, not from the distance of television. While she can talk with her relatives on the phone, she cannot see them in person as she really wishes to do. She finds that media is not a substitute for this copresence she desires. While she may be able to watch stories of other places and see other destinations in the world on television, it does not replicate seeing something for herself and having the full embodied experiences of travel. The easy but insubstantial connections of television and internet are poor substitutes for the face-to-face contact and first-person experience Jaclyn desires.

Staying Home and Mental Boundaries

In response to the confusion of how to stay home on vacation and distaste for it, a small industry developed to offer assistance and advice. This abundance of news reports, blogs, advertising, and books offering guidance on how to make do in your own home for a week of unstructured time underscores the novelty of the stay-at-home vacation for middle-class Americans. These instruction manuals usually include a set of rules that follow the same general format; building mental boundaries to prevent one from falling into the habits of everyday life and replicating the feel of a travel vacation. These rules typically include setting a defined beginning and end, planning an itinerary of activities, avoiding daily routines, not doing chores, and taking day trips. Essentially, they are trying to establish the cognitive work necessary for setting apart the time without the benefit of physical distance. One self-described "guidebook" for staycations offers advice on "creating mental distance."[15] Rule number one is "a staycation must be treated as a *real* vacation":

> [That] means that just because you're not getting on that cruise trip, you still need to do the same mental checkout of the real world that typical vacations entail. That means turning off your cell phone and not checking your email each day. It means getting all the household chores done before the start of your staycation.

It means not thinking, "If we leave right before the curtain falls, we can beat traffic; I'll be in bed before midnight and can get up early to mow the lawn." For any vacation—a staycation or something grander—you have to unplug. Unplug from work, from your chores, from the daily compulsion to get things done.[16]

Although the author reinforces the idea that a vacation without travel is not a real vacation, he still sums up the components of what this time off means regardless of location; to disregard time, to disconnect from work and social obligations, and to change one's routine in order to create the mental distance for identity shifts. At the same time, he suggests that by not traveling it is harder to resist the duties, obligations, and habits associated with home, and more conscious effort must be put into ensuring distance and creating mental boundaries between work and play. Other media outlets echo these ideas in their commentary on staycations, offering specific advice on how to eliminate or alter aspects of the everyday environment so as to imitate the experiences of travel. In addition to setting defined start and end dates, *Good Morning America* recommends that people take photos and videos to commemorate the time as they would on a trip; "declare a 'choratorium,'" meaning not do any chores; and "pack that time with activities."[17]

This need for mental preparation is supported by the perspective of ecological psychology. Roger Barker and Herbert Wright describe how different environments, and the people in them, mold how people act.[18] Certain actions are encouraged and others are discouraged by the social, physical, and cultural properties of an environment, or its "behavior settings." In their study of the children of a midwestern town, Barker and Wright argue that the situations and settings that the children were in usually influenced behavior more than any personal characteristics. A child in class may be still and silent, and on the playground she will be energetic and playful because she adapts her behavior to the expectations of the setting. Peoples' behavior is channeled in a way that is compatible with place, and it is difficult to break out of these patterns. Everyday life worlds are made up of these behavior settings that individuals pass through on any given day: home, the office, the grocery store, the library, the mall. Behavior settings have the benefit of simplifying social life by reducing cognitive dissonance as people move between locations and roles and by creating standard rules of behavior for any given setting.

Over time people learn to associate familiar settings with a certain range of behaviors into which they can quickly transition. Settings are therefore so powerful that people quickly come to associate behavior settings with different ways of being and doing. Museums and libraries are associated with learning. Playgrounds and theme parks are not. Because certain activities become so associated with particular behavior settings, they are facilitated in some places and inhibited in others. Context becomes important in how people switch between roles and adapt their behavior.[19]

Remaining in an everyday setting can therefore inhibit the alteration of identity facets or transitions into new and temporary roles. It can be difficult to break the learned or expected behavior for a particular place. This is evident when people compare their experience of vacationing at home, either their own or a house they grew up in and where they feel at home, with staying in a hotel. Jamie explains why she cannot fully relax when she goes to stay at her parents' house:

> [I] feel pressure to help with the cooking and the cleaning when I'm there. So, like, if it's Christmas or Thanksgiving . . . or even just going home for the summer, I kind of feel like I have to participate, rather than just lie on the couch. You know, when you go to a hotel, you don't think, "Oh, I need to clean the bathroom." But I do feel that way at [my parents'] home.

Jamie feels compelled to foreground aspects of her everyday identity, primarily obligations to the family, in this everyday environment. In the household setting it is difficult for her to switch into a more indulgent sense of self in which she is not responsible for the day-to-day upkeep of her environment. It compels her to prioritize aspects of self pertaining to being a responsible daughter.

Beth, a mother of two small children, enjoys vacationing at home because it gives her control over her environment that she would not have at a hotel. She has an experience similar to Jamie's, the feeling that she cannot put aside homelike responsibilities, but for her this is an advantage. In her experience, staying in a hotel with her small children was frustrating because it prevented her from providing childcare as she would have liked. She compares an overnight in a hotel with staying at home with her kids:

> With a house, it's different than a hotel room. You know, like in a hotel room you're kind of confined in the space, and you still make a mess, and you can't really stay on top of stuff. I mean, the house-

cleaning people come, but it's not the same. And when you have little kids—my kid's only . . . four, and [her sister is] two and a half . . .—you need to make accommodations with milk and food, you know what I mean? So sometimes it's just easier [to stay at home], and because we were out all day, I didn't really do a lot of house-work during the day.

Because of the persistence of an unequal division of household labor between men and women it continues to be more difficult for women to separate being home and away on vacation. Household-related work and child-rearing responsibilities, especially, travel with them whether they like it or not,[20] as illustrated by a headline from the humor site the *Onion*, "Mom Spends Beach Vacation Assuming All Household Duties in Closer Proximity to the Ocean."[21] This is also the case for fathers and influences their shifts in identity while on vacation, but women still do a dispropor-tionate share of housework, and this is reflected in their vacation experi-ences. Beth appreciated the ease that staying home offered as it made it easier for her to integrate the work of childcare and home maintenance, whereas Jamie was disappointed because she wished she could segment them more than she was able to. In contrast with all the guides that sug-gest putting off doing chores for the duration of the staycation, both were happy that staying home allowed them to stay on top of laundry, dishes, and cleaning, because otherwise they would have had much more work to do at the end. Continuing their daily chores may not have felt as much like vacation, but it kept their work load manageable.

Situating a vacation in an everyday behavior setting represents less of a burden in terms of preparation and return, but it also makes it more difficult to establish boundaries around work and play. Packing suitcases, buying necessary or wanted things, making lists and keeping track of what to do, canceling papers and the mail, or preparing the house for an absence are not necessary if one does not actually leave home. But these activities serve more than a functional purpose; they also help create the mental space that facilitates absence. While not having to do these things reduces the work load, it also makes it more difficult to mentally switch from reminders of everyday life.

At the same time, behavior settings can strategically create a quick change, and even a radical one, for someone who cannot travel far but still wishes to benefit from a leisure-oriented environment. A behavior setting exists regardless of who is in it. Behavior patterns persist year after year.[22] Before arriving in an environment and after leaving, a person can enter patterns and adapt to them with little relatively little transition. People take advantage of this as they easily move through the familiar environments that make up their day. A man may go to church on Sunday morning and behave in a way appropriate to the service and later in the day go to a drugstore and act accordingly. He knows what to do in each environment, and the physical setup and other inhabitants of the space facilitate his actions. Similarly, for my respondents, going to a water park for the day, a theme park, the beach, or a zoo allowed a temporary transition into a leisure space that they anticipated and took advantage of. Day trips and short overnights to a hotel were the most popular activities, allowing them to temporarily switch into a tourist role and enjoy the benefits of it. Patrice, a resident of Honolulu who rarely travels for her vacations to save money, will occasionally check herself into an affordable hotel in Waikiki for the night. In this way she can share the experience that visitors to her city have without traveling far or spending too much money. At the hotel she can swim in the pool with other vacationers and lie in the sun, walk downstairs to the restaurant to get dinner in the evening, get a free breakfast, and not make the bed or pick up after her kids. Since she is a local and not a tourist, it is not a perspective from which she would normally experience her own city, and she is surrounded by people on vacation doing the same activities as she is while in the hotel. It suffices for a mental break.

On the other hand, staying too close to home, with the reminders of work that are built into it, can make it difficult to stop working. Self-governance is necessary in this situation, especially for those who find it difficult to stop working. Selena experiences this when she stays in her apartment, which is located near her work space. It is easy for her to stop in as she likes, but she is strict about keeping the two spaces separate. She intentionally limits her work-related behavior at home so that she can leave those associations behind at her lab. "Being close allows me to stop by [the lab] if I need to. If I need to just stop by for an hour or two, I can do that, and then I can go back home. Being home is different from being here, I feel, because I'm not doing or thinking anything, the computer doesn't go on, I don't check email. . . . When I'm home, I'm home." Spatially partitioning home and work helps keep the two separate, leaving one clearly defined for labor and the other for leisure.

For people who have difficulty separating home and work, having the constant temptation of their office nearby can be challenging. Transitioning briefly to a different behavior setting away from the office and the home can help guide their minds elsewhere. Erik, the international graduate student who is limited to train travel, also likes to work a lot and finds it difficult to turn off this particular aspect of self when he is in the vicinity of his lab. Because of the demanding nature of his work and the lack of clear boundaries between home and the lab, he often feels compelled to work through his vacation time. His solution is to go see friends, go to his favorite bar in New York City, or take day trips to Baltimore:

> I know that I can never have a real break when I stay here because I'm always tempted to go to do something, to go to the lab and do something. So [being] there [in New York City], at least that erases the temptation of taking work home, because my work is not only in lab, but I do math modeling at the same time. So I only need a scrap of paper and a pen. So if I stay here [at the lab], I notice that I'm always up to something, even though it's not always productive [*laughs*]. But if I go to New York City or if I go somewhere else, at least I can take my mind away from it, so it does help.

Those who are able to set strict boundaries for themselves, like Selena, have an easier time negotiating the slippage between home and work. Others, like Erik, need to create some physical distance between the settings of their work and play identities to set bounds on the two.

Retreat and the Home

While some of my respondents struggled with the experience, others enjoyed their stay-at-home vacation. Those who are content with staying home find that it can offer valuable opportunities for self-directed identity work. While staying home can represent familiarity and routine, home is also a space that has been tailored to the self. It is a place where one already has the structure in place to indulge personal interests and where one can retreat into privacy. Vacationing at home can represent a practical situation to put in place some of the vacation ideals of self-directed action. The already-personalized flexibilities of home can allow a level of release that might not be possible when staying in a more public place. A travel editor writes:

> I love staying home. No holiday is ever as stress-free or feels as long as one in which I wear the same T-shirt for four days straight. If I wear one at all. No vacation is as hedonistic or self-indulgent as one in which my fridge and my TV remote present the only serious decision-making challenge of the day. No vacation can offer the

hermetic privacy or sociable gregariousness as one at home, surrounded by friends, or just your own four walls.[23]

In this space a person can enjoy the autonomy of personal choice. The enjoyment from retreat into the home can mean just watching television for a week or playing video games all day. But the home is also a site for enjoyment of hobbies. Hobbies aid in building separate mental realms of play and work in the everyday world, and they often take place in the home. If people cannot escape from their surroundings, they can at least escape the alienating activities of work life through involvement with a favored activity that reflects their personalized interests. For this reason homes are an example of what Stanley Cohen and Laurie Taylor label "free areas," or places that are relatively high in routine and low in the need for self-monitoring.[24] The mental realm dedicated to hobbies is generally made up of objects that the hobbyist can arrange, modify, and master. Gardening, collecting, video games and computers, cooking, embroidery and knitting, and carpentry allow retreat into one's home and interests.

Homes are already partitioned into separate rooms that are given particular meanings, such as those spaces we define for eating, sleeping, and playing. These spaces help us create distinctions for formal and informal and work and play.[25] Hobbies are often assigned to their own designated space—a garden patch, a game room, or the basement—where one can withdraw to and enter a hobby world. People essentially carve out their own free area in their home.[26]

Hobbies themselves are another example of the American proclivity for productive leisure. Coming into popularity in the nineteenth century, they allowed people to enjoy time off from paid labor while not being idle. They also had an advantage on the depersonalized factory work coming into dominance at this time because they were individualized and self-directed. They represented labor one could do oneself, in pursuit of one's interests. Hobbies are one small way of exerting autonomy in a mass culture.[27] In a postindustrial society, such leisure is not just a means of recuperating from work; it is an opportunity for identity enhancement and self-fulfillment.[28] People may turn to hobbies for the satisfaction and personal gain they do not get from their employment. Hobbyists partake in serious leisure during which they can engage aspects of self in fulfilling ways that they cannot during their work time, and they can do so in their own home or neighborhood. One of the key aspects of this serious leisure is that people identify strongly with it. Through their enthusiasm for the activity, they develop a clear identity associated with it that is reinforced in practice.[29]

Hobbies are also well suited to expressions of individuality because when engaging in a hobby in one's own home some of the impression-management work that is key in other types of vacations involving traveling into the outside world can be relaxed. One can ease up on the projection of identity to others when alone in the home and therefore more fully mentally immerse oneself in the activity and be oneself. Especially when enjoyed in a private space, a favored activity is easy to lose oneself in because there is no one else around with whom to interact or impress. The self-consciousness involved in so many activities of the outside world, where one has to construct and present an appropriate identity, can be put on hold.

People can happily suspend self-consciousness and create their own retreat when inside their hobby world. This is facilitated by the cognitive benefits that come from immersion in a favored activity that one is good at. When immersed in a hobby without stresses or distractions a person can reach a state of flow. According to Mihaly Csikszentmihalyi, flow occurs when a person has skills and abilities that are strong enough to meet the demands of a situation or goal and does not feel overly stressed or out of his or her depth.[30] Time passes quickly as the person enters an intense mental state that contrasts with mundane everyday life. When one loses oneself in an activity, one can similarly lose track of self-consciousness and immerse oneself in the task at hand. Csikszentmihalyi argues that having leisure time in itself does not necessarily lead to enjoyment or higher levels of satisfaction; it needs to be used in a way that encourages engagement in order to be "translated into enjoyment."[31] To get the most out of leisure time, the time should be used to expand one's capacities, not just passively consuming or observing. Not all leisure necessarily leads to flow, because the activity must be complex enough to fully capture one's attention and focus. An active hobby or home improvement activity can offer the ideal balance of challenge, enjoyment, and end goal to achieve this state. In a state of flow, that facet of identity related to the hobby or activity naturally becomes paramount, and others shift to the background as focus moves to the activity at hand.

A hobby in the home is a time to retreat from projecting identity to others, and it is also a time to more deeply engage with a particular facet of self in a concentrated manner. A reading enthusiast or at-home gardener, for example, can put in extra time, concentration, and care to a facet of identity that normally does not receive the desired amount of attention. Retreating to a hobby room, garden, or garage workshop is, then, retreating to a specific area of the home that has been reserved for that particular facet of self. Mark says:

I like to read, catch up with reading. I have reading projects. You know, when I read a subject, I try to get five or six books, both pro and con on that subject, so I have all these stacks of reading projects to be done. And then I like to go to . . . the backyard of my house, and I am a survival enthusiast, so I like to survive and practice survival skills. Stuff that I would do in the woods, but since I don't get to go to the woods all that often, I do it in my backyard.

A space in the home can therefore be transformed from an everyday utilitarian function to one facilitating a particular identity. When Mark practices survival skills in his backyard, he is transforming that space from one of family leisure and everyday chores to his personal space for skills that he highly values.

People who take stay-at-home vacations emphasize the cognitive basis of negotiating and bounding identities and demonstrate that a change in mental routine can be just as important as a change in place. While motivations range from not having the money for a trip to the responsibility and challenges of vacationing with young children making staying at home a preferable option, to wanting to indulge a hobby or get some housework done, the content of a stay-home vacation does not have to be all that different from one that involves travel. Sightseeing, eating out, shopping, relaxing and socializing with friends and family dominate both experiences. People find ways to match vacation time at home with the cultural scripts they have come to expect for their time off. Thus, they demonstrate what it means "to vacation" regardless of location; to disregard time, disconnect from work and social obligations, and change habits to create the cognitive space for identity shifts.

Mobility and leisure travel are patterned in a way that follows class structures. For some, staying home is facilitated by the tools in their cultural tool kit. For those accustomed to the experience, it is less challenging. For others, staying home is a new experience and one that does not fit with their image of what a vacation should be. They struggle with how to make it work and have it be positive. Because it was new to them, some of my interviewees needed a little help with a stay-at-home vacation. They had to figure out how to do it without either causing themselves increased stress, being too bored, or working too much. They struggled with how to vacation without traveling.

An important theme of this chapter is how similar a stay-home vacation can be when compared with other forms of vacationing. While staycations, tourism, and beach vacations can seem very different, they hold in common many formal properties that facilitate a person's identity shifts. Chapters 1, 2, and 3 explore the individualities of these three forms of vacationing. Chapters 4, 5, and 6 examine the similarities that bridge experiences. These include forming mental boundaries that define the parameters of the identity shift, navigating the spaces and places in which the identity shift is situated, and negotiating the temporal schedules that structure the performance of the shift. These factors are necessary across vacation experiences to create the flexible mental space for identity change.

4

Objects and Identity

Tanya, Jeff, and Jane return from a shopping trip at the market in Xi'an's tourist center. They go straight to their shared room and dump everything out on the bed. They spread everything out, inspecting the items as they go, reexamining their purchases. They then begin the process of showing each other what they bought and explaining where it is going to end up when they get home. Tanya bought a silk runner to give her mother for the family dinner table. It is in her mother's favorite shade of green. She bought a pair of chopsticks and teacup that she will give to a friend and some cheap paper fans that she can hand out to anyone she has forgotten. Finally, she pulls out a silk dress that she had tailored to fit her. She already plans to wear it to her brother's wedding and had it made especially for this occasion. Saying how excited she is for the wedding, she goes to try the dress on.

It is then Jeff's turn to show off his finds. He had an ivory stamp made with his initials. He bought several more bootleg copies of American movies and television shows to add to the collection that he is slowly amassing during his time in China, where they can be bought for a fraction of the original price. He found some fake ivory carvings he will display on his bedroom bookcase and some prints of Chinese landscapes that he plans to hang in his home office. He is not worried about how he will get everything home because he brought an extra, empty suitcase with him to China to fill with his souvenirs.

Jane then pulls out her favorite find; a jade bangle bracelet. She had been looking for one since they arrived and finally found one that was not too expensive but nice enough for what she wanted. She also found some chrysanthemum tea that blooms into a flower when put in hot water, which she is excited to share with her grandmother. Last, she pulls out a box of decorative painted chopsticks, explaining she does not know who it is for yet but that she will find someone to give it to. Tanya and Jeff both comment on how much they like it and say they will go back to the market tomorrow to get one for themselves.

The previous chapters discuss three representative vacations: beach vacations, tourism, and stay-at-home. These three types hold much in common. It is impossible to analyze in depth every kind of vacation people take because the individually satisfying nature of the experience means that the opportunities are almost infinite. It is possible, however, to extract structural similarities from different experiences to recognize the patterns among them. In the following chapters, I draw from these three types as well as additional experiences written up in vacation blogs to identify the cognitive patterns found among vacationers in the manipulation of identity. The following three chapters address how people use objects, space, and time to blend in or delimit aspects of their everyday life from their special vacation time.

The activities actors engage in, places they visit, and objects they surround themselves with not only create the mental space for a vacation but also highlight the relationship between practice and cognitive identity formation. Carrying out actions that one would not normally do creates a contrast, marking this time as exceptional to routine, daily existence.[1]

Patterns of identity change persist across substantively different situations, and thus people employ similar mechanisms regardless of the type of vacation they take. Participating in established or favored practices before, during, and after the occasion emphasizes the experiential foundation of constructing an internally coherent and externally discernable identity shift. This chapter examines the objects people surround themselves with, either in an intentional and instrumental way or inadvertently, that support flexibility in the organization of identities.

When getting away from it all individuals must negotiate their connections to home and their presentation of self to create and sustain a personally meaningful and externally validated identity. This process is inherently social because people use shared symbols, rituals, and systems of meaning to create boundaries, but at the same time it is individual because people pick and choose, embrace, and drop connections to fashion their identities. Vacations offer an excellent basis for a discussion of cognitive boundary work because they are created specifically by drawing distinctions between everyday life and time off. People must choose how they wish to connect to or disconnect from day-to-day experience to fashion their trip.[2]

Activities and objects help actors create these mental boundaries and highlight the relationship between practice and cognitive identity formation. Behavior serves a dual function in experientially reinforcing identity for the individual and externally corroborating it with others. Packing bags for a trip, buying and wearing particular outfits, or indulging in an extra drink or dessert allow the vacationer to create identities defined by facets of difference from everyday ones.[3] These behaviors are "sociomental"[4] signposts experientially underpinning their temporary identity shift.

Individuals construct and manage mental divisions between facets of self. These cognitive boundaries are then reinforced in practice through interaction with objects, enacting behaviors, and repeating routines. This is all part of a process of identity integration or segmentation.[5] While not everyone integrates and segments identities to the same degree, the practice itself is commonplace. Some people make strong efforts to mark off their vacations and separate them from their everyday lives, and others more willingly let the two overlap. At the same time, actors integrate and segment identities differently across circumstances. One would not necessarily always combine identities or always keep them separated, and it is not always possible. Different vacations and different objectives elicit different priorities. As structure and content vary, so too do aims and desires.

This chapter focuses on the objects people use and interact with while on vacation to construct and project identity. Clothes, accessories, souvenirs, and the ephemera of everyday life travel with people and help create identity shifts by facilitating the performance of a particular facet of self. Objects also talk about the self to others by showing observers how a person imagines him- or herself to be and in turn how to be treated.

Objects and Identities

For both sides, the visitors and the visited, culture is represented in physical forms. Much of tourism is composed of objects that are invested with symbolic meaning.[6] Vacationers actively use props in an instrumental way to generate personal conceptions of identity.[7] Props are critical to understanding and communicating identity because they convey encoded messages about a person or place to others who view them. Cultures, then, travel with objects. The symbols of a home culture move into a vacation through the clothes, books, cameras, games, and other items, both necessary and optional, people bring with them. They also travel home from the vacation in the form of souvenirs and mementos of a place.

George Herbert Mead argues that individuals develop a self that is inherently social by taking the role of others, or looking at themselves as they imagine others do. People achieve "self consciousness" by taking on the attitudes of others and imagining how they will respond to their actions. The self is shaped not only in interaction with others but in *anticipation* of how others will respond. Mead observes that, in addition to other people, objects can potentially spur human action in a similar way. People can engage in a kind of anticipatory role taking with nonhuman entities. A chair, for example, "invites" a person to sit on it, or a bed "invites" a person to lie down.[8] The objects around us therefore "call out" responses from us. Mead argues that if an individual is capable of taking the role of other people in interactions, he or she can also take the attitude of the chair. Although Mead does not elaborate on the potential for interactions with things other than other people, this potential suggests that objects are also important to consider in understanding the constitution of the self.[9]

Objects, then, influence the way people see us and the ways we are able to show ourselves to others. They mold the socially created self by offering both opportunities and limitations to the presentation of self.[10] Tourists almost inevitably bear the physical markers of travel, whether intentional or not. Throughout the vacation experience individuals surround themselves with items such as clothes, photographs, cameras, and accessories that shape how they perceive themselves and how others see them. When people wear or carry these items they serve as interactional hooks[11] that mark the tourists as tourists, mediate how the tourists are perceived by the people around them, and in turn, mediate tourist interactions. Bodily display of the visible signs of a tourist ensures the tourist will be treated as a visitor by locals and a fellow traveler by other tourists—to either associate with or distance themselves from.

Clothes powerfully convey identity. Dressing in a way that confirms one is on vacation is an outwardly oriented strategy in defining identity and soliciting the support of others in maintaining it.[12] In part, this is achieved through anticipated responses of others to the way an individual is presenting him- or herself. A particular style of dress announces identity to others, and people usually respond in a way that supports it. Dressing in a certain way cues others to how a person wishes to be perceived and treated, the way that supports his or her desired identity. When Marissa wears shorts and flip-flops to happy hour during her staycation instead of the usual slacks and button-down she wears on workdays, she is showing everyone around that she is taking the day off. Or when Selena, a stay-home vacationer who cannot help but stop into her lab on her day off, wears shorts and a baseball cap, she hopes to communicate to others through her casual dress that she is not there to get involved in extended office business.

Maria describes how she changes from her more formal dress back home, where she works as an office executive, to a more casual style that matches her new environment in Hawaii: "I put on what I want, when I want. I rarely wear a bra [*laughs*]. Hang loose, right? And just—I wear little short dresses a lot of the time, just kinda very casual. Just be more free and easygoing." At the beach she can choose to be more casual, comfort-able, sexy, or suggestive, and she can do it on her own schedule. Of course, it is more practical to wear casual things at the beach, things that can get dirty and are not too hot, but there is nothing inherent to the beach in not wearing a bra, or showing her body off a little more, or wearing a floral print. It is a socially driven choice. Being "free and easygoing" is repre-sented by the clothes, the feeling they give her, and the responses she gets from observers.

The interactive potential of objects assists in the process of segmenta-tion and integration of identities. Particular clothes can be used to elicit internal and external responses in support of desired identities. Maria wears clothes she could not wear during her daily life at home, helping separate work and play. At the same time, people who see her sitting on the beach relaxing in her casual dress can get a pretty good idea of her situational identity without a lot of effort put forth on her part.

Jeff, a college student, presents a more extreme, yet illustrative ex-ample. He intended to segment identities as much as possible to make his highly anticipated trip to China special. To achieve this he bought a new version of everything he needed for his journey, so he would bring as little as possible from home with him. He says, "Everything I have with me is new, . . . I mean, from my white T-shirts and my, like, ExOfficio underwear to my suitcase and my shorts and my shoes and my hat. It was all in prep-aration for the trip." Objects have the capacity to invoke nonpresent peo-ple and places, and Jeff made a very specific choice not to bring items that would remind him of home. At the same time, he surrounds himself with special, "travel-friendly" items, many of which have been marketed to be uniquely associated with travel.

The demarcation of everyday items as being specifically for travel highlights this phenomenon. Underwear is an everyday need, but ExOfficio underwear is designed to be quick drying and "long wearing," so a person can wash it in a sink and have it ready to wear again before long. The practical necessity of travel-friendly underwear is questionable, but it is useful in that it helps Jeff establish some difference from his everyday life through an object that has been given associations with travel.

Vacation styles of course differ depending on the location and purpose of the trip. Appearance is a way of demonstrating membership in a particular group, and by dressing in a specific way people can demonstrate their allegiance to a particular identity. Maria embraces a beach-themed look with her casual dress and lack of bra, dressing to display a specific type of casual identity. In Hawaii, clothing and accessories of an island style were worn by visitors who had little connection to the islands other than a one- or two-week vacation. This style includes bright floral aloha prints, leis with real and fake flowers, sandals and flip-flops, shorts, and T-shirts. Women often wore fresh or artificial hibiscus flowers in their hair, purchasable at the ubiquitous souvenir shops near the beach, and men wore brightly colored aloha-print shirts. The style is meant to convey a feeling of easygoing informality for men and exotic femininity for women. Couples and entire families dressed in matching aloha-print dresses, slacks, and T-shirts embraced the role of being "on vacation together in Hawaii." Contrasting these people on vacation with the office workers going about their day in dress shirts, slacks, and more covered bodies again demonstrates how these clothes are used for a particular situational identity.

In China people similarly wore trip-appropriate clothes, but instead of the bright colors and casual styles of the beach, clothing often conveyed a sense of adventurousness. With heavy-duty walking boots or sneakers, passport bags, old or sturdy clothes, and backpacks, visitors conveyed an image of the explorer, even though they had traveled to an urban metropolis.

While travel-friendly clothes, fanny packs, backpacks, brand-new sneakers, suitcases, and resort wear may seem the result only of function—one is traveling, so one needs a suitcase—they nonetheless are crucial to constructing identities. First, they help people see themselves as vacationers as they don the clothes and accessories of travel. These items usually differ in some way from everyday wear, if only in outward design, and offer an experiential reminder of changed situations. Wearing the loose dresses and losing the bra help Maria feel she is a vacationer in a Hawaii, in a way different from wearing an old pair of shorts. It reinforces her temporary identity shift. Similarly, certain "realm specific" objects[13] that will be used only during travel reinforce the sense of difference necessary for that identity shift. Instructions for getting by such as maps, guidebooks, and language dictionaries are needed only when outside one's everyday environment. People have an interactive relationship with these objects because they use them as both props in their identity performance and essential guides to get through their trip.[14] Similarly, travel-size toiletry bottles, portable alarm clocks, passports, plug adaptors, and converters are exclusively used during travel and reinforce for vacationers the new realm into which they have moved.

These items aid identity construction by communicating to others who a person is. People may assign personal importance to what they wear or carry, or these items may be convenient for a location, but nonetheless perceptions shape identifications. Objects specifically associated with vacations or travel are interactional hooks, and wearing or carrying them marks individuals in the eyes of others regardless of the intention when putting them on. Wearing a camera around your neck tells other people you are a tourist. The camera therefore helps define the traveler's social identity by communicating this piece of information about him or her to others who are observing.

This also works for stay-homers looking for ways to segment vacation identities from everyday ones. Wearing clothes that matched whatever they were doing that day meant variety and options as they moved between different experiences on different days and allowed them to dress in the intention for the day. While people at the beach tended to dress for the beach every day, and people in China usually dressed every day from a tourist-friendly wardrobe, the dress and appearance of stay-homers had more potential to vary depending on the activities of the day, because their activities were those of a longer vacation but on a shorter basis. A trip to the beach meant sandals and sun hats one day, and a trip to a museum later in the week meant comfortable shoes.

Obvious markers from home have a similar outcome in signaling identity. They show that someone is an outsider or visitor and shape the social self, because they influence how people will interact with them. People see the camera, assume a person is a tourist, and treat him or her as a tourist. They use these objects as visual cues to assign a social identity to others. These objects are therefore a nonhuman part of an interaction that signal how a person should be perceived.[15] Wearing sneakers and a passport bag may be functional when touring a foreign city, but they will also mark the tourist in the eyes of others who do not use such items in their workaday lives. Observers will instantly know the individual is a tourist and treat him or her as such.

In this way, objects such as clothes and accessories serve as the markers of travel that help impose an identity on people and influence what their interactions will be like. These interactions can be either positive or negative. Looking like a tourist can mark one as a target for pickpockets or scams. Similarly, prices may be raised for a tourist and lowered for a local. Or tourists can be the target of marketing. On the streets of Waikiki, vendors aggressively sell day trips to passersby, focusing on tourists and ignoring locals. All such interactions are based on purely visual cues that tourists give off through their clothing and the items they carry. Stay-home vacationers going on a day trip to the beach or city could have much the same experience, because they would temporarily don the clothes appropriate to the environment they are visiting, similar to being mistaken for a tourist in one's own city by a shopkeeper or wait staff when taking a day off to sightsee.

Alternatively, there can be benefits to being seen as a visitor or an outsider. Especially if a destination is particularly dependent on tourist dollars and the happiness of tourists is a financial benefit. In being understood as outsiders to a location, tourists may be given some slack in attending to local norms or rules. While this ignorance of local expectations can be one of the things that draw locals' ire to vacationers as they innocently or intentionally ignore local expectations, visitors can get away with breaking rules in ways that locals cannot. The amount of slack a person is given depends on how different they are. An American in Hawaii is expected to follow certain rules that a Japanese visitor to Hawaii might not be aware of, and Americans in China often are assumed by locals to be almost completely incapable of taking care of themselves. The difference here is stark between the tourists' self-understanding of being accomplished travelers and the locals' perceptions of them as not being able to do anything for themselves.

Others are obliged to dress in ways more dictated by local norms or mores. Dress is not always a matter of fulfilling personal wishes for self-presentation; in some situations travelers encounter local cultural expectations of self-presentation. While people do not always attend to these rules and sometimes rely on their outsider status to ignore them, sometimes norms are so strong they cannot be avoided. This in itself can strengthen a sense of differentiation in identity when the local norms being adhered to are very different from one's everyday life. Women traveling in Muslim countries, for example, who wish to respect local norms cover themselves with long-sleeve shirts, long pants, and scarves. This can be a strong experiential switch for Western women not accustomed to being obliged to present themselves in this way. It also demonstrates the importance of clothes in shaping others' perceptions and reactions and of the choices people make when deciding how to present themselves in a foreign environment. A tourist recounted a story to me of traveling in Egypt and taking a camel ride in the desert. A group of Frenchwomen were also present who chose not to cover themselves and instead wore shorts and camisoles with thin straps. The shorts presented modesty problems when the women climbed onto the surly camels. In response they were criticized and laughed at by the men who were leading the camels. The tourist women who had covered themselves did not receive the same treatment.

Others can also use objects associated with tourism to confer identity onto tourists; the things in an interaction mold the selves of the people in it.[16] Certain objects mark people as tourists, and then people respond to them as such. In a post on the now-defunct TravelPod travel blogging site, a tourist in Italy comments on her experience in Rome, "We liked the fountains, the Trevi, the Piazza Navona, Bernini, but they are so overrun with tourists, pushy foreigners, hordes of them following various umbrellas, giant flowers, radio antennas with colorful scarves." She is referring to the habit of tour guides in particularly crowded places to use some easily identifiable and unique object to keep their groups together and prevent members from getting lost. The use of these objects by the tour guides instantly tells this woman that the people following are tourists. The flowers and scarves confer on the group members a social identity of tourist, in particular a mass tourist, and one that is in need of special tending to. They give away the social status of those in the group to all who observe. Even a local who somehow joined the group, maybe hosting a family member who is in town, would get assigned the same identity by an observer.

Stay-homers draw on this to construct their vacation identities. Objects that are evocative of vacation time shape the social self of stay-homers. The consumerist marketing that developed around vacationers discussed in Chapter 3 and the compulsion to buy realm-specific objects can help them replicate vacation experiences while at home and reinforce identities. Buying pool and barbecue gear, splurging on an ample wine supply, buying trinkets at a local festival, or investing in new patio furniture evoke the experiences and attitudes associated with vacations and help constitute a brief shift in identity. These objects are not only some of the material things that make up a vacation; they "carry the attitude"[17] of vacationing. They can be strategically used to cultivate the attitudes and dispositions of a vacationer. Stay-homers making use of these objects in their vacation activities and performance are reminded or prompted for the ideal identity they wish to reach. The objects help them act in certain ways and therefore think of themselves in certain ways.

Bringing Home into the Vacation

In addition to travel-specific items, things brought from home, intentionally or unintentionally, have a similar effect. The boundaries of an identity are drawn by these kinds of signs, but similar to tourist objects that mark someone as an outsider, not all signs that communicate information about an individual are intentionally worn. In their everyday familiarity, people may disattend to objects they routinely wear or use, but these objects are still signs that communicate identity or membership in a particular group to the people interacting with them.[18] "Home" is usually written all over tourists' bodies and demeanor whether they are aware of it or not. A brand of jeans, a particular haircut, a style of shoes, or even the color of a shirt can give clues about otherness to people observing. On vacation, people are surrounded by innumerable objects from home that convey information about their attitudes and dispositions, and these objects organize the self and define identities through the actions other people take in relation to them, because they tell other people that one is a visitor. In China, for example, Chinese Americans were instantly identifiable to local Chinese by the American clothes they wore. Even without speaking or otherwise identifying themselves, their clothes conferred a social identity on these travelers.

The framing that defines a vacation as special means that these everyday items often get overlooked for their mundanity during a time of novelty, but they still compose a large part of the traveler's immediate environment. Electronics, clothes, books, and toiletries travel into the vacation with people, often without thought. They unintentionally surround vacationers with reminders of home and bring elements of it into a vacationer's trip. The way that these objects travel into a vacation demonstrates that travel is more than a binary relationship between home and away, the extraordinary and the ordinary, or hedonism and rules.[19] For many of my respondents, the idea of intentionally bringing things from home on a brief one- or two-week vacation sounded silly, but in reality they remained surrounded by these basics. When asked if he brought anything with him to China to remind him of home, Roger responded, "Not on purpose [*laughs*]. I have a laptop with several thousand pictures on it. But I didn't bring the laptop to have the pictures." Nevertheless, they traveled with him, along with the laptop itself and all the additional files it held.

Objects like laptops and cell phones serve more and more as traveling repositories of the self. These "totems" bring aspects of the everyday self into the vacation and conjure aspects of self.[20] Storing pictures, music, photographs, stories, work assignments, and games, they encapsulate one's interests and history. Entire music collections can be easily transported and played, as well as movies and television shows enjoyed at home. In China, as travelers who were previously strangers got to know each other better, they would regularly share photographs from home that were on their computers. Scrolling through images of friends, pets, apartments, parties, and past vacations conjured aspects of the self not currently on display on the vacation.

Laptops and other electronics were brought along as seemingly inseparable items from everyday life, and other objects were also used to conjure aspects of self from home and integrate them into the vacation in an intentional way. Jess, an American mother in her forties, brought a pound of Starbucks coffee with her because she was worried she would not be able to find it in China and felt she could not go without. Sarah, a nineteen-year-old college student, brought her pillow with her, and Carliegh, a German college student, kept a small travel alarm with her that she left set to Berlin time.

For stay-homers, being surrounded by everyday items could not be avoided or overlooked. The objects of everyday life were all around them. While they may have tried to introduce some difference into their experience by buying new items that carried with them the significance of vacationing, the majority of their environment was still formed by the items that made up their daily experience.

Souvenirs and Gifts

Perhaps one of the best examples of the importance of objects as nonhuman interactants in constructing the social self is the purchase and distribution of souvenirs and gifts. The heavily commodified nature of tourism allows individuals to easily transform their trips into objects and images that encapsulate their experience.[21] These mementos signal where a person has been and what he or she has done, and they make a small bit of the temporary into something permanent. These items bought both to keep and to give away were the physical, shareable objects of the trip that travelers would intentionally use to shape perceptions upon their return. The items were not taken lightly. The purchase of souvenirs meant bringing someone from home into mind and imagining his or her response. Their distribution meant sharing a representation of a bit of the self.

When someone purchases a souvenir, culture becomes "detached" from place and travels with the object, out of its original context and into a new one. In this sense, traveling objects undermine the "fixity of culture" to a particular place.[22] An aspect of culture, or at least its representation, associated with a place moves with the item. This includes making the intangible tangible and the inaccessible accessible. "Culture," an amorphous concept that people encounter when they travel, is objectified, made tangible and portable. Souvenirs, then, bring the significance of a particular place home with the traveler and, in a way, contract the distance from a vacation destination through their integration into everyday life. They allow cultures to move in an accessible format that can be held in one's hand or placed on one's shelf. A hallmark of the souvenir is to reproduce things in miniature form.[23] A tiny Eiffel Tower or Mount Rushmore re-creates the grand into something that can be acquired and brought home. As one man who went to Hawaii with a group of friends said in a post on his TravelPod blog, "After we all get home we can get together, eat macadamia nuts, drink Kona coffee, reminisce, and enjoy it all over again." These distinctly Hawaiian foods will be a tangible, sensory reminder of their trip when they gather at home.

Souvenirs come in two forms: objects that are specifically bought and purchased with the intention of being reminders of place and items to which people assign their own meaning. While many souvenirs are mass produced, others are everyday objects brought from their original location to home as mementos. These items are given new, personalized meanings and integrated into a narrative of identity that reflects the trip and the person.[24] This transforms the original meanings assigned to an object, because it is invested with reminders of past identity. A glass surreptitiously taken from a favored restaurant or a coaster from a bar is not initially intended as a souvenir but made into such by individuals who picked it out and saved it as a reminder of a trip. Similarly, natural objects such as a shell, sea glass, or piece of volcanic rock taken from a beach and put on a shelf at home are transformed through their travel from small elements of a more vast natural landscape to representations of an entire experience. When singled out and placed in a new context as representative of a place they become vested with symbolic value. All the meanings and associations of the beach are imparted to a shell as a synecdoche for the beach. Still other items have a particular everyday use value in their original environment that is transformed when the traveler chooses to keep it and take it home as a souvenir. A foreign coin or a bus ticket is thereby transformed from currency into a keepsake. The monetary value is disregarded because it becomes irrelevant to the object's new meaning.

Items people acquire may not be evocative of a particular place but instead create memories of the people with whom the experience was shared. Their association with the trip generates memories of both the experience and the people with whom one shared it. These items are meaningful regardless of the destination or type of vacation. A shell taken from the beach on a day trip to the Jersey shore is just as evocative as a shell from Waikiki. Gina describes a silhouette portrait of her two girls that she bought while visiting a local fair during their staycation:

> We bought [it]; we didn't do it purposefully to remember the vacation, but I'm sure we always will because of it. . . . At the Kutztown Festival, they had this man who using scissors . . . cut . . . a shadow picture, like a profile. So . . . Kelly sat on Jenna's lap, and he cut . . . out their profile, and we put it in a frame. . . . And we bought one for ourselves and two to give as gifts, so we'll always have that to remember the vacation.

Other items are manufactured and purchased with the sole intent of being souvenirs. They have no other value or purpose and serve no other function than to tell stories of a different place.[25] Such commercially produced souvenirs are made to represent aspects of local culture, or some idealized culture that may or may not have existed in the past, and to retain that same meaning after they have been purchased and taken home. The importance of the role these items serve can be seen in the ubiquity of souvenir shops in any location that has been designated for tourists. Souvenir shops in Hawaii are filled with items that signify local cultural stereotypes, many intended to be novelty or display items: grass skirts and coconut bras, carved tiki statues, leis made of fake flowers or shells, and many food items involving macadamia nuts or Kona coffee. This is also demonstrated in souvenirs available for purchase in China, most of which are replications of locally used objects not intended for actual use, such as chopsticks, teapots, hand-tailored silk clothing, hairclips, fans, musical instruments, paint brushes, carved seals with Chinese characters, Chairman Mao paraphernalia, and when I was there, anything with the Beijing Olympics logo.

While these may be intended to be representative of local life, many of the souvenir versions that tourists buy are different from what the residents actually use. Vacationers themselves were often uninterested in the actual objects of daily use available in grocery and department stores and instead preferred the replicas sold in the tourist shops. While many Chinese locals do of course use chopsticks, teapots, and hairclips, the ones used in everyday life are not the ones sold as keepsakes in the markets. The special versions sold to tourists in markets were usually more "Chinese" than the everyday objects sold elsewhere. They included more detailing, more color, and more decorations meant to represent the culture. Tea and chopstick sets could be purchased in tourist markets and came decorated in colorful styles and patterns representative of something Chinese, but they were not the same as the functional utilitarian items local residents would use in their homes.

These souvenirs re-create a time and place for the tourist, because when they are placed in their intended context back home, not as household items or items of use, they will be things to look at. In this sense, the manifest content of the object itself is not what is important. That the souvenir is a cup from which to drink or a fan to cool oneself with is secondary. Rather, its significance is in its ability to bring to mind a particular time and place once it has been brought home. This is the souvenir's essential purpose.[26] The significance of shopping for and acquiring these items is demonstrated by the habit of vacationers in China showing off their haul to fellow tourists after returning from a shopping trip. They would participate in something of a ritual, calling those present to come see, laying their new purchases out on a bed or a tabletop, and showing the people present what they got. They would point out particular features they liked, such as a nicely painted motif, or a characteristic that differentiated it from a nearly identical item someone else had bought. As part of the ritual, they would discuss who back home was going to be the recipient or whether they would keep it for themselves, sometimes even specifying where in their house it would go once they got back. Travelers reported a similar ritual of laying out all their purchases once they returned home to show to family or just look at once again themselves. Jeff reports:

> The first thing I'm going to do when I get back is unpack my souvenirs and then go over them with my mom. Because I always buy a ton of souvenirs. Like, every souvenir I see, I buy it. And I always—

because everyone wants something, and I don't know what they want—... me and my mom always go through it and think of who I'm giving what and what she wants out of it all and what I really want. And then we'll go over pictures together. . . . Normally I get back at two in the morning, and we'll stay up until, like, five looking at all my pictures and souvenirs and everything.

Jeff anticipates not only the response of recipients to his gifts; he anticipates this ritual he will enact with his mother. These items play a crucial role when he reconstitutes his identity for his mother.

Souvenirs are purchased for two purposes: either to be kept for oneself, or to be given away to others. These objects are important, then, in creating both personal narratives of the self and the social self in interaction. They highlight important events and activities and give tangible evidence, to oneself and others, that one has gone somewhere and done something. When kept for oneself, they are integrated into daily life and used as personal reminders of an experience. They give physical form to the experiences that make up the salient events in one's personal biography.[27] Returning home with a souvenir allows people to integrate the exceptional into their everyday life and reflect on it.

Additionally, souvenirs, as reminders of time and place, encapsulate the identity taken on during that period, which is then shared with others. When people give souvenirs as gifts they confirm their identity by presenting it in object form.[28] Buying a gift for someone not only shows loved ones that they were thought of while away but also involves sharing an identity with someone who was not there to witness it.

A fundamental element for identity construction is that the purchaser conjures up an idea of the receiver in his or her mind and imagines what the response will be. Buying a gift for someone contributes to the construction of identity by both setting up a future interaction, when the gift is given, and looking back on past interactions to determine what the recipient would like. We set the stage for an interaction with other people whose responses we can anticipate.[29] The souvenir is an intermediary by which individuals can create future interactions that will narrate and demonstrate their trip to others. The object itself ties action in the present with interactions in the future and therefore helps shape the self through the anticipation of the receiver's response.

Buying gifts involves thinking about people on the basis of prior experiences with them, imagining what they would appreciate, what their personalities are like, and what they might need. A carefully bought gift can require devoting a good deal of attention to the receiver. When shopping, the giver often envisions the receiver and the story that will be told of the trip that goes along with the object. Luke illustrates how evocative shopping can be when he bargains with a salesperson over a novelty Mao pocket watch that he noticed and wants to buy for a friend. "I ended up paying fifty [yuan] for it, and I tried getting it down, tried getting it down. But they could see me holding it, rolling it in my hand thinking, 'Oh, Liam's really going to like that.'" Luke mentally conjures up his friend as he sees this trinket and imagines his response. Betty comments on the amount of time she spends thinking about others while she is away:

> [What reminds] me of home? Shopping. Because I have to think, "Chris is thirty-one; what size T-shirt is he going to wear?" And I have two grandchildren that live in California, and that's the biggest thing that I spend time on. . . . I kept thinking, "How can I go back without getting something for Joe and Jenny?" That's their names. And I must have made four or five trips to the Muslim Quarter [a district of Xi'an with a large market for tourists], and I walked through and walked through, and that really made me think about home.

People like Betty spend a lot of time thinking about what to get others and what they will like, making multiple trips to find the right thing or always keeping an eye out for something a particular person might want.

Shoppers take on the role of the other to imagine what friends and relatives back home might want and how they will respond to the gift. The shoppers speculate on what they will like, what they might be impressed by, or what they could find amusing. In addition to the pocket watch, Luke spent several hours looking for the perfect wok to give to his brother in cooking school back in the United Kingdom, and Linda spent the first week of her trip searching for the right Chinese-motif cloth for a friend who enjoyed quilting. Travelers would also speculate on what those back home would not respond well to. Roger explains that he has chosen not to buy anything in China for his parents because he did not think it would meet their upscale tastes. His relies on his prior knowledge of their attitudes and dispositions to determine that the knickknacks widely available in the Chinese tourist markets would not meet their standards:

> I haven't bought my parents anything. Mostly because it's just crap. You know, they have crap here. And I don't mind having some

crap that looks kind of fun, but I'm not going to buy my parents that. Maybe I will buy them a little joke that costs nothing, just as a thought. But they also specifically said, "Do not buy us anything here," and part of that is because they know it's just crap, and I can't buy anything that they're really going to love.

Roger is concerned about the way that a cheap gift would reflect on his self. He anticipates that the items he sees will not be appreciated by his parents, and he does not want to invite the discredit that a cheap gift would bring. He also distinguishes between giving something cheap as a "joke" gift to his parents versus giving them something that could be considered cheap but doing so with sincerity. The latter is not possible in his view.

People buy two kinds of gifts for others: specific items they have put thought into and generic gifts, usually for larger groups of people. The former, requiring more effort, tends to combine the identities and interests of both the giver and the receiver, and the latter is more impersonal. Putting thought into a good gift shows the receiver that he or she was kept in mind while away and that the giver made an effort to find something that would please. Owing to the amount of work and intimacy this involves, most seek these specific, thoughtful gifts for only a small number of people.

The more general gifts to distribute to others do not receive the same degree of attention and thought as the personalized ones. Shopping for these items was not evocative of particular individuals but of a generalized group that needs to be seen to in order to make up for one's absence. While the personalized gifts take into account a mutual consideration of the identities of both giver and receiver, the more impersonal gift is used in a more unidirectional manner to share a memento of a particular experience. Jackie says:

> Since I've been here I've bought presents for everybody. But I've been quite lucky because I've bought a lot of Beijing [Olympics] stuff. Like, there's been Beijing stuff in all the stores here. So I bought Beijing pencil cases for the kids and stuffed them with Beijing pens, pencils, and loads of sweets and stuff like that. And I've bought some T-shirts. I've bought cushion covers. I've bought some table runners as presents . . . and two silk dresses. And quite a few silk bags and purses. And I've been buying bracelets for people and putting them inside a silk bag or bag with Chinese writing on it or something like that. And chopsticks.

She was fortunate that the Olympics were taking place in China at the same time as her visit and she was able to buy something many people would find interesting without having to put too much thought into it. In addition, silk products, cheap and readily available in any tourist shop, are an instant signifier of China, as well as chopsticks, and of course, anything with Chinese characters on it. Rather than having to spend time deliberating on specific gifts, Jackie is able to buy these mass-produced items that quickly bring to mind the time and place of China and satisfy a large group of friends and family. While her friends and family receiving them may not have gotten the same level of attention from her, they were still remembered and included in the experience.

Upon return home, these souvenirs, even if kept for oneself, continue to shape the identities of the people who brought them back by communicating information to the people who see them. Most are displayed somewhere in the home, put on a shelf or in a special place in the house dedicated to displaying the objects of travel. Jackie has a specific room where she will put everything. "Most of the Chinese stuff I've bought I have got places for, because I've got a Chinese bedroom at home. My spare double room is where I keep all my Chinese stuff." Jeff has an office in his townhouse where he displays all his travel mementos. When integrated into the home upon return these objects serve to hone social status by communicating information about prior travel experience and locations visited.

Entering and Leaving

Interaction with objects also helps people prepare for a trip, gain new knowledge about a place, build excitement, know what to anticipate, or otherwise ease a transition, including returning home. Interactions with objects and the routines around them create mental boundaries around the vacation, or "brackets in time"[30] that mark off the temporal space. Stopping and then restarting the mail, packing and unpacking luggage, dropping off and picking up a pet with a pet sitter form the brackets within which the identity shift will take place.[31]

For many the trip to China was a once-in-a-lifetime experience that they devoted considerable time to preparing for in order to make the most of their trip. Linda did a lot of pretrip research, immersing herself in the possibilities of her destination before she even left. She bought tour books and maps of Chinese cities in the region she would be traveling to, read fiction books set in Xi'an, and did extensive reading on the internet.

Literature, guide books, websites, maps, and itineraries allowed her to indulge in some mental travel before she left home. Through preparatory work people can become aware of the parameters for their identities in advance. Through her reading Linda became quite familiar with her future environment and all the things she could do there, and she made lists of what she would see and do that would shape her days in the future. Before she left home she already had a detailed plan for all the museums and cultural sites she would visit and how she would fit them into her full itinerary. This work is emphasized for any trip that is particularly valued or unusual. Selena, who usually stays home for her vacations, had the opportunity to go to Puerto Rico for a friend's wedding. Because it was an unusual and highly valued event for her she prepared meticulously for her six-day trip, taking months to plan and days to pack. She explains, "I wanted to see as much as possible, since I don't really get the opportunity very often. And plus I was very excited, so I was always reading up on it and going, 'Oh, I can go here! I can go there!'"

On the other hand, people put less effort into bounding a vacation that is more routine or mundane. A once-in-a-lifetime trip has more significance and therefore is invested with more effort than a trip that is repeated often. To frequent travelers, the act in itself has less novelty. When asked how he prepared for his trip to Hawaii, Rick replies, "Just packed my stuff and left, really. That's about it. . . . I've been here lots of times. I pretty much know what I want to do before I get here." A lot of anticipatory planning was not necessary for him and probably would not be as interesting as it would be for a first-time visitor. Francine, another frequent vacationer in Hawaii, says about her preparation, "I come so often that I kind of have a routine. It's almost routine to me. I just throw everything in a suitcase." This is a very different experience from those who spend days making lists, shopping, and packing and unpacking their suitcases in anticipation of an exciting trip.

Pretrip shopping allows people to not only buy necessary items but also equip themselves with the props they need to live out their desired identity. Most respondents reported putting a lot of care into the items they brought with them, shopping for things they needed, carefully selecting the clothing they wanted with them, and creating detailed packing lists. Such shopping is effective not only for people who travel somewhere but also for those who stay home and seek a way to establish a sense of difference in their everyday environment. Part of one couple's staycation planning was buying items, similar to what they would use in a new place, to help them plan and discover their local environment. "We went to the bookstore and bought a guidebook for our area and a hiking trail guide-book for nature trail options. We live within commuting distance of Manhattan, but there are also plenty of places in New Jersey we had never been to and decided this was the time to discover them."[32] Much like Linda buying a guidebook for China to build her anticipation, this couple staying at home bought a guidebook of their local area in advance so they could plan new things to see and do.

Because the suitcase is particularly symbolic of travel and movement, it is not uncommon for travelers to put extensive attention into the details of packing. Packing and unpacking means interacting with the objects of travel at crucial points of the trip, and so they often received special attention, first while packing to leave, and then unpacking on arrival at the new destination. Then, in a complementary way, objects are returned to their permanent places while packing up to leave the vacation and unpacking one last time at home. This action that is singularly associated with travel is therefore an effective means of establishing and playing with the boundaries separating the vacation and day-to-day life. Some vacationers reported being reluctant to unpack and thus bring their experience to a close. Anna comments, "I usually wait a day until I unpack. 'Cause you're on vacation, and you come home, and all of a sudden you have to unpack and get back to your life. So I like to extend that a little bit and wait a day before I unpack." The association with travel gives her packed items a special significance. She makes a choice to keep her things in her suitcase for an extra day to extend the special feeling of vacation a little longer.

Luke also hesitates to unpack, but for different reasons. For him, unpacking is a chore associated with return home that he does not want to deal with. He just wants to get straight back to everyday life. "Unpacking usually takes about a week. Or a week and then I decide to unpack. I just leave it. Just fall straight back into the routine of things and feel like you never left." He associates his suitcase and the things in it with travel, so they are no longer relevant once he exits his trip.

> I guess one way of looking at it could be saying, like, as soon as you're back, you just don't need to look at the time you spent away, which is what is still in your bag. So that just goes to one side, so when you're eventually forced to do it, it's not like you're unpacking; it's just like you're doing laundry, and it's not anything related to the trip still. It's just that you have a bunch of stuff in this box, and you have to spring-clean it. As soon as you get back, it's not

your vacation anymore, and you don't do stuff vacation-like. There's no down-briefing at the end of my vacations. It's just like, okay, let's get back to work.

While it may be just an excuse for not getting around to unpacking his bag, for Luke these physical reminders of vacation become less important over time. Once the associations with travel have receded, he turns his attention back to putting away what have once again become everyday items.

Packing and planning can be an exciting way to build anticipation, but it can also be an additional task that adds stress to the experience. For Gina this was a benefit of the stay-home experience. She was not limited to the select items that she had chosen to bring with her on a trip. This was especially advantageous as a mother of four:

> I felt like it was—it was nice to be on vacation but have your own home amenities, you know what I mean? Just to have your own stuff. To not have to—you know, if I want to wear the same pair of pants again, I can just go wash them. If it's bad weather, I don't have to worry that I have to wear the same jeans all week long because I only brought shorts. Those kinds of things. Less planning, and when you have little kids, there's a lot of packing involved that is really overwhelming, with, you know, how many diapers do I take? You know, do I take shampoos, and do I take four pairs of clothes for one day or two pairs of clothes? In that sense it was just a lot less stressful.

Not having to pack eliminated the stress of having to worry in advance about bringing the right things with her, not having something she needed, or not bringing enough of something.

Electronic Devices and Home

The now near ubiquity of electronic devices makes them a necessary consideration when understanding the role of objects as facilitators of interactions or even as interactants themselves. Their capacity to draw people who are far away into the immediate present makes them particularly important in the shaping of identities while away from home and increasingly introduces a hindrance to identity flexibility.[33]

Sitting on the beach with her friends, a young woman takes out her camera and turns on the video function. She points the device at each of her four companions and directs them to say hello and introduce themselves. When they all have finished she reviews what she has just recorded. She turns back to them with a dissatisfied look and instructs them all to do it again but more cheerfully. When they complain, she responds she is going to post the video to Facebook when they get back to their room and she wants it to be just right. They sigh, and one by one repeat everything they just said but with bigger smiles. Elsewhere, two men relax by the hotel pool. It is a very hot day and one jumps into the water to cool off. The other sits in a deck chair and starts playing with his smartphone. The man in the pool yells to his friend, "Are you letting her know that I'm floating around in the pool like an orca right now?" His friend responds, "No, but I will," and raises the phone to take a picture of him. The man in the pool pauses to pose for the shot, and his companion lets him know he is sending it to their mutual friend. A few moments later he laughs at her response.

The woman creating the video wants a positive, happy image of herself and her friends, and she makes sure they get it right before she shares it with the audience that will be viewing it in the near future on Facebook. Her friends become props in communicating her message effectively. The two men include in their fun a friend who is far away, momentarily drawing her into their vacation through the synchronous interaction that is made possible through the immediacy of texting. Both groups are managing presentations of self to an audience that is not present with them on their trip but observing nonetheless.

Advances in communication technologies have enhanced the abilities of people to connect with others across distances in space and time. The ubiquity of these communication devices also means that vacationers now have an additional nonpresent audience for their identity shifts. Because devices have made it possible to have meaningful interactions with others without physical copresence, they have effectively expanded the number and variety of generalized or specific others who influence the construction of self.[34] Individuals now actively imagine, interact with, and respond to individuals and groups who are nearby or far away. The potential for simultaneous interactions through phones, tablets, and computers means that individuals on vacation are creating an identity in response to others who are not physically present. People back home being so easy to reach enables making them an additional, distant audience familiar with the vacationer's actions. Instead of having to wait to return and retroactively reconstruct the experience, vacationers could present their self to this nonpresent group and modify it in real time. This is demonstrated by

Jeff's reluctance to wear the same shirt twice during his trip because "every day is a Facebook picture." These vacationers were very aware of friends and family back home who were only a phone call, social media post, or email away.

Today's communication technologies make the process of updating others easier and faster, but performing and presenting identity for an absent audience is not new. Tourist photography has long been performed and framed by those doing it for acquaintances at home who would see it in the future.[35] Choosing what to take a picture of, who to include in it, and what to include in the frame has been an effective method for sharing with others a specific story about what one did. Telephones similarly connected people to home, voluntarily or involuntarily. The nature of these communications was different, however. Although people certainly stayed in touch through postcards, letters, and long-distance phone calls, in the past the vacationer had more control over the exchange, and the one-way nature of the exchange ensured it would be limited.[36] Travelers would get in touch with home if and when they could find a phone. A phone in the hotel room would allow connection only while one was in the room. A call made from a pay phone could not be returned at all. Letters could be delivered to a hotel address if known, but the traveler would need to be there long enough to receive them. The traveler therefore had much more control over when and how often he or she would be contacted.

Today email and cell phones allow people back home equal and reciprocal opportunity to locate and communicate with those who are away. Wireless connections are increasingly available around the world, which creates the expectation in people left at home that one will reply to emails. Cell phones similarly allow ready access to the traveler, since they are usually carried at all times. It is no longer the case that someone must refrain from communicating with travelers until they are on the receiving end of a call. With this increased ease in communication comes an escalation in the implicit and sometimes explicit responsibility of the traveler to respond and keep in touch. This introduces an element of social control into the experience as "greedy"[37] institutions from home reach into the vacation and demand attention. Family, work, and friendship obligations pull people back into daily experience and prevent them from moving too far from the obligations of everyday life. Rather than waiting for people to return from their trip, obligations demand attention while people are away and become more and more difficult to evade.

This ease of connection can at once be a hindrance and a benefit. For someone experiencing homesickness or a bewildering foreign environment, effortless contact is welcome. Easy access to home shrinks the feeling of distance between people. Anna appreciates the internet while she is far away from home in China: "I think that one thing that is essential, that reminds me of home, is the internet. It makes me feel like I'm not completely detached from the States or my friends and family. Because I can contact them on email or Facebook." David, who feels a little isolated in China, echoes this as he sits in front of a computer and says to the entire room, "I love the internet! It's like my only connection to the outside world right now." The result is an experience of physical disconnection from home but with the possibility to remain mentally and socially integrated.

How people connect depends on the social relation and their personal inclination for the integration of work and play. In everyday life, individuals are always negotiating their social accessibility with groups of people, both online and in face-to-face communication. In day-to-day interaction we choose to make ourselves more available to some and less accessible to others. People establish a range of accessibility based on the nature of their relationships and their differing requirements and expectations.[38] People therefore draw different boundaries around whom they wish to speak with and whom they do not and what kind of news they wish to share when communicating with home while they are away. Some are happy to speak with friends and family while away, and parents will usually insist on keeping in touch with children not present on the trip. Others see a vacation as an opportunity to limit interaction with a particular family member who remains at home, and still others choose to focus all their attention on family accompanying them on vacation and so intentionally limit interactions with friends and acquaintances at home. Many like to leave work behind and cut off all interaction, but others check in with colleagues, perhaps sneaking off to answer emails while a spouse is not looking.

Communication technologies such as the internet and cell phones make maintaining connections with home easy for identity integrators, but they introduce complications for segmentors that must be managed. Steve expresses growing frustration with his girlfriend and parents back home when both insist on speaking with him every day of his vacation in China. He usually had several calls every day, at least one in the morning and one in the afternoon. For his loved ones back home, the call was an easy way to keep in touch and stay connected to him while he was far away, but for him the frequency of the calls became an intrusion on his trip:

If I don't call [my girlfriend], I can pretty much expect to get a phone call. But it's like I don't like to feel obligated. You know what I mean? Like, I want to call someone because I want to call them. I want someone to call me because they want to call me. Not because they feel like, "Oh, I have to talk to this person every day." And . . . because it's so new here, there's a lot of things that I want to see and do. It would be nice if I could have that kind of flexibility.

Steve's challenges demonstrate the tradeoffs people make when using devices to negotiate relations with people left at home. To some degree it is of course a choice whether to stay in touch with home, but it can come with costs if one chooses to separate too much from the people left behind. Steve resented the connections that kept him on the phone with home every day of his trip and prevented him from going out as much as he would have liked, but he chose to maintain the connections because they people who were allowed the most accessibility. Since having his cell phone made it so easy to locate him and talk, he remained accessible, and he felt he had to reciprocate. While he could have not answered the phone and waited to return their calls, or not returned their calls at all, he felt compelled to answer. Although he felt his everyday life was on pause, the expectations placed on him by others were not necessarily similarly on hold, and not responding would not have been acceptable to those loved ones to whom he had to return at the end of his trip. Steve realized that segmenting them more, as he desired to do, would have negative consequences when he returned, because they would be upset with him. His desire to create these boundaries around his vacation would then spill over into consequences in his everyday life whether he wished them to or not. His anticipation of the future influenced his actions in the present and encouraged him to answer the phone. In a cost-benefit analysis of the gains of segmenting identities, the advantages of completely taking off when on vacation become moderated by the disadvantages of alienating one's loved ones. Ultimately, he opted to call his girlfriend or be sure to answer the phone when she called because he wanted to have the relationship in good standing when he returned. In light of maintaining the commitments of his everyday self, his temporary freedoms lost out.

While Steve ultimately bent to his loved ones' expectations, others set firmer boundaries and did not allow the flexibility of communication devices to increase intrusions on their time. When in Hawaii, Maria demonstrates a true segmentor's attitude about communicating with home. She draws firm boundaries about communicating with home, and she expects friends and family to respect them. If they do not, she simply does not respond:

> Maria: When I'm on vacation or when I'm off, I always tell them, don't call me; I don't want to know anything until I get back, fine.
> Me: And they respect that?
> Maria: They do. You know, I have a friend, and she's texting me, but she knows I'm not going to answer. It's just like, I'm on vacation, don't bug me. . . . I am not answering any emails. I am not even checking emails or anything at all. No phones, no nothing. That's the way that I like vacations. No contact with home. Or work.

Maria enforces the strong boundary she draws between home and vacation. If people do not follow her wishes, she just ignores them. This is effective in part because her friend back home accepts it. She knows she will probably not get a response, even though she keeps sending text messages. Maria's boundary work is successful because she is resolute but also because the people on the other side respect her decision to segment, and their demands are not that urgent. In an effort to keep home and vacation separate, Jodi has a similar message for people back home:

> For me this is very much like, I'm on holiday, and unless something really awful happens and I can do something about it, then just leave me alone. And that's what I said to people. Because I've got quite a bad experience of being away when my dad died, and I sort of left details, contact details, but I said, look, unless someone's ill and it looks really awful and I can see them before they've died, then don't bother. Which is kind of a blunt statement, but it's sort of the frame of mind that I'm in at the moment.

People can also use their devices to help them set boundaries. To enforce the segmentation she sought and ensure that people complied, Jodi used the ease of technology as a tool. She wrote one email that detailed everything she had been doing and sent it to everyone who was interested in an update. This kept them involved in her trip and prevented them from feeling overlooked while also limiting her time spent communicating.

Setting an email away message is another tactic that tells colleagues one is out of the office for a set period and also offers a small vacation-specific ritual that sets the opening and close of the experience: setting the away message on the way out and removing it again upon return. A stay-home vacationer used this as a tactic to help reinforce for others that she was on vacation—despite remaining home: "Even though we weren't going anywhere, no one else knew that. We told our friends and family that we were going on vacation. We set vacation responses on our email and voicemail. We decided that computers and iPhones would be restricted to vacation-related activities. No checking of work emails was allowed."[39] She used the devices both to limit access (by not allowing herself or her family to use them to connect) and to create a feeling of break (by letting people know that she would be inaccessible for a time).

Disconnecting like this is easier for some than for others. Some use the ease of connecting as a tool to lessen their workload when they return. The accumulation of email, updates, and issues one has to deal with can be overwhelming and seem to negate the benefits of being away at all. For some, using a smartphone to check in with work while away can help keep this pileup to a minimum. Gina explains that her husband kept his phone with him at all times during their staycation, as he does on any other vacation the family takes. "I mean, my husband always had the Blackberry with him, but he does that on any vacation. We could be, you know, five million miles away, so that's ever present. But it makes life for him a little easier when he returns to work to stay on top of things like email." For others who have trouble disconnecting from work, phones and email allow them to easily check in from afar. For Connie, a high level of responsibility at work as well as big events going on in her organization kept her mind at least in part directed toward what was going on in her absence:

> Well, I missed it at first, so I wanted to make sure everything was going smoothly. We have summer camp in full swing, so we have fifty-four kids there every day. And we've had a lot of turnover with personnel lately. We just finished this major renovation and hired a new artistic director and hired the new managing director. He started three days ago. So lots of turnover, and I just want to make sure they're doing it my way. You know what I mean?

Communication technologies have made it easier for those like Connie, who "can't stop" working, to continue to connect while away. Linda, the traveler discussed earlier in the chapter who spent a great deal of time preparing for and thinking about her trip, ended up contacting work while she was away. Her coworkers incorrectly completed an assignment that she was ultimately responsible for, and she decided to do it herself and then email it back to them. She did not mind being contacted by work, because "they messed up." She said, "You know, I really want the opportunity to straighten it out. I don't want it to stay messed up for the entire time I'm away." In the same way that Linda was flexible before leaving about integrating her travel into her everyday life, she was also amenable to allowing her daily obligations into the vacation. Her flexibility extended both ways and was facilitated by technologies that allowed her to indulge in pretrip mental travel on the internet and connections with home during the trip via email.

Jodi did make an exception to her segmentation, however, for very bad news. Having learned from previous experience, she makes an exception for emergencies. Beyond who is doing the contacting, the content of the message, then, can also be considered more or less welcome. Contacting a loved one from home with good news may be a welcome interruption of one's vacation. Bad news, however, may or may not be acceptable contact. It can change a positive mood of the trip, but one also does not want to be inaccessible if something truly unfortunate happens. Margaret, an older snow bird in Hawaii, resented an intrusion on her time away when a relative insisted on calling her with bad news about a family member who needed to go into the hospital. She had told her family and friends not to bother her and resented the intrusion of problems that she felt were beyond her capacity to help with while she was away. "You know what really gets me? What the hell am I going to do about it? What are you telling me for? You know, why do they do that? I keep telling people, don't call me. Don't call me. You know, like, Jesus Murphy, don't call me here and tell me about it. Wait until I get home." Margaret was attempting to firmly demarcate her vacation from her everyday life and to keep upsetting news away for a little while by asking people not to contact her. That people did not respect her request illustrates how easy it is for daily experience to intrude in the vacation against one's wishes. Her family back home felt it was more important to include her on the bad news than follow her directions to be left alone. Like Steve, she felt compelled to answer even though she did not wish for the connection.

Objects both reinforce identity for individuals wearing, carrying, and using them and communicate identity to others observing, thus giving cues for how to interact with a person. Clothes and accessories are one of the most powerful ways to accomplish both these things. While something as simple as an outfit can seem like a basic choice of wearing something to fit an activity, it also helps a person embrace an identity and tell other people how that person wants to be seen and understood. Sometimes these messages are intentional, such as wearing a full aloha-print outfit for a day in Waikiki, and sometimes they are perhaps unintentional, such as when that same outfit communicates that one is a tourist and outsider.

Individuals are surrounded by objects besides just the clothes they wear. Some of these objects are intentionally brought on a trip, like a camera or a guidebook, and sometimes they are objects from everyday life that travel with a person without much thought. Regardless, they are a reminder of everyday life and everyday identities that are welcome or unwelcome to the traveler. While these unavoidable everyday objects have always made maintaining strict boundaries between home and away difficult, communication technologies make these lines blurrier than they have been before. A smartphone brings easy access to family, friends, and coworkers, as well as pictures from home, music, videos, and internet access for even more connectivity to everyday experience.

Souvenirs also demonstrate the porosity of boundaries and the ability of everyday life to travel into the vacation and the vacation to travel back out again into day-to-day life. Souvenirs bring reminders of the trip back home in physical form. They also help in sharing the experience with others, thus highlighting the significance of identity changes in the need to commemorate and share the identity shifts with others once one gets back. The spaces and places that people travel to similarly create and reinforce boundaries of the self that demarcate and influence identity shifts.

5

Space and Place

Patrice is excited to be spending the evening out at a hotel. She has rented a hotel room in one of the nice hotels near the beach, an area she does not usually visit as a tourist. She sees the ocean every day in her job at an aquarium, but it is not somewhere she goes to relax. Her home in the suburbs of Honolulu on the island of Oahu is far from the beach, and her neighborhood in a subdivision similar to one in the U.S. mainland definitely does not feel like a resort. She has rented this room as a way to treat herself during her time off work. She does not have the time or money to make a longer trip, but she will still feel she is away from home for a bit. She and a friend rented this room to enjoy the amenities of the hotel.

Several aspects of the trip excite her. Even though it is not far from home, it is still a hotel room, and so it will feel like a vacation. She will not have to clean up after herself, someone else will wash the sheets and clean the bathroom, she will have a nice cable package on the TV, she will be able to walk downstairs to the restaurant to get her dinner, and she will get the complimentary toiletries. At the same time, she gets to enjoy for herself the experience that she has seen so many people having all around her. When she looks out the window to enjoy the view of the ocean she will be doing it from the perspective of someone on break, rather than someone working at her job. She has also not invited her husband and kids to come along, so she can spend the time with just her friend. The break from her daily responsibilities will be even more complete, even though they are just a few miles away.

When asked to define what a vacation means to them, people usually name two primary criteria: a change in routine and a change in place. This suggests the identity shifts made on vacation have a distinct temporal and spatial character. It is not only a change from one's everyday schedule and routine; it also requires a change in one's everyday environment. People interact and make sense of their world in and through the arrangements of space and place. A setting, as well as the other people who occupy it, both channels and encourages the identities of the people in it. Because the creation of identity is a reflexive social process, identities cannot exist independently of one's environment. "*Who* one is depends, in part, on *where* one is and *when* one is. Identity resides not in the individual alone, but in the interaction between the individual and his or her social environment."[1] Sites and times are therefore "identity settings" guiding how to feel, how to act, and who to be.

The identities of people in a space share a sense of meaning derived from place. This is reflected in the varied identities expressed in vacation spots. The identity shift of a vacationer at a family beach will differ significantly from that of someone at a beachside singles resort. Similarly, the identity shift of an ecotourist in Costa Rica will differ from that of a camper at Yellowstone, and that of someone at Epcot Center at Disney World will differ from that of someone with a Eurail Pass. In each situation the meanings and physical arrangements of the destinations shape the way the people in them conceive of, prepare for, and enact identity.

Traveling to particular places can help people play up their identities in a desired manner. Some may move to an environment because it is arranged in such a way that it allows them to express a specific identity in what they feel is a more deep or authentic way. In his study of gay men living in the suburbs, Wayne Brekhus found that identity "chameleons" intentionally move, changing to locations where they felt more comfortable foregrounding and expressing their gay identity, while in other locations they moved this highly salient identity to the background.[2] David Grazian similarly found that people who go out to Chicago blues clubs temporarily reorganize their sense of self to foreground a "nocturnal identity," based on the consumption of urban nightlife.[3] For the tourists and suburbanites who travel to the city to frequent them, these blues clubs inhabit "a rustic urban playground set half a world away from the reality of their everyday lives."[4] These bars are tourist draws and have become places to which people travel where they can embrace a slightly more edgy identity than usual. They can also experience a piece of the blues world in a way that has been constructed to meet their expectations. It is created to be as they imagine it should be. In both these situations, the physical change in location and the arrangements of material culture facilitate the identity shifts. Thus, certain aspects of space are organized to aid the performance of specific identities. In these areas, people share the same specialized identity, and dedicated displays of it will be encouraged or supported more than in other areas.[5]

This interactive relationship with physical environment shapes and is shaped by cognition. Built environments are created by people and in turn contour the actions and perceptions of the people in them. "We mold buildings, they mold us, we mold them anew."[6] People continuously interact with their environment in a dialogue that is shaped by formal space and the people in it.[7] The identities that people derive from place reflect the patterned behaviors the site elicits, the cultural meanings objectified in its structures and organization, and the expectations and perceptions of other people who inhabit that space. Moving to and between environments, then, allows for the expression of corresponding identities. Some may move to a particular location because it allows them to express a desired identity; others move through locations during the course of everyday life. This allows the short-term reorganization of identities because space and place draw a boundary around where identity shifts may begin and end.

Distance and location are used strategically by vacationers to create a sense of break, whether they travel many miles or stay close to home. But the extent of this change depends on the individual. For some, distance may mean going to another continent; for others, traveling to a nearby city is sufficient. The degree of familiarity with an environment dictates whether the change will be enough. Being in an unfamiliar place can create a mental sense of separation regardless of physical distance. Perception of distance is composed of two cognitive categories rooted in space and place: "near and far" and "familiar and exotic."

Experiencing Near and Far

For many, the first step in establishing the mental space for identity shifts is establishing a sense of distance from everyday life. Introducing some cognitive space from one's day-to-day experience allows one to enter a new setting in which to situate identity shifts. People use differentiations of physical space to reinforce mental distinctions. Just as people use desk drawers or the rooms of a house—kitchen, bedroom, or office—to organize and sort information or domestic activities, they use different locations to organize and sort different facets of self.[8]

Creating distance does not necessarily have to be about traveling far away. "Near" and "far" are cognitive categories that are defined more by an individual's sense of familiarity and difference than any concrete geographical measurement. People experience distance topologically as well as metrically.[9] A topological understanding of space looks at the distance between things in terms of the similarities they share or the boundaries that separate them. Distance is more a matter of meaning than of measurement. The existence of boundaries often shapes our sense of distance more than physical space does. People perceive more distance between things that have a boundary of some kind separating them. That boundary can be physical, symbolic, or experiential. A visit to the city can seem more of a journey if one has never been there before, while a trip to the beach becomes less significant if one goes back and forth all summer. Therefore, some can define "far" as a nearby city, while for others it must be outside the borders of the country.

For those who feel stress from their everyday obligations, travel can create not just physical but also mental distance between their vacation and everyday identities. This sense of distance from everyday life is imperative to becoming the more relaxed person they wish to be during their vacation time. Celeste has four children and seven grandchildren at home who live near her and make constant demands on her time. Their mere proximity is a source of stress she escapes at her vacation home in Hawaii. "We all live close, and when you live close, you're always hearing and seeing, and things annoy you. When I come here, I don't even think about it. I'm totally relaxed. I think that distance helps me to get into this relaxation mode that is more difficult to do when I am at home." While being a mother and grandmother is an important part of her everyday self, traveling to another state provides some distance to temporarily background these facets of self and let others come forward.

Jamie shares the sentiment that it is the distance itself that creates a mental space for relaxing that is not possible at home. Jamie attempted a staycation with her husband and young children and was disappointed with the result when she found herself doing the same chores and housework she normally would do during what was supposed to be a break from the roles of domesticity. Without traveling somewhere new she was not able to get the sense of release from responsibility that she was looking for. Traveling gives her a feeling of release from her family-oriented responsibilities:

> Having a husband, and having children. . . . It's just a lot of work. . . . I think, well, if I don't cook tonight, what's he going to eat? What are the girls going to eat? You know what I mean? So to me the getting away takes you out of all that home stuff. But also I think getting away for me is like a mental thing. You know, I want to feel that sense of space. Like, I don't have to go home right away or tomorrow, and I can't even get there. This is what I really liked about our honeymoon, is that we got on a plane and we flew. And I knew we were going to be there for a week and a half, and that was a long time. We were totally exhausted from all the wedding stuff. So yeah, I just really liked that—mentally, that sense of being away from home and not ever having the responsibilities of home again. 'Cause they're fine, you know, it's good, but, like, [I need] a temporary reprieve from the responsibilities of home.

Jamie clearly experiences the sense of break that physical distance can create. In addition, being able to go away on her honeymoon, at a distance far enough that they had to get on a plane to get there, helped give her a "temporary reprieve" in her day-to-day responsibilities, even though one of them, her new husband, came along with her.

At the same time, people can use long distances to consciously sort and separate identities. A long commute from one identity to another can help keep them distinct and prevent undesired overlap. In this way, an aspect of self can be bracketed into existing only in a faraway place.[10] For people who travel to indulge in out-of-character behaviors or aspects of identity they prefer to keep submerged, this technique is particularly useful. They can travel to an experimental identity while maintaining a steady everyday self. The successful advertising slogan "What happens in Vegas stays in Vegas" plays on this tendency. Visitors travel to a bounded space where they can indulge certain aspects of self and then return home, hoping for no overlap.

Jeff is a traveler who put a lot of effort into segmenting his home and away identities. At home, he lives a very studious life as a prelaw college student. He explains that when he goes on vacation as a tourist he lets loose in a way that he does not at home. In China he went out to bars and clubs where he drank a lot and stayed out late with other tourists he met on the trip. He explains what motivates his behavior: "I'm a nerd during the school year. A big nerd. I don't do anything but schoolwork. And I—whenever I come here, I come to party a lot, to drink a lot, because I don't do it during the school year at all. So it's completely different." As a college student, Jeff would have the same opportunities to drink and socialize in his hometown, but he chooses not to. Instead, he geographically separates his more extreme behavior from that of his responsible everyday life. While traveling, Jeff allows himself to indulge in the behavior that he usually denies himself.

From Space to Place

The difference between space and place is important in understanding how identities are channeled by their environments. The two concepts are fundamental for understanding social life because they shape how people make sense of their world and their place in it. Space is a more abstract concept than place. Space is made up of structures and forms. It is the distances between objects, the locations of things, and the directions between them. Place is a location that has been provided with meaning by the people who inhabit it or visit it. Rather than a geometric abstraction, place is invested with values. Place can be as small as a corner of the room with a favored chair or as large as a city. Space becomes place as people get to know it and give it value.[11]

Groups existing and interacting in the same spaces and places cannot be expected to perceive and respond to environments in the same way. With the increasing mobility of modern life, aptly demonstrated by tourism, people interacting in the same space may be drawing from different histories or cultural understandings. Each group can hold its own ideas of what gives a place significance. Thus, an area in the countryside is a scenic or quaint destination for city day-trippers but a quotidian site for local residents. Many sites that become tourist attractions are the result of a "historical layering of human effort" in which different groups have used them for different purposes over time.[12] In many cases the tourist attraction is just the latest outcome of power struggles, preservation efforts, and changed cultural values.

The varying historical, social, and economic purposes of a location ensure that meanings and interpretation will not be consistent. Hawaii, for example, is a popular vacation destination for Japanese and American visitors. This is certainly reflected in the built environment of ubiquitous hotels, souvenir shops, and beach resorts. But the two groups do not perceive the environment in the same way and hold different meanings for it. Americans experience the islands as a destination culturally distinct from the mainland United States, one that is derived from and reflects a Polynesian heritage. This is reflected in the islands' theming of space. Japanese tourists, on the other hand, experience and consume Hawaii as an American destination.[13] This is perhaps best demonstrated in the shooting ranges that can be found around Waikiki. Marketed solely to Japanese tourists, they offer the opportunity to have the "American" experience of firing a gun for recreation—something most American visitors would not associate with their dream trip to Hawaii.

A group can bestow its own meaning on a specific site, in addition to larger areas. Elmina Castle in Ghana is a five-hundred-year-old structure used, among other purposes, for its dungeons during the slave trade. Visiting African Americans experience the site as part of a search for roots and historical insight. Local Ghanaians perceive the site in its guise over time as a trading post, slave dungeon, military fortification, colonial administrative center, prison, school, office, and now, tourist attraction. This difference in perception extends to the identities of the individuals in it. African Americans traveling to the site for heritage tourism think of themselves as returning to an ancestral home, while the Ghanaians see them as foreign visitors.[14]

Tourism and vacationing have the capacity to change meanings of place. In one sense, space becomes place as people "discover" a destination and invest it with meanings congruent with being a tourist attraction. In another sense, tourism can change local meanings of place as new groups of people visit an existing place and give it their own meanings. Certain locations undergo a "social spatialization" in which they acquire a shared social meaning.[15] For example, the beach has been transformed into a collective "pleasure zone," and rural areas have been constructed as "the countryside" for urban residents in pursuit of leisure.[16] In the same way, nature has been constructed as a leisure destination that is considered to be pure and authentic, in contrast with urban modernity, but notions of natural beauty are not inevitable and have not been perceived in the same way by all groups.[17] "Wilderness" is a state of mind for those people perceiving it that is defined in contrast with "civilization." The definition is necessarily subjective.[18]

On vacation people move to places that have been collectively marked as desirable locations for leisure. Daniel Boorstin spoke of the creation of the "attraction."[19] An attraction is anything deemed interesting or amusing enough to draw people in large numbers and that could be easily commoditized and sold to visitors. Now, in addition to attractions, people colloquially speak of "destinations." Defined as something that is set apart for a particular use, purpose, or end, tourist destinations are cognitively "set apart" from their spatial setting by visitors and already commodified for tourist consumption.[20]

The meaning of this chunk of space becomes transformed as it is redefined as a destination. It is set apart from its surroundings and isolated in space as a place to buy a particular experience. Once a swampy area of the island of Oahu set aside for farmland, then a leisure spot for Hawaiian royalty, and then a residential area of Honolulu,[21] Waikiki is now an international beach destination exemplifying a commodified Hawaiian culture. Surfing lessons; menus at bars and restaurants selling local dishes; stalls offering island tours, cruises, and time shares; outdoor markets selling souvenirs; convenience stores with rattan beach mats, suntan lotion, and sunglasses in the front windows; and souvenir shops with leis, plastic ukuleles, macadamia nuts, and tiki statues create a sense of place associated with a Polynesian beach destination through the consumption possibilities available in the streets in this area of the everyday urban space of Honolulu.

Consumption itself is a "place-creating" activity,[22] which is particularly important in transforming locations into tourist destinations. Consumer landscapes are built on the "aura" of all the goods and services that are available: the souvenirs in the shops, the contents of window displays, and the mannerisms of service personnel all provide material for the creation of place.[23] Tourism creates place through a specific form of leisure-oriented consumption that can be seen not just at the beach but in ski towns like Aspen, Colorado, or Killington, Vermont, or in urban areas like Times Square in New York, Piccadilly Circus in London, or the Las Vegas strip.

This intentional construction of place results in an environment that supports and channels identity shifts for the people who travel to it. Resorts, cruise ships, and theme parks are group-specific enclaves designed to accommodate people who are on vacation and seek to act in a certain way. The "default setting" for such environments is a concentrated display of a specific identity, in contrast with a diffuse display that would occur in more diverse environments.[24] Interactions are often limited to like-minded travelers who dress the same, go out to the same bars and clubs, eat and drink similar food, and participate in the same set of activities. People are not only guided into foregrounding particular aspects of self but encouraged to do so by the uniformity of their surroundings.

This can be good if it is something the traveler wants to do, but if the design of a place does not correspond with the facets of identity a person wishes to foreground, being trapped in such a highly defined environment with few escapes can be an unpleasant experience. Anna discovered this when she was forced into going on a family vacation to Pigeon Forge, Tennessee. This is a resort area in the Smoky Mountains designed around a rustic, family-oriented country theme, embedded in Appalachian Mountains history, and highly commoditized as a down-home family vacation destination. Her aunt chose the location for a family reunion:

> She made us go to Pigeon Forge, Tennessee, and it was awful. It's up in the mountains, so that part's kind of pretty. But it's this huge tourist trap with fudge shops and, like, oh, what is that? Ripley's Believe It or Not! museum, the weird thing. It's by Dollywood. It's terrible. That was definitely my worst vacation ever. It was like a family vacation from hell.

This was a vacation experience that Anna did not wish to have, and the commercialized, enclavic nature of the environment aggravated her discomfort. The location was geared toward supporting particular facets of identity that she was not interested in, leaving her few options for enjoying her time that were not in line with the rustic Pigeon Forge atmosphere.

Over time, the effects of mass tourism have a homogenizing effect as generic qualities overwhelm the specifics of place.[25] This can be seen in the standardization of architecture and landscaping in tourist areas and the introduction of multinational companies and chain stores. A backpacker's disappointment, as expressed in a post to the now-defunct TravelPod travel blogging site, when he visits a coastal region of Belize that has been transformed into a resort area to appeal to high-spending international tourists illustrates the interchangeability of location:

> The Lodge at Chaa Creek was exactly what we were not looking for in a hotel in Belize. The grounds were expertly manicured, all of the staff wore identical polos tucked into their pants, the thatched roof huts contained single rooms and each had their own surrounding "lawn," the bar and restaurant were filled with expensive looking furniture, and it was filled with mostly middle-aged "explorer" tourists types with white beards and younger couples who were obviously on honeymoons or just plain rich. For about $320 a night, you can pay to stay in a place that looks more like it belongs in Maui than Belize and get none of the local flavor or culture.

His description picks up on some of the transferable characteristics of a resort-style vacation destination. It is this uniformity and the way it can erase place that creates his distaste. The meanings of place disappear as they are replaced by generic signifiers of the corporate resort experience like neatly uniformed staff, expensive-seeming furniture, and diligent maintenance of the lawns and grounds. Local flavor and culture is what defines place for him, and whatever he was expecting to find in Belize that matched that description was not present at this resort. The particular resort that he visited is a highly regarded international destination that advertises itself as offering eco-vacations to the rainforest and the "heart of Maya civilization" offering "unique adventure travel experiences for thousands of visitors looking for an in-depth yet civilized Belizean vacation."[26] It includes a spa, Jacuzzis, and thatched-cottage-style suites in the middle of the jungle. By importing the globalized notions of an upscale resort to rural Belize, the local meanings and cultural identity are taken away and replaced with a set of signifiers found in similar locations around the world. The resort's architecture, landscaping, apparel of the staff, and even the groups of people that made up the clientele were all "out of place" in coastal Belize in the perception of this visitor.

While this backpacker was not happy with the division of place from space, for some vacationers the cultural specifics of place are not as important. For other North American and European vacationers who travel to beach-resort spots, local meanings of place are overlooked in pursuit of a particular transferable ideal of sun, sand, and sex situated in a not-too-alien environment. The "place" for them is the destination that can offer these things. The specifics of local culture are less important than having the comforts of home reproduced alongside the hedonistic liminal opportunities of the beach.[27] The resort-style destination offers an expected standard of luxury and comfort to the degree that localness becomes less important. Many seek out this standard, and the local meanings that may contrast with it are secondary. A woman at a resort in Cancun, also posting to a TravelPod blog, has the opposite reaction from the backpacker in Belize when she arrives at her chosen vacation destination:

Vacation has officially begun—we were really there. The pool was massive, surrounded by flowers, giant palm trees lined the walkways, there was one massive beach with no end in sight. . . . Happy music came from the loudspeakers and wonderful smells found their way into our noses telling us it was time for breakfast/lunch/dinner or something. Paradise has been found!

Pools and the beach, flowers and plants, even the colors and scents create a welcomed sensual environment that signifies paradise, which could be found in Mexico or any number of beach locations around the world. The meanings that define the writer's destination are drawn from these features. These associations are so primary that seeing them signals to her that the vacation has officially begun. Specifics of Cancun or Mexico are not important and are overlooked entirely in her description. In other entries in her blog she details her travels around Cancun as she visits and compares other resorts but does not leave the enclavic resort area. For her, the place she has traveled to is the resort itself, not Mexico.

A cruise ship, which is all space and no place, imports décor and associations with place to create a sense of somewhere else. While not necessarily accurate or authentic, decorations and design lend meanings to the location. A passenger on a cruise ship describes how each floor of the vessel is decorated in a way that is reminiscent of exciting or exotic locations elsewhere. Whereas a resort or hotel usually limits itself to motifs reminiscent of the local culture and environment, a cruise ship does not have such limitations. Onboard, passengers can travel through an approximation of continents and time periods as they move around the boat. As one TravelPod blogger on a Pacific cruise says:

> Although it might be blasphemous to compare our ship to a European rococo cathedral, I was left with the same feeling—where should I look first? The nightclub has an Egyptian motif—golden mummy cases line the entrance way and the curtains, upholstery, and carpeting is peppered with cartouches and hieroglyphics. A smaller club a floor below is decorated to look like a French palace. A floor above we can order an overpriced drink from a Chinese lounge redolent with the red, gold and black colors that country favors.

The designers of this boat chose themes to distinguish and make special areas of the ship that otherwise would have no meaning. Meaning also is added in locations that are specifically developed for a leisure purpose but had no prior local meaning because they were undeveloped before their invention as a leisure destination. Architectural and retail elements brought into these themed areas make them very much a "place" that has importance and meaning to the people they draw.[28] The beachfront areas of Miami, for example, were developed from rural lands, and the fantasy architecture that now defines them was intentionally selected and imported but is unrelated to anything inherent to the locality. Built in a style borrowed from Latin America and the Mediterranean, the architecture was meant to be reminiscent of a supposed Spanish past. Houses, hotels, and country clubs were built in a style that borrowed a vernacular for a space that did not have one of its own. Ski resorts such as Vail similarly import an alpine look, completely disconnected from the local environment, that imparts a self-conscious and commercially driven sense of place reminiscent of ski resorts elsewhere.[29]

A cruise ship or undeveloped area imports meanings from other locations as a way of creating a sense of place that did not exist before. In other, more permanent locations, importing meanings can eliminate or alter local meanings of place. Existing meanings are superseded or replaced entirely by visitors who seek comforting associations of home in what become enclavic areas that attract travelers of the same nationality. Beaches in Thailand that are known as Little Sweden or Little Germany[30] or Spanish resort towns where British visitors can eat British foods, watch British TV, and socialize only with other British tourists[31] illustrate such replacement. People travel to them because they are like home, only in a nicer climate, and people can have a comfortable experience there without venturing too far from the familiar. The result is an easy integration of the social identity of nationality and the material reminders of it into a vacation. For those who choose to prioritize this or are not comfortable with too much of a change in this aspect of self, these environments facilitate the overlap of home and away.

These places not only allow an easy integration of the everyday and exceptional; they also speed the transition into a temporary organization of self arranged around leisure, relaxation, and fun. One does not have to worry about speaking to locals in a new language, trying new foods that may be unpleasant, or negotiating unfamiliar cultural norms, because these complications have been eliminated. The risks and challenges of vacationing are reduced. One can go straight to leisure in a manner that is scripted and expected. The path to drinking pints in a pub and lying on the beach is direct and simplified.

Daniel Boorstin noted that the mid-twentieth-century American traveler wanted to feel as if he or she had experienced the exotic while having the comforts of home at hand.[32] Conrad Hilton had just this in mind when designing his hotels. Around the world, regardless of location, he claimed, "Each of our hotels is a little America."[33] Travelers are made to feel as if they are still in the United States but with a "measured admixture of carefully filtered local atmosphere."[34] The overall effect is to re-create a feeling of home during travel, no matter how far one goes. This style is now the standard for the corporate hotel chain. They follow a standardized design that is more or less the same from Washington, D.C., to Beijing, with some allowances for local flavor. The traveler staying in one of these places will know what to expect and what is expected. This concept has extended beyond hotels to chain restaurants, around the United States and often around the world, that offer the same experience, regardless of place.

As travel and tourism change places, spaces gain meanings that coordinate with desired identities. Some vacationers want to experience an exotic or authentic culture and thus travel to locations such as China or rural Belize where they hope to encounter local culture. Others wish to relax and unwind by a pool, and for them local place becomes irrelevant. Others want to travel somewhere new, but not too new, and so go to tourist enclaves where they can find reminders of home in a new environment. Others, no matter where they are or why they are traveling, want to stay in a familiar, or even identical, room. For all, place supports identity.

The Familiar and the Exotic

Conrad Hilton understood the tension between the familiar and the exotic that people feel while traveling. They want to experience something new but in a comforting environment. This is an experience that transcends tourism. Zygmunt Bauman used this fundamental challenge the tourist faces as a metaphor for a form of postmodern identity when he described tourist spaces:

> You recognize the tourist haunts by their blatant, ostentatious (if painstakingly groomed) oddity, but also by the profusion of safety cushions and well-marked escape routes. In the tourists' world the strange is tame, domesticated, and no longer frightens; shocks come in a package deal with safety. . . . Having a home is part of the safety package: for the pleasure to be unclouded and truly engrossing, there must be somewhere, a homely and cozy, indubitably "owned" place to go when the present adventure is over.[35]

This view emphasizes the need to balance the familiar and the exotic in constructing identity, between wanting to do or be something different and having the reassurance that the comfort of stability and familiarity remain. It also illustrates the places for identity shifts that the tourism industry creates for travelers, where they can try out new things and play at risk, freedom, and change in the comfort of a familiar environment. Knowing one has a safe "home" to return to makes adventure more palatable because it is not permanent. It makes risk more doable because the stakes are not as real. Adventure is easier to undertake when it is temporary and its risk is not as consequential. It is something to be played with and then left behind. In these spaces, when the unusual is introduced it is cushioned and made easy. There are always ways to exit and return to a state that offers stability through familiarity. In Bauman's view this state defines not only tourism but the experience of everyday life and the identities that people shape in it. The placidity of home can translate into a monotony that compels people to do new things but at the same time offers people a base of stability they can return to. "Home" is a mix of both "shelter and prison."[36]

As discussed in Chapters 1 and 2, adventure and risk are a part of the identity work and identity play that make up identity shifts. Adventure is a part of an experience that introduces controlled risk. Accommodation for this is built into many vacation and touristic destinations where people play at the limits of their everyday identities. It is buttressed by the design and layout of spaces.

To appreciate the change and novelty of visiting a new location, many must experience it from a base of familiarity. A familiar microenvironment allows them to feel secure enough to enjoy the strangeness of their new macroenvironment.[37] Something that reminds people of home must be present, such as food, newspapers, or a familiar living space. The hotel becomes a familiar and comfortable base grounding exploration for the tourist who goes out to experience the exotic. He or she may then experience "home" while away.[38] Home is embodied in the comfort and safety of the hotel, and one's company there, and is contrasted with the uniqueness of the environment outside it. Hotels have recently begun expanding on this concept of mixing home and away by allowing customers to request personal preferences that make the hotel feel more like home, including a favorite newspaper, customizable pillows and mattresses, custom food and drink menus, and even temperature controls set before arriving.[39]

The identity shifts done during tourism echo this basic existential tension between wanting both the familiar and the unusual. While aspects of the exotic may make a destination more interesting or appealing to the potential traveler, they can also be threatening and introduce uncertainty into the experience. Regarding her trip to China, Connie sums up how the exotic can feel threatening: "This is so foreign to me. I am the quintessential foreigner. I try to blend in and respect the local customs and traditions here, but it's been very eye opening. Certainly not like Europe, which is—I used to think Europe was scary, but this has been very eye opening." Something that is too different can be frightening. Her anxiety comes from her relative unfamiliarity with the culture and context. In comparison, Europe with its familiar architecture, cognate-heavy languages and Latin script, and recognizable food and drink is within the realm of the accessible. Because it is her first time to China, these differences are intimidating. Europe at first was similarly so, until additional travel gave her the cultural competencies to understand it.

Travel is a skill, and the savvy of negotiating the exotic that is built through repeated trips signifies status. This is expressed in one's definitions of the familiar and the exotic. The experience of the two is relative. What is different, new, scary, or intimidating for one person may be run-of-the-mill, everyday, or enjoyable for someone else with a higher degree of familiarity. Connie followed a fairly standard process for American international travelers. First, she left the United States for Europe or Mexico, and eventually, after developing the requisite comfort and curiosity, she moved on to non-Western destinations.

This need for familiarity that many vacationers experience creates enclavic areas where linguistic and cultural differences isolate people in space. Lack of confidence in successfully interacting with others; practical concerns of how to get by when one does not know the language, customs, or transportation system; and a general feeling of helplessness in an unfamiliar environment often limit activities and interactions to environments where one can be confident of a successful interaction. This success is usually facilitated by the efforts of someone else. Japanese tourists in Hawaii primarily travel in large groups, stay in hotels that are Japanese owned, and attend Japanese-language shows, events, and tours. A significant infrastructure accommodates Japanese tourists and makes the trip easier but also confines their visits for the most part to the island of Oahu and a "Japanese bubble" in Waikiki.[40]

Similar to these Japanese tourists, many American and European visitors to China find the language barrier an intimidating, and at times even debilitating, impediment to touring the country. This limits their visits to heavily traveled tourist cities like Beijing, Shanghai, and Xi'an or to a guided tour that escorts them. For the volunteer tourists much effort was put into ensuring that the comforts of home were re-created for a group of curious but intimidated and sometimes reluctant guests. They stayed in apartments that were better than the local standard instead of hotels. Computers, internet access, and mail service ensured visitors could easily communicate with home without even having to deal with the local post office. Televisions with DVD players were set up with a large selection of American television shows and movies available to watch. They were not set up to watch Chinese television, which the tourists were told they would not be able to understand. Home-cooked meals were provided that combined new Chinese flavors and ingredients with the option of familiar foods from home. A typical meal would include dumplings, stir-fried Chinese vegetables, sweet and sour chicken, and bread and peanut butter.

Linda explains why she chose to come to China as a volunteer tourist and reflects on what adventure means to her in her travel and in her self:

> It's worth considering whether you think of yourself as an adventurous person or not, in general. And then from that, whether you choose adventurous vacations or not, you know? Because I don't normally think of myself as an adventurous person, . . . I thought this was a very safe way to do what other people thought was an adventure [*laughs*]. You know, for me it wasn't threatening. I mean, the worst part was arriving in Xi'an; after that everything's taken care of. But other people see, you know, just, the whole concept of staying in China [as] an adventure.

This tension between the familiar and the exotic can be equated to a tension between adventure and security that transcends location. Campers who take with them complex equipment for the outdoors make adventure more accessible from a secure and comfortable base at the campsite. Gear can range from the basic to the elaborate, including portable chairs, stoves, and dishes and even kitchens, inflatable mattresses and beds, knives and tools, GPS, two-way radios, lighting, heaters, and generators and portable power kits. All these objects moderate the relationship with wilderness in campers' outdoor adventure. RVs and RV parks similarly replicate the comforts of home with amenities ranging from the basics like electricity, bathrooms, and showers to bonuses like air conditioning, DVD players and stereos, wide-screen televisions, tile and hardwood floors, skylights, swiveling recliner chairs, and even fireplaces.

While people prefer to have their experience of the exotic made accessible, an exotic location cannot be too familiar or it will lose its appeal. In a balance between expectations and security, a location cannot be too familiar or too different. Marcia exemplifies this attitude in her description of Vietnam: "I found the people friendly. *I found it exotic but not grating.* You know, it's colorful, it varies from place to place, the architecture's interesting" (emphasis added). For her, Vietnam is different enough to feel exotic, but not so much that it is uncomfortable or irritating to be there.

Whereas the tourist staying at a hotel goes *out* to experience the exotic, for the vacationer staying at a resort, which is often the destination in itself, select elements of the exotic are brought *in*. The attention of visitors is distracted from elements that do not fit with the theme or may appear to be extraneous and is directed to a few key elements and images of the locale outside the grounds. Thus, limited motifs are displayed that channel attention to a particular vision of the culture that is based on a stereotyped ethnicity or national identity.[41] Among these design components intended to evoke the outside world are simulacra of aspects of local social and natural life.[42] The fixtures characteristic of many Hawaiian resorts—for example, volcanic rock, pools, and fountains—encourage guests to feel they are having an authentic Hawaiian experience without having to leave the resort grounds. These simulacra attempt to not only represent the local reality but enhance it, and the result is something somehow more real than what exists outside. The representations meet the expectations of the visitors more than the actual spots around the islands. They are also much more elaborate and extravagant than any of the natural formations that exist, distorting the relationship between the natural world outside the resort grounds and what is represented within. These reproductions include mock volcanoes and rock walls with trickling waterfalls, pools of koi fish, live tropical birds, and other flora and fauna. The result is the production of a "real Hawaii" that is difficult to find outside the hotels and resorts.[43] At Waimea Valley Falls Park, for example, visitors hike a mile-long paved road to see a naturally occurring, small waterfall. When a mother and daughter arrive at the end of the trail they pause to look, and the daughter says, "It's not that great. The one we saw in Africa was a lot bigger." The waterfall in the lobby of the Waikiki Marriott, on the other hand, is three stories tall.

In this way the abstract concept of the exotic is put into object form for the consumption of visitors. In addition to the simulacra that fill public spaces, Hawaiiana souvenirs, furnishings, and decorations also encapsulate Polynesian exoticness and surround guests. Tiki statues, grass skirts, ukuleles, leis, koa wood objects, and muumuus take an idea of Hawaii that may have existed in the past and turn it into a salable artifact for tourists. They make the exotic accessible and available to bring home. But much like the simulacra of the resorts, tiki statues and grass skirts in their present form bear little relation to the extant culture of the Hawaiian people; rather, they are representations for visitors looking for a souvenir.

Another part of the decoration of many of the larger resort hotels in Waikiki is museum-like displays of objects of Hawaiian heritage and culture that historicize the exotic and attempt to lend a sense of authenticity to the souvenirs and decorations and link them with the past. They build credibility by bringing elements of the real into the representation. These objects are different from the simulacra in that they do actually represent what was real; it just no longer exists. The authenticity that people look for in these situations usually has little to do with actual present-day life. Instead, the authenticity is a representation of a remembered past they desire to exist. The artifacts on display give authority to that constructed authenticity.

Attending and Disattending to the Environment

The construction of culturally desirable vacation spots requires that visitors selectively attend to and disattend to particular aspects of their environment to meet their expectations of place. People are socialized into particular "optical communities" that teach them to attend to certain features of their environment and not see others.[44] They learn to pay attention to events and phenomena that are considered relevant and to ignore others deemed to be irrelevant. Thus, much of what people "see" has been socially conditioned because they adopt the outlook of their community. Once individuals have learned what to ignore, the irrelevance of those events and phenomena seems natural or logical. Peoples' decisions about the places to travel to and what they notice while they are there are shaped by these cognitive traditions of perception. Optical socialization is so strong it influences not only what they see but what they anticipate while planning the trip and often what they remember when they return. This socialization can also be rather overt. Guidebooks, informational plaques, and tour guides carefully point out what to pay attention to and leave out what is not considered worthy of being seen. A tour guide will pause for a moment to point out something visitors should photograph.

Attending is key in appreciating vacation spots. Enjoying nature as a pleasant destination often involves overlooking undesirable or unpleasant aspects of the experience or those elements that do not fit the ideal. Visitors to the countryside attend to particular elements like local architecture, winding roads, and minimal development while ignoring other features of the landscape. John Urry describes how the "tourist gaze" focuses the attention of urban day-trippers to the countryside on those aspects of their environment that they want to see and that support their expectations and turns their attention away from those things that do not fit:

Such a "rural landscape" has erased from it farm machinery, laborers, tractors, telegraph wires, dead animals, concrete farm buildings, motorways, derelict land, polluted water, nuclear power stations, and diseased animals. What people see is therefore highly
selective, and it is the focused gaze that is central to people's appreciation.[45]

The beach is another natural environment where evidence of social in-
tervention such as beach erosion, pollution, and overcrowding are disattended to, as are undesirable environmental conditions like uncomfortably
hot temperatures and overexposure to the sun, blowing sand, and potentially dangerous animal life. While Hawaii has been constructed as an idealized beach vacation site for Americans, it is also a prominent and strategic
location for the U.S. military. Army bases, warships, and even weapons testing and practice on less populated islands are rarely thought about by vacationers, if they are even aware of them. While locations like Pearl Harbor
are memorialized and included in the tourist experience for nationalistic
purposes, functioning everyday sites of the military are disattended to.
    Many vacations are spent not in highly specific enclaves, like resorts
and tourist towns, but in an environment that combines vacation and local accommodations. In these hybrid areas hotels and tourist attractions
intermingle with shops, businesses, domestic housing, and the public and
private institutions of everyday life. Vacationers are surrounded by people
there to support their identity shift and those who are indifferent to it.
Other tourists, staff, and locals all mix. Markets and bazaars that draw
tourists out into the city are examples of these hybrid spaces,[46] as are
European and American cities, the countryside, and functioning everyday
sites for which tourism is a secondary purpose, such as Saint Patrick's
Cathedral, Notre Dame, or Oxford University. It is easy for tourists to
disattend to the primary purpose of these institutions because it does not
match with their intent for being there.
    This disattention also manifests in asymmetries in perception by
groups that interact in the same environment. Members of the military
are very aware of the leisure definition of Hawaii, while visitors are not
always aware of the military. Farm laborers are very aware of insects, pes-
ticides, or dangers of farm machinery, while visitors to the countryside
see fields and vistas. Fishermen pay attention to weather, tides, and sea
life, while swimmers admire the blue ocean.
    In a country that was overwhelmingly different from their home and
in a role as visitors having an authentic experience, volunteer tourists in

China at times seemed almost incapable of seeing the significant tourist infrastructure and accessibility of Western-style comforts that was around them. At the same time that they complained that the city was too westernized, they missed the amenities from home. This lack was something they complained about often, but in the tourist-friendly city of Xi'an they were surrounded by familiarities from the West. Chain hotels, including Hyatt, Sheraton, Hilton, Holiday Inn, Sofitel, Crown Plaza, and Westin, offered Western-style restaurants, bars, souvenir shops, newspapers, candy and snacks, beer and wine, and other amenities and reminders of home that the tourists claimed just were not available in Xi'an. Familiar stores and restaurants were also readily available in the downtown shopping districts. In one example, despite all the hotels having well-stocked bars, Mona frequently lamented her inability to drink a glass of red wine while in China: "It's like being in detox. You can't get anything you want. I'm like, 'Oh my god, I want a glass.' So I told my husband, 'Please bring me a glass of wine at the airport.'" She could have alleviated her frustration and enjoyed a glass that evening by going down the street to the Hyatt.

At times the expectation and what people see are so different that anomalies to the culturally articulated scenario cannot be overlooked. It is difficult to act out an imagined self when the supporting environment for it does not match the stage set in one's imagination. This leads to disappointments when an environment does not live up to an ideal. "Paris Syndrome" afflicts visitors, especially Japanese tourists, who have gone to the city and experienced shock when it does not live up to their idealization. While this disappointment happens with many destinations, Paris, in particular, has been profitably represented in advertising, film, and the public imagination as "quaint, friendly, affluent—and likely still in black-and-white."[47] Once arriving, these Japanese tourists cannot overlook the racism, dirtiness, crowdedness, and other assorted disappointments of a typical modern city that they were not expecting to encounter.

An anthropologist experiencing a similar cognitive dissonance between her expectations and reality describes her search for the real Tahiti that she was expecting. She arrives in Tahiti expecting to see Polynesian life and instead finds herself in an "inauthentic" resort. In frustration she leaves her resort to find the real culture that she is looking for. Walking down the road into town, trying to ignore the traffic and dust around her, she thinks to herself, "Once in town I'm going to just sit outside a beachfront café, drink an exotic cocktail under a palm tree, and watch the people stroll by." She explains:

We were sweaty and covered with dust when we finally reached the downtown. [The capital city of] Papeete was like a miniature Paris: dirty, expensive, busy, and a bit rude; no beachfront boulevard dotted with cafés. Instead, Western popular music blasted from the stereo speakers outside tacky souvenir shops. As we walked, I could feel my shoulders burning red under the merciless tropical sun. It was suffocating walking on the hot pavement of the noisy, crowded streets. City life in Tahiti was as uncomfortable as the debilitating summers of New York.[48]

On her trip into town she is thwarted time and again as she tries to experience the "real" Tahiti and "real Polynesian life" that she believes is outside the boundaries of her planned resort. Neither place was what she expected, the resort too commercial, the city too urban. She gradually comes to realize the problem is not that what she sees is not real (of course it is), it is that everyday life in Papeete is much closer to everyday life in New York than she anticipated or wanted. The problem was more her own misconceptions about what a place *should* be.

Waikiki is a section of Honolulu that is arranged almost completely to satisfy visitors' expectations of a tropical paradise. The rest of the city is less enclavic, and vacationers mix into the everyday urban environment and confront the realities of a modern American city in their idealized tropical paradise, including crime, homelessness, and urban development. In a TravelPod blog post, a cruise ship passenger, on a daylong stop in Honolulu, is disappointed that the city is not natural enough:

We can't help feeling that Honolulu is a paradise ruined by concrete and steel—heaps of towering office and accommodation blocks with only a few palm trees around to remind you that you are on a Pacific island. Of course we didn't make it too far out of the city itself so maybe the other side of the island is more natural.

Hawaii, and especially Honolulu, also has a large homeless population. They are very present and visible in the city. The pleasant climate makes it possible for people to live year-round in the outdoors, usually in the public parks. This inevitably causes concern for visitors. On a typically sunny and mild day in Waikiki, a homeless man sleeps under a lamppost in front of a church and across the street from a popular coffee shop. A clerk from the coffee shop comes out to watch as a policeman wakes the homeless man and makes him move from his spot. The clerk says to a man sitting at one of the tables on the patio, "Thank goodness. I thought he was dead." The man responds, "Yeah, I saw him move earlier. It's a shame because it really spoils the atmosphere." The clerk tells him that homeless people sleep all over the beach area at night, but police keep them moving throughout the day. Although local authorities make an attempt at it, the realities of urban life cannot be completely shielded from visiting tourists. The homeless population is one of the uncontrolled, unplanned elements of everyday life that enter into the carefully constructed and maintained environment of Waikiki, disrupting the intended effect of idyllic Polynesia. Unlike controlled private spaces that seek a similar effect such as Disney World, where such evidence of conflict can be "designed out,"[49] the realities of life sometimes seep into the fantasy.

Marcia had a reaction similar to the coffee shop customer when she went to Puerto Rico with a group of friends for what she thought would be an idyllic island vacation. Once she left the small planned space set aside for visitors she discovered that she found the realities of everyday life for the local Puerto Ricans unsettling: "[I and my friends] went to Puerto Rico many years ago, and I hated it. We all hated it. . . . It was a long time ago, and it was very unattractive down there. We rented a car and we went from San Juan. We drove around the island and found just a lot of poverty and nothing redeeming."

These encounters with what is actual everyday life can thus be dismaying and can undermine the identity shift that visitors had hoped to make. The irony for people seeking authenticity is that very often the realness that they seek is in fact very much like the everyday life they have left behind, including ranges of poverty and wealth, natural landscapes and urban development, and small-town familiarity and urban alienation. This realness is more true than the vision they have been socialized by their communities into expecting to see. Often the authentic experiences tourists are seeking do not match environments, because they reflect an unrealistic, outdated, or romanticized vision of what a place is. The culturally defined "vivid scenarios"[50] vacationers hold for their destination may not match their physical reality and thus must be reworked, through processes like attending to and disattending to, or dismissed altogether when cultural ideals do not match built environments.

A key aspect of the freedom gained from identity shifts done on vacation is the difference created with everyday life. Some aspect of day-to-day experience must change to feel as if one is on vacation. Many people create this difference for themselves by changing locations. This feeling of being away is important. Some sense of distance between the realms of home and away has to be experienced. Space becomes a crucial variable in constructing identity. The arrangements of space and place undergird identity shifts, and people use specific locations to facilitate the changes they want to make. Whether it is to a faraway location that has been made to feel like home or somewhere they expect to be completely unlike home, places have meanings that help define identities. In turn, people traveling to these destinations can change meanings of place. It is an interactive cycle of meaning making, interpretation, and reception.

Local environments and the people who design them are essential in creating spaces for identities. When Hilton creates identical hotels, resorts follow a standardized architecture, or tourist towns import meanings or themes from other spaces and places to create or re-create place, they form an appropriate or desirable environment in which people situate their identities. They create the identity-specific locations in which it is easy to match one's comportment, appearance, and activities to the surroundings. In other circumstances, people travel to the extant environments, like cities or the countryside, that they believe will provide the backdrop for the identity they desire.

Environment does not work alone in manufacturing cognitive realms for difference. Space and time interact with each other to create a sense of contrast and distance. Moving to a different place usually means disruption of one's normal experience of time. In a new environment, with its own temporal norms, individual schedules and routines change to adapt to local expectations for attending to and organizing time. Local temporal patterns are an important element of environments that help structure identity shifts. Chapter 6 explores the importance of time as a guide in shaping shifts in identity.

6

Temporality and the Self

eslie and her husband sit by the hotel pool most of the morning and then much of the afternoon. She is tanned a dark brown from sitting in the sun every day during her three-week vacation. To pass the time she reads religious-themed pulp novels, which she describes as "clean and no thinking involved." When she is not reading she takes naps or chats with the people sitting around her on the pool deck. Usually her husband goes to a nearby convenience store later in the morning to pick up some beers to drink with their late breakfast. The Kilauea Hotel is casual, moderately priced, and no one notices or cares what they bring in and out from the pool areas. They eat lunch when they feel hungry at the hotel's restaurant, sometimes late in the afternoon or sometimes when they have finished their beers. Sometimes they skip it altogether if they do not feel like eating. Leslie tells me she is concerned about the recent management change at the hotel. She is worried they will become more strict about meal service times at the restaurant. They have come to this hotel for years and do not want it to change. They go for dinner in the evening when they get hungry, but usually not before the sun goes down. That way they can enjoy the full day the way they like. They do this day after day during their three-week vacation away from their retired lives in Pennsylvania.

While they could also live this way in Pennsylvania, because they are well into their retirement, at the beach it is different. Their children and grandchildren are not here. Leslie's unwell brother-in-law is not here. The church they regularly attend is back in Pennsylvania as are the golf club and the book club. Moreover, nobody at the pool cares what they do. Surrounded by strangers, except for another couple who traveled with them, they have no one to account to and no one to monitor their behavior. Leslie and her husband have created their own routine that is independent of the clock and its conventions. They eat when they want, sleep when they want, and drink when they want. While they more or less follow a pattern, it is dictated more by the sun—sunup and sundown and the full heat of midday—their own hunger, and their interest in today's book or a stranger's conversation.

Vacations have the capacity to alter perceptions of time. Individuals removed from their usual routines and schedules experience modes of time alternative to those that structure day-to-day life.[1] This is possible because the temporal dimension of experience does not always coincide with socially determined clock time.[2] On vacation, individuals can have "freedom from time"[3]—freedom from pressures or feeling rushed and the need to meet obligations. The flexibility of time during periods of absence or escape was first observed by Georg Simmel, who noted that "the adventure" is separated from the usual continuity of life.[4] It is an experience that is "out of time," not defined by the regulations that structure everyday interaction. If time structures the self, the removal of time, or at least the social structures of time, truly introduces an opportunity for play or at least change. The rigidity that is introduced by schedules is eliminated, allowing for looseness. People on vacation often travel to new places where they will likely encounter different tempos and different ways of experiencing time. People live, work, and play at different paces in different places.[5]

Time can be thought of in two ways. There is clock time and there is social time. Clock time is astronomical and based on the division of the day into hours, minutes, and seconds. Social time, on the other hand, is qualitative and based in experience. These two forms of social time, unrelated to the hours marked on a clock, "reveal the rhythms, pulsations, and beats of the societies in which they are found."[6] Examining contrasting experiences of social times uncovers more than just different approaches to temporality; it offers insights into the cultural contexts that form the temporal scaffolding for living out identities and shifting among them.

Day-to-day experience is moderated by contrasts between action and inaction.[7] The juxtaposition of the two creates a rhythm that is a fundamental feature of social life and is based on an alternation between activity and rest. A "cultural arrhythmia" has developed, however, out of the acceleration of tempo in modern, especially urban, life.[8] In Western societies time is considered to be valuable and filled with activity; it is regimented, organized, measured, and scheduled.[9] People are expected to maximize their active time and minimize any periods that are empty or unaccounted for. The tempo of our daily lives is now set by numerous advances and inventions meant to eliminate wasted time: microwave ovens and instant foods, jet airliners and bullet trains, journal abstracts and the computers they are written on are all viewed as time-savers.[10] In this climate, doing nothing or pausing is dismissed as a waste of time.

The activities that make up this rapid tempo often must conform to a fixed order and duration and be performed within a certain time limit. The creation of fixed routines that come with repeated action built into a scheduled day, week, or year has the effect of robbing everyday life of spontaneity. Having to conform to a schedule eliminates many opportunities for unplanned action or improvisation, and temporal rigidity amounts to a form of social control, because people must follow the strictures of routine laid out for them by the clock.[11] Built into this system, however, are periodic "remissions" that provide relief from the discipline.[12] During breaks and pauses for time off the limiting aspects of scheduling and routinization may be subverted. These "stoppages, breaks and hiatuses in activity" introduce a downbeat of contrast to the rhythm of everyday life.[13] Pauses are valuable in that their inherent discontinuity adds multidimensionality to experience.[14]

Vacations are defined in part by their distinct temporal characteristics. They are short lived and set apart from the usual flow of everyday life. They are periods in which social rules are inverted, but they also conform to normative conventions of frequency and duration that make them acceptable remissions from society.[15] Analysis of vacations, in their unique position of being constitutive of everyday life yet set apart from it, can illuminate through contrast the social dimensions of time and the ways that these dimensions structure the self.

People alter the concentration or dilution of identity facets. People's self-identities are made up of many "ingredients," and "density" refers to the volume of any particular identity at a given time.[16] A person can be 25 percent sister in one situation and 75 percent in another. Identity density demonstrates the commitment to a particular identity at a given point in time. A person on a yoga retreat is turning up the volume on that identity facet during the trip. For an identity facet, that may be difficult or undesirable to do at full capacity in the course of everyday life, whether it is too expensive, time-consuming, or strenuous, the limited time of the vacation offers a manageable opportunity to turn up the density of that facet and then turn it down again when the vacation is over. In the break itself, a shorter trip allows, and sometimes demands, increased identity density, and a longer duration permits more diffusion. People will choose not to waste a minute to get the most out of a short time. Depending on the identity being indulged on vacation, this can look very different; increased density could mean trying to see and do as much as possible, but it could also mean spending as much time as one can lying by the pool.

This chapter examines how the social experience of time, as a constructed and constitutive element of people's environment, influences identity shifts. Local, culturally specific temporal regimes determine when people will take on roles and alter identities and for how long. By regulating the duration, ordering, and salience of roles, temporalities fundamentally influence the self. They determine what people can do, how often, and in what order. They therefore shape how people will act in given contexts and how they will respond to others.

Time and the Shaping of Identity

The self is shaped by temporalities. Part of its basic organization is a division between a public side and a private side. The public side is shaped by a temporal regime that is shared, and the private side by one more idiosyncratic.[17] The public self must synchronize with other people and conform to a shared experience. It is necessarily regimented and scheduled so that it may operate in accordance with a given culture and its demands. While social time is a purely qualitative experience, there must also be a shared system of timekeeping that allows people to be organized and in sync with each other. Georg Simmel identifies a will to connection among individuals that drives the tempo of public life, especially in urban areas. For people to connect there must be coordination of time and place. Precision in timing is necessary to tie together the many relationships and activities the typical person is involved in. Without punctuality there would be chaos. A standard time that is organized and shared beyond subjective experience is a bridge that enables individuals to connect with each other.[18]

This shared temporality patterns the public self when it seeks connection with others. People must adapt, on an hourly to a yearly basis, the publicly shared aspects of their self to conform to schedules. The private self, on the other hand, can have no such constraints. In this realm, individual desires and personal routines shape the self and personal identity shifts rather than collective ones. People frequently switch between personal and private selves in the course of everyday life, juxtaposing periods of temporal regulation and autonomy.

Within this framework, vacations organize privacy and accessibility. On a break, many of the scheduling demands of everyday life are reshuffled, and priorities may be rearranged. During the working day, most people must remain accessible to their boss or coworkers in order to properly fulfill their role, putting children, family, and often friends in abeyance. Once the work day is over, this accessibility changes, prioritizing more personal connections over the public ones. On vacation the hierarchy may be flipped, prioritizing contact with friends and family at all times while allowably neglecting coworkers and supervisors. This temporal reshuffling allows reprioritizing facets of self.

Public and private time are not the same thing as leisure and work time. A vacation is not in itself totally private time since there are still various audiences with which one interacts. These two elements should be understood as more of a continuum than a dichotomy. Some audiences, such as a spouse or close friend, may be more equated with privacy than one's coworkers but still are not equivalent to being alone. Rather, almost every moment of one's time is characterized by some combination of private and public, allowing degrees of social accessibility.[19] Further, moments of private time must be scheduled in accordance with the demands of public time. They operate only in relation to each other. A vacation usually respects the demands of work flows.[20] It is restricted to a set number of days and, often, a certain time of the year.

Émile Durkheim was the first to observe that time functions as an ordering principle that keeps events apart.[21] He noted that the organization of institutionalized holidays segregates the sacred and the profane so that the two do not overlap and cause cognitive confusion for celebrants. Since holy days often have special rules, including a reordering or flexibility of the norms and regulations observed on profane days, they must be distinctly separate in the minds of individuals so that activities meant for the sacred do not overlap into the profane, and vice versa. These differences are substantiated through behaviors such as eating special foods, wearing more formal clothes, and participating in certain religious rituals. There is therefore a social need to keep these two realms, and their corresponding norms and behaviors, separate, lest the indulgences and excesses of one period spill out into the other. This temporal segregation is a fundamental feature of social life. The basic cultural contrast between the ordinary and the extraordinary is necessarily divided and segmented in time.[22] In the same manner as holidays, vacations are temporally bounded and confined to specific days off that segment this period of lax regulation into a defined moment in time.[23]

While confining holidays to particular days helps organize experience, it also contributes to the rhythm of life. Although in Western societies we tend to think of time as having a linear nature, always moving forward, with no opportunity to go back, there are other ways of experiencing time. The repetitive nature of annual events such as holidays or vacations or other marked occurrences contribute to a cycle of recurring experience. For example, the weekend forms a regularly occurring "pulse" in the endlessly repeated cycle of the week.[24] Holidays work similarly on an annual scale. Henri Hubert noted that all social rhythms are the result of alternations between certain critical days and the time between them. Time then alternates between these rare special days and the plentiful mundane days.[25] The critical dates of events such as holidays and the unexceptional time between them give a rhythmic spasmodic nature to time. Building on Hubert, Edmund Leach interpreted the passage of time as not continuous but rather a repetition of alternations and full stops between these critical days.[26] In this view, instead of moving in a straight line, time operates more like a pendulum, oscillating between the short, marked intervals of exceptional time and the longer, unmarked expanses of everyday life that occur between.[27]

A vacation replicates many of the exceptional or unusual aspects of a holiday, and it represents one of these marked contrasts that set the pace and tempo of the year. The annual summer vacation or planned time off around the holidays in November and December represents points at which the pendulum swings toward the unusual and the infrequent. The time between is the standard. Since these events tend to occur with regularity and are thus anticipated, they create a repeated cyclical nature to annual time rather than a linear progression. Not as long as a sabbatical but not as short as a midday nap, vacations offer an extended period of release from the flow of everyday life that permits extended rejuvenation and refreshment.[28]

The timing of trips conforms to the norms of the annual alternation between time on and time off. The passage of the year has a rhythm that is moderated and punctuated by the seasons, school schedules, holidays, and work demands. In this cycle summer is often experienced as a standstill or pause in which the pace of life slows down and people choose to leave town or take time off work.[29] Summertime is a broad switch of the pendulum to a down-tempo period of the year. While this pattern made sense when it was created for a society oriented toward the demands of agricultural schedules, vacations no longer have a practical reason, in a time of air conditioning and office work, for conforming to this rhythm. Yet the annual summer vacation remains as an expected escape route built into the structure of the year. School schedules still generally follow a fall to spring calendar, thus determining in large part the timing of family vacations, but this schedule is mostly a normative leftover from earlier years, when extra labor was needed for the summer farm work. The growing popularity of winter vacations[30] emphasizes the cultural nature of taking time off in the summer and adds emphasis to the critical period of seasonal holidays around the end of the calendar year.[31]

The infrequency of these vacation times in part marks them as exceptional, which in turn allows the cessation of strict regulations on behavior. Not all time off shares these characteristics. A two-day weekend, while enjoyable and highly anticipated, is not invested with the same significance of a vacation because it recurs in every seven-day period. It is an expected part of the temporal structure, not an escape from it. The weekend instead represents repetitive, scheduled leisure that is provided with regularity.[32] This frequent repetition makes it conventional and therefore less special than a vacation or holiday. Alternatively, using a sick day to play hooky or receiving an unexpected snow day from work or school, although short lived, can give the feeling of a minivacation because these events happen only occasionally and irregularly.

Regardless of cyclical contrasts, not all vacations are experienced in the same way. Because these breaks reliably punctuate the passage of the year, they become a routinized part of the cycle in themselves. Certain experiences have more frequency than others, and this invests them with varying degrees of importance to the individual. Repeating a particular type of trip makes it less unique, and possibly less special, than doing something new. Thus, the vacation itself becomes part of the annual routine at the same time that it is an escape from it. It is constitutive of the cycle of time. The annually occurring summer vacation becomes mundane because of its repetition.[33]

Then there are trips that are once-in-a-lifetime or dream vacations to somewhere far away or very expensive. In contrast with the circular annual vacation, these trips mark out time in a linear manner over the life course because they are infrequent and mark rites of passage, such as a backpacking trip after college or a postretirement trip abroad, or are so special that they become milestones in themselves.

Vacations and Time Tracks

Being a temporary experience, a vacation by definition is limited to a fixed-term "time track."[34] Social behaviors take place on these predetermined time tracks that sequence and organize experiences and that may range from the brief or episodic to the long-term and continuous. These time tracks act as the containers for identity shifts. Time tracks are set apart from the daily flow of life by investing them with particular meanings. The time track of the vacation is a chunk of time endowed with special permission for flexibility and release. This is all the more reason why it must be contained within a period defined as finite.

Ideas about the proper duration of these time tracks are normatively binding and influence how people structure their identity shifts in them. The rigidity placed on ideas of duration is primarily due to convention,[35] however, and it is difficult to apportion what can be considered the correct duration to define something as a vacation. A three-day weekend can qualify as a vacation for one person, while another needs two weeks to properly get away. This is further complicated by experience of duration being subjective and often distorted depending on the context a person is in.[36] This variability of duration as a defining characteristic of a vacation is demonstrated by factors including nationality, social class, age, and gender affecting the availability and the use of vacation time. What is considered to be an appropriate length for a vacation also varies sharply across countries, with the U.S. standard being one to two weeks and most European countries' being four to six weeks.[37]

The conventions of time tracks, such as the duration, frequency, pace, and sequence of events, guide identity shifts. Duration, for example, influences the ability and interest to draw boundaries around the identity change. When the time away is shorter it is more permissible to cut off contacts with people back home. When leaving for a long weekend it is usually more acceptable not to remain in touch with friends and family. Alternatively, if one is leaving for a month, it is expected that one will stay in touch in some form. Duration similarly influences the degree to which a person may be willing or able to segment or integrate identities. A short trip that does not demand as much absence from everyday life can allow more segmentation. It is easier, and possibly more desirable, to set up firm boundaries when the absence is short, while a long trip usually necessitates more contact with the life left back at home. Normative guidelines help direct behavior. An absence of a month must be accounted for in some way.[38]

Duration influences the experience of the trip because levels of activity and expectations of novelty expand and shrink to fit the time period. There is an inverse relationship between duration and pace. Longer trips tend to have a slower pace because there is more time to see and do what one wishes. Conversely, shorter vacations often have a rapid pace to fit everything within brief temporal boundaries. Jeff traveled a long distance for his relatively short trip to China and spent a lot of money to get there, so he intensifies the density of his tourist identity while he is there:

> Sightseeing is the biggest thing. Trying to do everything that I can, even if, you know, I'm so worn down that I don't want to do it. Like, I didn't get home until five last night, this morning. And then I had to wake up at seven thirty so I could do my acupuncture. So I'm tired, but go hard or go home.

Jeff's enthusiasm to do and see as much as he can during his limited time in China means that he tries to pack as much as he can into his days. He likes to do his identity shift at a high level of intensity, and this is reflected in the way he schedules his time. Rather than relaxing, his days and nights are filled with activity. Similarly, Luke describes a sightseeing trip he took through Italy, stopping in several cities over the course of a week. He describes how it was good to be able to see a lot in a short time. He notes that he was able to do a lot this way, but it took effort because time moved quickly:

> When I went to Italy, it was an arranged thing. It was kind of traveling from the north to the south and jumping through different cities on the way. So that was really good. Just to see more in less time. But it's difficult to do that kind of thing. It has to be really arranged. You don't have enough time. It just flies by.

Those like Jeff and Luke, who have invested a good deal of money and vacation days into a big trip abroad, want to make the most it, fitting as much as they can into a limited duration so as to get a lot out of the experience. In this situation the nature of time as a budgeted and finite commodity becomes apparent. People invest in the trip in terms of the money spent as well as possibly lost wages for days not at work. In exchange they want to get as much out of the trip as possible. The limited time also means that it becomes a constraint on the freedom of the vacation. Since there is only so much of it, individuals must maneuver within its restrictions. They use their agency to do "time work" and get the most out of the experience.[39]

A chief constraint on the duration of vacations in the United States is the expectation that work takes precedence over leisure. The amount of time an event lasts is symbolically associated with the significance that is attached to it.[40] When we devote more of our time to something, we indicate to others that we value it more. Many Americans demonstrate that they value work by confining time off to brief intervals and not making use of all their vacation days. Unused vacation time reveals that one prioritizes the job over leisure.[41] Joanne's former high-stress job at an investment bank fostered this attitude, and she felt she could not take time off, even though it was promised to her:

> It was hard for me to [stop working] unless I was really far away. Part of that was because I had to plug in with my portable computer. I was required, even at the beach. You have to be a workaholic to be a banker because you work every weekend, every night, all your life. That's all you can do. . . . When I went to the Jersey shore, I ended up being in the [hotel] room the whole time because I had to work.

Even though she was given a good deal of vacation time as a job benefit, she was not expected to use it. The expectation of employers that employees be available can be as limiting as not even being given the vacation time. Before Joanne left her job as a banker, the implicit and explicit expectation of her coworkers that she be accessible and productive limited the amount of time that she was willing to spend away from work. This shortened the length and frequency of her vacations, as well as her activities while away.

Taking longer vacations may elicit negative reactions from friends or family in addition to colleagues. Attitudes about the importance of time devoted to work and the indulgence of too much free time extend beyond the workplace. A vacation that is too long is viewed as a luxury or even as selfish. Since vacations can be expensive, in terms of the assets of money and free time, long vacations signal to others that one has the available resources for an extended absence. Cindy, a college student from Alaska on vacation in Hawaii with her boyfriend and his two kids, was reluctant to tell friends back home that they would be gone for a month because she had gotten negative reactions and teasing from friends who knew and called her "spoiled." "I almost feel bad to say we're here for a month. . . . But we're just going to get a condo, which is a lot cheaper than staying at a hotel." She feels the need to justify the length of the trip by noting how they made it more affordable.

Durations of social relationships allow greater or lesser satisfaction before the relationships are finished. Longer durations allow more ambivalence and more negotiation for periods of personal dissatisfaction. Robert Merton uses the example of a long-term marriage versus a short-lived affair.[42] Because of the extended duration of the marriage there is more room for frequent, as well as more intense, ambivalence. Even if one feels unsure occasionally, the marriage can endure. In fact, the extended duration of the relationship makes ambivalence an expected reaction. The short-term and impermanent nature of an affair, however, leaves less room for indecision. It is expected to be exciting and not tedious. If it becomes tiresome, it may be terminated.

In the same way, when expectations for a trip do not fit the time track to which they have been assigned disappointment and ambivalence occurs. People have apportioned a certain amount of their valuable leisure time to the experience and so hope to get the most out of it. With more time comes more room for ambivalence. While longer vacations introduce opportunities for ambivalence, they are generally more in line with the affair than the marriage. They are short term and expected to be enlivening. Expectations for pace, activities, and durations must be properly matched. In a post to the now-defunct travel blogging site TravelPod, a woman on a bird-watching trip demonstrates the importance of matching duration and pace when she expresses her dissatisfaction that planned activities were not enough to fill her fifteen-day trip: "Eleven days would have been enough. Fifteen is too much, at least the way they planned this. It seems like the trip was actually planned for eleven days and then we have three days kicking around to different spots that aren't really different at all." For someone seeking difference and novelty in her travel, there was too much repetition in her trip. Similarly, Mona, a vacationer in China, stayed put in the city of Xi'an for what she felt was a week too long:

> I'm here for three weeks. I would have been done at two. . . . The adrenaline of having it all be new and going someplace, seeing all this different stuff, and having all these sensory experiences, that kind of really dropped off. Like, I had felt like I had gotten all of that after two weeks, and now I just feel like I'm hanging, waiting to go to Beijing and try something new.

In both cases the travelers were frustrated when the length of their vacation outlasted the novelty and they had an unwelcome sense of idleness. The birdwatcher is just "kicking around," and Mona is "hanging." Both are waiting for the new experiences that they feel should make up their trip. They apportioned a certain amount of their free time to their vacation and they wish to get the most out of it. They experience a sense of waste that comes from not optimally making use of their leisure time. These tourists are trying to fill time. They want to keep busy on their trips. They do not want idle time, and to some extent they feel their agency to make that happen has been taken away. The woman on the organized bird-watching trip has to do preplanned activities. Similarly, Mona, as discussed in Chapter 2, feels a little inhibited by the foreignness of China and depends on others to make things happen for her. Neither feels she is adequately filling time, but they both, for their own reasons, lack the agency to fix the problem.[43]

While a shorter time track carries with it expectations of novelty and stimulation, a longer one comes with expectations of establishing a routine, with more room for downtime. A longer vacation with more time to relax will likely have a slower pace than a short vacation filled with activity. Francine, who is on vacation in Hawaii, contrasts her earlier weeklong trips with the month that she is currently spending in the islands:

> I thought, "What would I do here for a month?" And you just live. You just, you get up, and you take a bath, and you go shopping, and you come to the water, and you make it a lifestyle when you're here for that long. In a week you just want to do everything, the luaus, the cruises, and I've done that too. I've come here for a week before, and that's been really fast paced [snaps fingers]. It's different than coming for a month. A lot different vacation.

Celeste similarly describes the typical fast rhythm of a weeklong vacation: "By the time you settle down, three days have gone by, and before you know it, within a few days you're packing and going back to where you came from. So it's a really short period of time that you really get to do everything, and then you're going back." Staying for a relaxed month rather than a rushed week creates a situation in which it's desirable for the novelty to go away. The goal is to create a feeling of living in a different way and adapt to the rhythms of another lifestyle. Travelers of this sort taste a lifestyle in a way that a rushed tourist moving from spot to spot and trying to fit it all in cannot. They relax and enjoy rather than maximizing limited time in a cost-benefit approach.

Marking Time

Whether a vacation is long or short, it has distinct boundaries that mark its beginning and end, and fluctuations in activity reflect the significance of its start and finish and the transitions gone through. People substantiate the beginning and end of their trip through their behavior. Position in the time track—the beginning, middle, or end—influences behavior because people mark out the temporal dimensions of their trip through activity. Behavior follows a pattern that begins with the initial splurge of eager activity, transitions to a less active period in the middle, and ends with a final peak of high activity at the end as they prepare to leave.[44] These changes in activity and behavior over the course of a vacation illustrate how time and position in a time track affect construction and performance of identity.

The beginning of the vacation time track is usually marked by a period of high activity that is spurred on by enthusiasm or excitement to experience the new environment and opportunities available. Often one has anticipated the trip, and arrival at the destination signifies achievement of this desired goal. Although this initial enthusiasm usually wanes a few days into the trip, excitement marks the beginning of a novel experience. Maria comments on her initial enthusiasm on arriving in Hawaii for her vacation and its lapse: "The first day I was so tired, but I got off the plane, and I dropped off my son and my luggage at the hotel, and then I went everywhere. Yesterday, I just slept all day. That's all I did." On her first day in Hawaii she ignored her tiredness and jet lag to go "everywhere"; by the third day she was more inclined to sleep on the beach. Many visitors to China had a similar reaction upon their arrival. After an on-average thirteen-hour plane ride and twelve-hour time zone switch, they were eager to meet fellow travelers and explore the city without a break to rest. Their enthusiasm would wane only after they became more familiar with their new environment. Many tourist itineraries similarly institutionalize this midtrip lull by scheduling some downtime of an afternoon or day off at the midpoint.

The beginning of a trip is exciting and highly anticipated, and the end of a trip also means completing a favorable and highly anticipated activity and returning to everyday life until the next such event is possible. Activity speeds up again as people mark this transition by trying to fit in last-minute activities, revisiting favored sites one last time, buying last-minute souvenirs and gifts, or planning celebrations and goodbyes.

Because people are running up against the boundaries, they push back an extra bit before they must return to the limitations of everyday life. While the majority of the vacation experience is organized around indulgence of some kind, at the end of the vacation people often indulge an *extra* bit because it is their last chance. They embrace the freedoms a bit more when they realize they are coming to an end. This is a final opportunity for indulgent enjoyment before return to a more abstinent everyday life where control over things like eating or spending may be more strict. This is different from the indulgence that marks most of the trip, because it is done in such a way as to intentionally mark the closing of the trip. Two women at a theme park on Oahu loudly discuss ice cream on their last day on the island. They yell to each other over the din of the cafeteria at lunchtime. The first woman asks her friend, "Are you getting ice cream?" Her friend replies, "Oh, I don't know." The first woman responds, "You're still on vacation; do it! One more day!" And her friend replies, "One more day! It will be my last hurrah!"

This woman conceptualizes her indulgence in a temporal manner and thinks of it as acceptable because it will be her "last hurrah," or last indulgence of her Hawaiian vacation. On his last night in China, Xavier organized a night out to his favorite nightclub during which he intended to stay out as late as possible and get very drunk before his trip ended. Brenda, on an eight-day tour of Hawaii with her family, booked front row seats at an elaborate luau on their last night in the islands, splurging on table service so that they would not have to wait in line at the buffet with everyone else. She explained it was all very expensive, but because it was her last night in Hawaii she wanted to do something special.

At the end of the trip people will also plan particular events or activities intended to celebrate the experience with others and in some way thank them or acknowledge their role in the vacation experience. On her last night in China, for example, Jodie planned and executed a large dinner, inviting all her fellow tourists and program staff members that she had befriended during her trip. Others distributed small gifts or treats, like a round of drinks at the bar or a popular ice cream, to say thank you and goodbye.

At the end of the vacation, schedules and routines may also be altered to expand the amount of time available or the sense of the available time. Said one visitor in a post to a TravelPod blog, "My last day in Hawaii . . . I get up before dawn to get my last thrills." Getting up very early on the last day, running through activities quicker than usual, or cutting out regularly scheduled activities or activities that seem too mundane, such as meal times, create the perception of more time for the vacation and fitting in as much as possible before it ends.[45]

Orientations to Time

On vacation people are separated from the temporal structures of their everyday life and sometimes from the cues to clock time that are around them. But this depends on environment. People experience time on a

continuum of freedom and constraint. In some situations of rest and relaxation people may ignore clock time and the constraints it imposes.
Time becomes flexible and is adaptable to one's interests and desires, and
the routines that structure one's behavior may be subverted. People may
lose track of time and ignore its passage because standard clock time is
altered. In other situations, such as tourism, close attention to time is
very important. Rather than disregarding the clock, visitors must adapt
their behavior to an existing temporal order. Especially for those who
move from place to place, the pace of a vacation is much faster.[46] In these
situations individuals are responsible for their well-being and the success
of their trip. This requires close attention to time. The phenomenological
experience of time while traveling can be jarring and shows that travel
still has distinct, localized properties despite globalizing forces. Cultural
and normative time use vary and visitors must be attentive.

There is, then, a difference between vacation time and everyday time
that echoes the temporal differences between the private and the public
self. Vacationers may ignore everyday time and immerse themselves completely in the inversions of the vacation, neglecting the schedules, clocks,
and timetables that form the temporal logic of the world around them.
Instead, the norms and routines of everyday schedules are altered *for* them.
Temporal organization of everyday time does not offer this luxury, and
people must instead pay close attention to it if they want their trip to be
successful. The everyday environments to which they travel make no attempts to alter temporal norms and conventions to suit them as visitors.

Constructed temporalities thus influence identity through freedom
and constraint, and autonomy and security. Some identities are highly
routinized and subject to external regulation; other identities are more
temporally loose. Those on vacation time have an autonomy and freedom
in their identity that is lacking for those subject to external regulation.
For the most part, they can do what they want when they want, and they
lack many external time constraints. The social construction of temporal
rhythms specifically enables this. The freer identity is made possible by
the freer environment. The second type loses some of this autonomy. Their
busyness aids in their active identity shift at the expense of the personal
freedoms that come from liberation from clock time.

Ignoring Time

Cindy comments on how her days on vacation in Hawaii are removed from
the routines that delimit her everyday experience: "Well, we have no

schedule [*laughs*]. We're just on vacation, so we're being really—just relax and do whatever. There's no plan, versus when you're at home, and you have things to do like school and work. Here we're just hanging out." She and her boyfriend can do what they want when they want, without worrying about quotidian demands regulating their day. Celeste similarly describes a typical morning in Waikiki:

> I am not an early starter. So I typically get up around eight thirty, quarter to nine, open the shades, and look out onto the beautiful harbor, boats, and ocean. And I sit there, and I really stare at the ocean. I sit there. Which is something I can never do at home; get up, sit, and stare at something. I mean, that's unusual. So I look at the ocean and the boats coming and going.

Celeste may structure her days as she likes, including spending long periods doing nothing but looking at the ocean. She eats breakfast when she chooses, rather than quickly getting it in before work and errands, and then spends her entire afternoon sitting on the beach.

In trips to natural destinations, cues to social time are eliminated by virtue of the environment. When camping or renting a country home, for example, people may invert or ignore schedules, routines, or responsibilities. This may happen consciously because they seek to forget time or inadvertently because they lose track without the ubiquitous cues to time otherwise available in the city. Thomas Hylland Eriksen analyzed perceptions of time in today's information age and found that the experience of time changes on a typical Scandinavian family vacation to a cabin in the woods that leaves behind everyday technologies:

> One puts the watch in the drawer and leaves it there until it is time to leave for the city. In this context it is not the pressure of the clock that regulates activities, but the activities that regulate the organization of time. The children go to bed an hour later than usual, dinner is served as the result of hunger, berry-picking and fishing last as long as one feels like it, and so on.[47]

Physically taking off one's watch and putting it out of sight is a symbolically significant aspect of liberation from the constraints of time. Instead of orienting activities to fit into a predetermined timetable, the activities and desires of the individual fashion the passage of the day, while physical demands such as hunger determine when meals will be eaten and when activities will end. Schedules are lived out around individual wishes rather than adherence to the hours of the clock.

Temporal flexibility allows people to play with the norms of deviance and acceptability. Much of what is considered deviant is constructed and rests on the contextual factors in which the act is situated. Drinking in a bar is acceptable, but drinking at work is not. Along these lines, many activities are considered deviant depending on their place in time.[48] Drinking is usually acceptable after five but not at noon and only within a defined container of time, such as during happy hour or when having after-dinner drinks. But on vacation, people more generally do things when they want, for as long they want, and in the order they want. People not only have the flexibility to consume alcohol in the afternoon or with their breakfast; they may also do so *throughout* the day, not limiting their consumption to scheduled slots at mealtimes. This attitude is exemplified by Kelly, who frequently spends her vacation time at a lake house in the country where such conventions become very flexible: "I allow myself to drink beer really early in the morning—in the day, I should say, not morning. I try to wait until noon. I sleep in later than I normally would allow myself to, and I go to bed earlier than normal." Kelly has a general rule for herself about not drinking beer before noon, but this applies only to beer and not necessarily Bloody Marys, mimosas, or other breakfast drinks that can be consumed at brunch or anytime before midday.

Kelly's vacation indulgence extends from drinking more alcohol to reshaping her daily routine. Durations of events become more flexible as they expand or shrink according to her preference rather than social convention or a work schedule. In addition to extended time allotted for sleep, her lunch may go on for two or three hours instead of being a fixed one-hour break, or her usual quick breakfast may be expanded to take up much of the morning.

The seven-day work-rest cycle is what gives contemporary life much of its temporal structure. The beat in the rhythm of the week that the weekend introduces makes it easier to keep track of the days. Without an experiential difference to distinguish the marked days from the regular days, such as the contrasts between work and play or labor and relaxation, days begin to look and feel the same and can easily become confused.[49] As a result people may more easily lose track of time, forgetting not just the hours in the day but also the day of the week. A description of a road trip through the American Southwest demonstrates that experience of clock time is contingent on cues that organize and separate days: "The journey took on its own dimension of time as all journeys do. Sleeping aboard the bus and roaming the open terrain of the southwest soon removed the memory of the calendar and, before long, we were asking each other what day of the week it was."[50] When every day is more or less the same, the days seemingly slide together.

Resorts, cruise ships, and other total institutions of the vacation industry seek to replicate this experience of natural ease and release from the stresses of the modern city in their more controlled environments. A total institution, an organization that separates itself and its members from society, encourages different dress, different ways of thinking, and different behaviors. Members of a total institution tend to be very similar to each other but different from the outside society. Vacation destinations thus encourage temporary movement into a voluntary total institution.[51] A primary method of achieving this is by removing the cues to shared time and helping customers forget about schedules and the Monday-to-Friday routine. Every day in resort-type hotels is made to feel like a holiday. This is in contrast with hotels for business travelers, where things can be much more quotidian and temporal reminders are frequent to help keep travelers in line with the demands of home. In resort-type hotels not only are days alike, but each is special. Patricia and Peter Adler describe how a group of Hawaiian resorts intentionally alter the experience of the week for their visitors:

> Each day at the Ali'i resorts was contoured to make guests feel as if they were free from the weekly time treadmill, especially from the morose Mondays and the sad Sundays that preceded them, signifying the end of the weekend and the return to labor. Ali'i guests were liberated from the fetters of the week by being encapsulated in a world of service and luxury, where everything they wanted was available any day they wanted. They could create their days as they desired, without the rhythm of the week impinging on them.[52]

Cruise ships illustrate that much of a vacation is oriented toward eliminating or altering schedules and constraints. A cruise ship passenger sums this up in his idealized account in a TravelPod blog post: "The days seem to be falling astern with great speed. It seems that we rise for breakfast and in the blink of an eye we find ourselves sitting down to a wonderful dinner. Where does the time go? So much to do, and it seems, so little time in which to do it." The days are filled with pleasant and relaxing activities, and passengers hold little responsibility for making things go smoothly. Everything is done for them so that they may relax and enjoy the experience. This contrasts with the mismatch between agency and temporal experience that Mona and the bird-watcher, discussed earlier, experienced. These people have also handed over a lot of their self-direction to the cruise operators and in return are experiencing a balance of activities and leisure that make the time pass quickly. Meals are prepared and offered in several dining areas throughout the day in addition to around-the-clock room service in cabins. Activities, both enriching and diverting, are scheduled back-to-back during long days at sea to keep customers entertained and are followed in the evenings with performances, dancing, and availability of onboard bars. Housekeeping discreetly enters and leaves the cabins while people are out, leaving their spaces tidy and clean, but invisibly so. And long hours may be spent on deck by the pool. Effort is made to ensure that days are both full and effortless. As a result, people easily lose track of time.

A conversation I had with a woman and her husband who had just disembarked from a seven-day cruise in Hawaii reveals how people lose track of the days. Sitting at a bus stop outside where the cruise ships dock to unload their passengers, an older couple waits for their bus to arrive to take them into Waikiki. As we wait for the bus, I ask how long they had been on their cruise. The woman thinks for a bit but cannot answer; she really is not sure. She pauses and checks with her husband, who tells us both that today is Friday and they have been on the cruise for a week. "I'm so lost for time," the woman says several times, unable to keep track of the days since her vacation's start.

This effect is also achieved on an hourly scale. At the Club Med in the Turks and Caicos Islands, for example, two clocks hang above the reception area. One is set to local time, the other to "Club Med Time," an hour later. The second clock represents the official time of the resort, shared everywhere so that guests can enjoy an extra hour of sunlight.[53] When everything in the grounds is synchronized, it does not matter if this does not match "real" time; guests can adapt.

Much like casinos without clocks, which distorts perceptions of time and causes people to lose track of the hours, resorts attempt to capitalize on vacationers' flexible approach to their days. By expanding the time for socializing and consuming into the night, resorts blur or eliminate altogether the temporal boundary between day and night that usually divides experience.[54] Dining is available throughout the day and late into the night, retailers are open extended hours, and room service may be available twenty-four hours a day. Not only does this alter guests' experience of time in their days, but it also extends the hours during which a resort can be making a profit. Changing the clocks at Club Med coordinates better with the hours of daylight and expands the time during which customers will be awake and consuming. Resorts have around-the-clock hours because people arrive at all times from different time zones, and people have an expectation that service will be available at all times.

The luxurious perks of vacation time alter feelings of synchronicity with clock time. Vacationers in these environments do not need to comply with the temporal norms of their everyday life or of the place to which they have traveled. But this is possible only because temporal norms have been changed for them by the individuals and organizations that frame the environment. There is still an everyday time that employees and local residents adhere to, and thus visitors and locals represent two different temporal orientations that overlap in space, with the latter enabling the timeless experience of the former through their work.

The locations of an organization and the service it provides affect the temporal expectations that are put on it, as a busy kitchen in a restaurant must organize and manage the flow of work time according to mealtimes.[55] Because vacationers will inevitably leave the resort to explore their new environment, this temporal flexibility extends beyond the confines of the property. A restaurant or bar in a tourist area must adapt its workflow to suit the needs of visitors and often has extended operating hours. Bars, restaurants, attractions, grocery stores, and convenience stores open every day of the week and for extended hours. One popular tourist bar in Waikiki broadly advertises its hours as "serving daily from 7 AM to 2 AM"; a visitor can get a drink or a local dish virtually any time of day.

Break times in these organizations do not conform to the usual patterns of work and rest, because leisure-based businesses receive most of their business during traditional rest times. The temporal rhythm from the alternation between weekday and weekend is out of sync for these businesses and the people who work in them, because they tend to close on slow weekdays, rather than on a weekend. Museums, for example, which cater to visitors looking for productive leisure, often alter the standard weekly rhythm by closing on a Monday or Tuesday to accommodate weekend crowds.

There are limits on the ability to escape time in this way. Even in an environment that facilitates it, other actors and obligations can pull one back into attentiveness. Children, for example, can require an attention to time and routinization that might otherwise be forgotten. Joanne compares two trips she took to Hawaii with her husband. The first was about fifteen years ago, before they had kids. "We did what we wanted. We did more sports activities. So we did scuba diving, and we just did what we wanted, where we wanted, and we didn't have to worry about lunch schedules or this or that." Joanne and her husband could enjoy the freedom promised by Hawaii when they traveled as just a couple. On the second trip, with their three young children, however, their activities had to become more routinized. Today in Waikiki

we had breakfast in our room because we're too cheap to eat breakfast here, because it's so expensive. And then the kids decided. I said, "Do you want to go out?" They usually like to come out early here because of the sun. But today they wanted to play in the room this morning, probably because they've been doing so much stuff. So they played pretend, . . . and then we had a snack lunch in the room again, because we're cheap. And then we've been down here [on the beach] ever since. And then we'll probably go in because we'll probably start burning this afternoon. So we'll go in this afternoon, probably like two or three o'clock.

Joanne's day is ordered by the needs and interests of her children. Since their play and meal times are prioritized, those are the events that organize her time. She spends her morning in the room and her afternoon at the beach because it is what they choose to do. The ultimate goal is to keep the kids happy and entertained. To a degree they are still organizing their activities around the natural environment. They go to the beach in the morning to avoid the sun and leave the beach early so that they do not burn, but this is a natural influence of time that is very different from the ability to put the watch away and do what one wishes.

A second loss to Joanne's temporal freedom comes from no longer having the financial resources to do as she wishes. Since Waikiki is such an expensive destination, she must organize her time to be able to provide cheap meals to her family. When she and her husband had more money for just the two of them, they had more freedom to indulge in expensive activities and eat when and where they wished. This is a constraint that may not be as much of an issue in cheaper environments, like at a cabin in the woods, but since everything in Waikiki costs money except sitting on the beach, this becomes a key constraint on her autonomy. It is also one that she is very aware of.

The demands of others are not limited to just children. Connie's vacations change according to her traveling companions. With her own family she can relax and be laid back, but with her husband's she cannot. During a vacation at a lake house that should be free of the stresses of time, Connie describes how difficult vacationing with her husband's family can be, because she feels she cannot be herself around them. She uses temporal terms to describe the feeling of having to impress them. "You have to be on twenty-four-seven when you're with your husband's family. When you're with your own family you—depending on how you get along with your mother and father and siblings—you can just let it all hang out." Connie is staying with her in-laws and spends all her time with them. This turns out to be even more demanding than the temporal restrictions of everyday life because she does not get time off at the end of the day but is on at all times.

When she says she is "on" twenty-four-seven, she invokes Erving Goffman's[56] dramaturgical metaphor for identity and roles. The identity she must present when with her in-laws is that from a more regulated environment with a "front stage" that she has difficulty getting away from. Front stage and backstage combine spatial and temporal imagery for situating identity, because a place can be front stage at one time and backstage at another time.[57] Connie, on vacation with her in-laws, loses control over the amount of time that she is front stage, where much more regulation of the self occurs.

Attending to Time

In other situations that are more regulated or involve more immersion in an everyday environment, people must pay close attention to clock time instead of ignoring it. Identity shifts are adjusted to fit into the schedules, timetables, plans, and temporal expectations of others. Expressions of self are regulated to fit into a local environment rather than an environment changing to accommodate a freer self. The tourist experience has a diurnal nature.[58] People leave their hotel to sightsee and then return at night to the comfort of their temporary residence. Time oscillates between security and independence as people move between their obliging hotel and the less accommodating outside world. At a resort the diurnal split is lessened with the compliant accommodations of the incessant organization, always open and disregarding the delineation between night and day,[59] but in tourism this transition is highlighted. During the periods when they are responsible for themselves, tourists must closely attend to the clock for their trip to be successful. A European tourist's blog post on TravelPod highlights an attention and sensitivity to time that was missing from the beach and resort vacationers' accounts:

We had plans to land at 10:00, hurry to check in to our hotel, and make the 11:00 train to Birmingham for the soccer game which started at 12:45. We were ahead of schedule during the flight and landed an hour before schedule. Unfortunately our gate was not expecting us so we had to wait a little. We made it to customs by 9:20 and we were so excited thinking we could make the 11:00 train to Birmingham for the soccer game. Alas the entire nation of Zimbabwe was in front of us in the passport check and there were only 5 checkers. . . . We caught the 10:35 train from the airport to Victoria Station. At 11:05 we were still aboard the train waiting motionless on the track for our turn on the platform. We navigated the tube like pros and found our hotel with record speed. Our room was ready so we left our bags and hustled to the train station. It was 12:45 when we arrived at the station and looking at the options we decided that waiting 15 min for the next train, riding 90 minutes, to watch the last 15 minutes of a game was ridiculous.

His attendance of a soccer game demands that he not only closely monitor British train schedules and subway patterns but also rely on local organizations and employees to be ready for his plane to arrive, move him through customs efficiently, and have his room ready for him. Ultimately, this tourist cannot do as he wishes because the timing did not work out.

The consequences of not being on time can ruin plans or just be anxiety provoking because tourists depend on highly routinized and scheduled organizations like trains, buses, and timed tours for the success of their trip. In contrast with the relaxed customer on a cruise who lost track of her days, a couple wishing to leave the security of their ship for an onshore excursion get annoyed when the staff is late with a meal. They feel, as expressed in their TravelPod blog post, that this will throw off their planned schedule for the day:

We ordered a 6:30 AM room service and it arrived at 6:45 AM. We are particular about our time because we are aware of what time the ship departs and we know the amount of time we need for our excursion. Today they [sic] ship leaves at 2 PM. We need to be on board at least by 1:30 PM. The ship will not wait for us if we are late but it is ok for the crew to be late with their services?

Because of the "total institution" nature of the cruise ship, this couple has lost almost all autonomy over their time and with it a good deal of the agency they sought. They are completely reliant on the timing of one section of the cruise ship's staff to keep them on schedule to align with activities with another section. Time is paramount for them because if they lose track or spend too long doing something, they will be left behind. While a fifteen-minute delay may not be a big deal for someone starting a relaxing, unscheduled day aboard the ship, for this couple the delay causes anxiety over the disturbance it will create in their day's schedule. They are leaving the effortless bubble that has been created for them aboard the ship and transitioning to an independent area where they must be responsible for minding schedules and departure times. The stress over potentially being left behind contributes to the anxiety that compels them to plan and apportion activities in advance and then rigidly watch the time throughout the day. Their scheduled security has been compromised by the ship's staff.

Tourists must also conform to the rhythms and demands of the everyday environment into which they have traveled. On trips that involve visiting a city, schedules must correspond with the conventional daily and weekly organization of local time because tourists are visiting the everyday space of another group that is operating on its regular schedule. Major cities are not as dependent on tourism as are places like Honolulu, Las Vegas, or Orlando, and their organizations do not need to adjust schedules according to the needs of tourists, since they have other bases of revenue. A couple on vacation in London finds out the importance of understanding local norms when they finish a long day of sightseeing only to discover that they cannot find anything to eat in the city late in the evening. As they explain in a TravelPod blog post:

> One really odd thing about London is that it shuts down fairly early at night. You can't get food past 10:00 in most areas, and the majority of pubs only stay open until 11:00 during the week. We explored the area looking for dinner, but to no avail. Defeated, we took the tube back to our hotel and I wandered around our area looking for food.

Accustomed to American cities, where incessant institutions have taken hold, and expecting the city to suit their wishes as tourists, these travelers are caught off guard when they cannot find a late dinner to end their day. Being out of sync with local time can end in frustration and even, in this case, inability to meet one's basic needs.

Similarly, in countries that observe a siesta, or downtime in the middle of the day, visitors must observe this break themselves, even if they do not wish to. Planned activities often must be put on hold until things start up again. For people accustomed to making the most of their time, or who wish to get as much as they can out of the short time available in their trip, this pause can be exasperating, as one couple visiting Spain express in their TravelPod blog:

> After the fortress we tried continuing our sightseeing but were frustrated when everything simultaneously closed at 2 PM and the Spaniards, after four hours of work, had a three hour rest. This is annoying when you only have a couple of days to see a place but we could do nothing but embrace it by grabbing some lunch and heading back to the cool of our hotel room.

Trying to take advantage of the freedom introduced into their days by their vacation, siesta is inconvenient to vacationers because it is just one of the ways that the local schedules do not comply with their personal flexibility. The two are not always compatible, as a TravelPod blogger in Europe explains:

> We went to Pinor but it wasn't really much . . . and since we went during god damn siesta everything was closed. Siesta is the biggest nuisance in the world, especially when you're waking up at 11 AM each morning and shops close at 1 PM and don't open again until 5 PM and everything is closed on Sunday except for the market.

In addition to the course of a day, weekly or annual temporal norms can also frustrate travelers who are out of sync with or unaware of them. A traveler in Paris has a similar experience to those thwarted by siesta when she tries to visit a museum on a Tuesday. The problem is not that she has missed closing time but that she is unaware of the local norm for all organizations of this type to be closed on that day of the week. She explains in a TravelPod post:

> Rick and I decided to go to the museums today. That turned out to be not a good idea. We got to the Louvre. Closed. We went to the Musee Pompidou. Closed. Then we made our way to the Picasso Museum. Closed again. We had thought Monday was the day museums were closed, obviously we were mistaken. They are all closed on Tuesday.

Holidays can be similarly problematic if tourists are not aware of local conventions. Two friends looking to celebrate New Year's Eve in San Salvador did not realize that most businesses in the city would shut down for the night, as expressed in their TravelPod blog:

> Now it is New Year's Eve and we have been saving a local bar with music for this occasion but San Salvador was closed for New Year's Eve. Only one bar in a whole street of bars was open and that wasn't inviting so we headed off in a taxi to find a bar in the up-market part of town. . . . Nada, everything was closed. We rode around for ages in the cab and finally admitted defeat and were back in our room at 9:30! No big New Year's celebration for us.

In this case the cultural norms for celebrating a shared holiday were different, which led to an unexpected early night. For other travelers, such as a TravelPod blogger in Indonesia, not being aware of a local holiday altogether creates problems from disruptions and crowds:

> The hotel turned out to be full, as was every other lodging in town. . . . [W]e were unaware of the fact that an island-wide sports festival called "Pordafta"—the Olympics of Flores [Indonesia] was being held in Ruteng that week. There was literally no room anywhere and it was too late to move on to the next town.

In addition to hours and days, temporal patterns differ by season. Tourist spots that are based on seasonal patterns, like beaches, fluctuate between a tourist orientation and a local one. During peak tourist months organizations respond to the flexibility of tourist desires and then the rest of the year return to a locally based schedule. Janet discovers the difference time of year can make when she visits a beach town during the off season. "We didn't get to try too much because during that time all the good restaurants and many of the hostels and hotels were closed. They won't do business until, like, April, so it was two months away." Two friends in Greece had a similar experience, as described in their TravelPod blog, when they tried to visit an island during the off season:

> When we booked our ferry ticket to Ios we were told that it would be quiet this time of year. When we got off the ferry in the afternoon we discovered that quiet meant closed. We struggled to find accommodation but a lovely lady put us up in her guesthouse. We

are probably the only tourists on the island which makes it difficult to find food.

Local temporalities can therefore create challenging obstacles or just
frustrating mismatches for travelers in what the social psychologist Robert Levine refers to as "intercultural struggles over tempo."[60] These mismatches in pace are not limited to just international travel; the tempo of
life can shift dramatically within a country as well—for example, between
New York City and the Deep South.[61]

Some try to avoid the challenges and inconveniences of negotiating an
unfamiliar environment by signing up for group tours that take care of
these arrangements and thereby somewhat accommodate cultural expectations of tempo. However, while group tours reduce the discomforts from
not knowing local rhythms and norms, travelers yield their temporal autonomy to the tour operator, who is given authority to set the pace for the
trip. Melissa describes her experience on a vacation in Italy, where she and
a friend took part of their trip on their own and part with a tour group:

> The tour was structured, and we didn't have to worry about, like,
> hotels or certain meals, or getting anywhere, but we felt very con-
> fined, limited by Contiki [the tour group]. They only let us have like
> an hour by ourselves in Florence, or a couple hours here and there.
> Whereas if we were on our own, we could spend however long we
> wanted. So it was really hard for us to switch from being on our
> own to being structured.

Joining the tour was a trade-off between autonomy and security.
While they did not need to worry about making arrangements or looking
after themselves, they gave up the independence they had when they were
on their own. Instead, their periods of freedom were slotted into scheduled breaks in the tour itinerary.

On such tours and group activities, individuals not only yield control
over their own schedules but also rely on the temporal autonomy of their
fellow travelers. When they join the guided tour time is not their own. It
becomes shared with a group that must be synchronized. Booking tours
and activities ensures that one's day will be structured and that that
structure will be coordinated with others. In addition to being busy, one
must also be on time or risk disrupting the plans of fellow travelers. Being
late creates inconvenience and may provoke negative reactions. Maria
chose not to take a guided tour for her vacation because she had found the

expectation to participate and to stick to scheduled activity times to be too demanding:

> Last time, I went to do tours. I had to be up at six, five in the morning to go do a tour, and this time, no. Not this time. . . . I mean, you work the entire year, and then you decide to go on vacation, and then you have to get up at five in the morning. You have to follow a whole entire schedule, . . . because you have to get up early, or else you'll be late and everyone's looking at you like "You're late." Nicely, but "You're late" [*said in a scolding tone*]. So no, I prefer to be totally free.

Maria chose to reject this type of vacation because she resented the regulation it brought into her time off. She had to get up early, participate in a schedule, and face others' disapproval if she did not keep up. This was too much like her daily work experience, and she chose to enjoy her freedom on her vacation instead. The same is true for individuals who chose to attend all-inclusive resorts so that they did not need to worry about paying as they went or minding the details of their time. The trade-off is usually that they must stick to a rigid schedule for meals and activities. They are able to give up control and let someone else do all the planning, but they give up their freedom of choice. Accepting security and ease usually means trading freedom and autonomy. The tension between the public and the private self comes to the fore again. Individual activities are linked with the temporalities of the people around them. A waiter should be on time with room service, a person joining a group tour must be on time for activities, and it must be the right time of year, or a business may not be open.

On vacation, actors are negotiating a temporal order at variance with their everyday life. The frequency, duration, and sequence with which they do things are all subject to rearrangement. This has implications for the temporal organization of the self. Identity-affirming activities may be prioritized and given more time. A valued activity that usually gets pushed to the background may be moved to the forefront by being done more often and for longer durations. Time spent in unvalued activities can be minimized or done away with altogether.

While one's subjective experience of time may change from that of everyday life, other temporal aspects of the vacation remain tied to normative and conventional constraints. Because vacations provide a socially permitted break from the routines and structures of everyday life they must conform to certain expectations of duration. One cannot be away for too long before it becomes problematic. To be allowed to exit in the first place, a prompt return is expected. At the same time, a vacation that is too short may not feel like a vacation at all to the person trying to get away. In this way, the temporal aspects of breaks are limited by social constraints established through the conventions of time use, including the sequence, duration, and frequency of events during breaks.

People's overall approaches to time are also shaped by their environments. Some may be able to relax and lose track of time; others must pay close attention to the clock and comply with the schedules of others. These differing orientations are important because they demonstrate the essential role of time and autonomy over ability to fashion identity shifts. Some people may do what they wish when they wish. Freedom of time enables this. Others compromise this freedom, either for security or in a rational choice-based decision to make the most out of their time, and encounter much stronger constraints on the freedom of self. Time introduces an external control on what they can do and who they can be. For either group the temporal shifts of vacationing demonstrate that time takes a central role in the shaping and organizing of personal identities and identity shifts.

Conclusion

My research objective is to understand how people use breaks in the social structure of everyday life to alter identity and to understand how people change roles and construct identities when they have an added element of agency that is not usually available to them. I also look at how people negotiate the demands of multiple identities in new contexts and during identity transitions. The research in this area usually focuses on long-term social identities, such as those associated with race and sexuality or with work and home. In tourism studies, the focus is on the identity work done during long-haul travel. This study examines how people manipulate identities as they move between and alter salient identities. I seek to broaden the scope of study on identity changes done during vacation time and focus on identity shifts, or the temporary alterations or reorganizations of identities during these delimited moments of enhanced flexibility of the self.

As society becomes more complex and fragmented, peoples' identities follow suit, becoming increasingly multidimensional, flexible, and fluid to match the competing demands of contemporary life. Modern complexity means that individuals have more role requirements to meet, more group affiliations, and more need to organize competing identities. One's set of routinized, expected everyday identities is not always adequate. Occasionally, demands, obligations, or personal needs and wishes come up that are not met by an existing set of everyday identities. A temporary reorganization of self-identity may then occur to meet these requirements. In contrast with standard, more long-term conceptualizations of identities, these temporary shifts are, by definition, ephemeral. They have beginning and end points and an expectation of impermanence. In a shift an individual takes on an identity that supplements, complements, or diminishes his or her everyday identities and set of counterpart roles or adjusts the salience of existing identities, making an identity weaker than usual or more central than in everyday life. The individual takes on a new set of roles and meanings that are different from those of everyday experience and that will usually be put aside once the temporary period is completed.

This book examines one of these commonplace, but academically overlooked, moments during the course of everyday life during which these shifts take place. People take vacations with the expectation that they can reshuffle priorities. Whether this break is a dramatic change from everyday roles and routines or a more mundane shift in schedules and obligations, some kind of change takes place that allows individuals to temporarily and, one hopes, positively reorganize self-identity. This is what vacations have been designed to do: give people a break from the demands of everyday duties and allow an interruption during which the rigidity of self-identity can be relaxed and rearranged. People do not have to feel guilt or anxiety over putting aside everyday expectations, because it is a time when they are permitted to do so. Vacations are a socially accepted and anticipated break from everyday life.

On vacation people can exploit the mutability of self. One way they do this is by bringing favored identity facets that may usually go underemphasized to the forefront. People can briefly be who they *want* to be rather than who they *must* be. They can indulge in things and ways of being that they value but may not be able to devote time or attention to during the course of their everyday life. Whether this is family, friends, hobbies, or interests, they can refocus their attention and briefly reprioritize this valued aspect of self. At the same time, this means that they also have the freedom to shift other facets of identity temporarily to the background. Whether this is a part of life they do not value but feel compelled to attend to or just something they would like a break from to return to later, the option is available to put less emphasis on certain identity facets or put them aside altogether for the short term. In this way, a vacation can mean many things. For example, it could be simply not going in to work for a week and staying home with the kids, it could be touring Europe with one's partner and trying new foods and activities every day, it could be setting out on one's own and exploring a new city, or it could be attending a convention related to one's interests.

This study also examines the stability and durability of everyday identities—how they yield and flex. Some aspects of everyday self-identity are voluntarily brought into the vacation. Some can be put away entirely until return. Others, individuals might like to leave behind but do not have the option. Children are an exemplary challenge in this regard. Many parents do not have the option of leaving kids at home while they go on vacation, and if they could, they would not choose to. The parental identity and its accompanying obligations are a rigid facet of self that travels along on a vacation. Even those with older children or who leave kids with a caretaker keep their children in the fore of their thoughts while they are away. Work is also complicated. Some easily forget about work the moment they walk out the door to begin their vacation; others fret and call in, unable to leave behind their sense of responsibility for what is happening in their absence. Still others wish they could leave work behind but are concerned about the repercussions for doing so on their return.

Most people also do not want to entirely leave behind their everyday selves and enter permanently into a vacation realm. The return to everyday normality at the end of the trip can be just as highly anticipated as the break away was at the beginning. Part of the appeal of the break is its limited nature. The heightened identity density[1] of the experience means that although fun and enjoyable while it lasts, a vacation is not sustainable over the long term. The limited time allows more: more indulgence, more commitment, and more attention. In the long term this also means more expenditure: of time, resources, and focus.

Building cognitive boundaries around a vacation and the identity shifts made in it separates the everyday and the extraordinary and confines these indulgences to a temporary mental realm.[2] These boundaries are permeable and idiosyncratic. Some people may wish to separate vacation time as much as possible from day-to-day life, keeping their concurrent cognitive routines separate. Others blend and blur these boundaries, allowing overlap of the two. Most people fall at some point in between, letting some aspects of everyday life into the vacation and keeping others out. This in itself is inconsistent among people because different types of trips call for different applications of this process of segmentation and integration of identities. Although the changes being made are not permanent, identity shifts do not neatly start and stop with the trip's beginning and end. Identity facets overlap and compete with one another in ways that extend beyond the boundaries of the vacation. The degree of overlap must be mentally managed before departure and after return. In addition to the boundary work that is done while away, identities must be cognitively organized before and after the official temporal boundaries of the experience. People must manage the degree to which they will plan, prepare, anticipate, and daydream about a vacation and then how much they will remember, relive, and evoke their experience once it is over.

The methods of integrating and segmenting illustrate how opportunity costs influence identity shifts. Integrating elements of everyday life into the vacation is a way of mitigating the costs that vacationers face when they disengage from daily responsibilities. While people may or may not wish to do so, connecting with home makes it easier to negotiate the absence and return. Responding to work-related emails, dealing with crises from friends and family, and buying gifts and souvenirs for people bring home into vacation, sometimes undesirably, but in a way that eases relations and responsibilities temporarily left behind. This integration can constrain freedom, but it makes life easier when people get back. A vacationer may not have wanted to deal with her friend's hospitalization, especially since she felt there was nothing she could do from a thousand miles away in Hawaii, but to ignore it completely would be a challenge to the relationship she ultimately was not willing to make, and so she took his calls, listened to his concerns, and complained about it later.

Although people can consciously keep different identities separate by using mental boundaries or allow them to overlap, home and away can never be divided up and compartmentalized entirely even for the strictest of segmentors. The concept of home permeates everything we do and how we interact with others. Home is the place that defines and situates our knowledge of ourselves and of the world. It is also the place with which new experiences are contrasted. It is where we are socialized, the culture that shapes our thoughts, and the set of communities that guide our perceptions. What is new to us must necessarily be understood and interpreted through this framework. While we may seek to move away from it, and sometimes crave to, it is usually the place offering safety and familiarity and to which we want to return.

Vacations have often been described as liminal moments of flexibility and contrast. Liminality is defined by the absence of structure, yet connections to everyday social structure permeate the vacation, some voluntarily and some not. The roles and responsibilities of everyday life, themselves defined by and tied to social structure, do not disappear while on vacation. Instead, they become more malleable, some more so than others. Vacations are infused with aspects of everyday life. Even if these elements are disattended to they cannot actually be left behind. Overlaps extend from role responsibilities to material objects, routine activities, and embodied reminders. "'Tourist escapes' are full of everyday practices such as eating, drinking, sleeping, brushing teeth, changing nappies, reading bedtime stories and having sex with one's partner, as well as cotraveling mundane objects such as mobile phones, cameras, food, clothes and medicine. Even when a traveler leaves home, home does not leave the traveler."[3] Home is therefore inevitably a part of the vacation experience and performance.

Vacations are often used to reaffirm, replenish, or rebuild social ties. Family is a primary example. While family members, either immediate or extended, are often one of the stressors of everyday life, they are also a significant component of many vacations. Associated identities of mother, son-in-law, spouse, or sister are pushed to the forefront. Most trips are not experienced alone or with strangers but are enjoyed in the company of family and friends. They are a tie from everyday life to the experience. Shared leisure can be significant for developing these relationships to the extent that family roles are often defined in leisure contexts.[4] For example, middle-class American mothers and fathers often feel an obligation to be a "good" parent by taking their kids to Disney World. The quality time of an extended period away from outside demands can be quite different from the harried pace of day-to-day interactions that separate family members. Vacation activities, while they may be temporary and only occasional, contribute to core identities. In this ephemerality and density, they become marked with a special significance for working out family roles.

People can also embrace or indulge aspects of self that are present throughout everyday life but are put second to, for example, financial or temporal demands that prevent those aspects from being expressed as much as they would like. People can play up and immerse themselves in a facet of identity that may be backgrounded during everyday life—for example, a golf buff who can only occasionally get to the course and then goes on a golfing tour; a yoga enthusiast who practices at her gym each week and then goes to a weeklong yoga retreat, or someone who knits to relax in the evenings and then attends an annual knitting conference. These people are not using their vacation time to be something new or different but to emphasize valued facets of self they feel do not get adequate attention during the course of everyday life.

Making a crisp distinction between the extraordinary world of vacations and the ordinary world of everyday life, then, overlooks how the two may combine. Identities overlap and intersect in a more complex fashion than is conventionally realized; the out-of-the-ordinary world of vacations

is permeated with the social obligations, significant others, and role performances of everyday life. Many of the mundane elements of day-to-day
experience are, in fact, unavoidable during this liminal period. They are
just disattended to in accounts and fantasies of the experience because
they do not fit in the dominant schema of vacations.

Schemas themselves are cognitive objects that do much to define and
delineate how people perceive their world. Schemas filter perception by
making certain elements of one's environment seem more germane than
others. The irrelevant elements are then disregarded.[5] On vacation people
are focusing on the unusual, not the mundane. The perceptual bias this
creates allows people to ignore the omnipresent reminders of home while
away, but the reminders continue to influence identity and role performance. Self-schemas and group schemas similarly act as cognitive short-
cuts that organize information about the self and one's social positions.[6]
Although identities are context dependent, schemas do not dissolve while
people are in a liminal state but rather continue into it and influence individuals' perceptions of their environment and their place in it. Identity
shifts cannot be completely free because they occur in this lattice of social
structure and cognition. Modifications of identity across gender, sexuality, social class, citizenship, and race and also more mundane switches
such as hiding particular details of everyday life, lying about one's age, or
dressing for a particular environment require tapping into these extant
schemas. Identity shifts illustrate how agency marshals identity to best
meet contextual demands but also how social scripts and cultural schemas can limit identity performance and negotiation by minimizing what
alternative selves are plausible for a given situation.[7] One can choose a self
to project in a given interaction, but it must meet specific expectations of
others to be accepted by them as legitimate or real.

What emerges from this analysis is that while identities shift and
change depending on context, the mutable self overlaps between and extends into different situations to a considerable degree. Acquaintances,
responsibilities, and interests are not left behind; they often travel with
the individual and influence sense of identity, either voluntarily or involuntarily. Followers of Erving Goffman have compared his version of the
self to an onion. Each facet is a layer that can be peeled off and discarded,
but if you peel away all the layers, there is nothing left. Others compare it
to an artichoke, with a core beneath those layers. The experiences of the
people in this book show the self is more than either one. Both metaphors
are inadequate. The layers are not so discrete that they may be peeled away
and discarded without disturbing those remaining. They overlap, com-

bine, and persist. But they can be subject to a provisional reorganization. People can put aside some facets of self and return to them later, but they are still there in the background.

Freedom and Constraint

With freedom comes options and then also a need to manage those options. Part of the modern dilemma with identity is that we have too much choice and many limitations on making that choice. People cannot do or be everything that is reasonably available to them. Attempts to do so can result in being overwhelmed, uncertain, or exhausted. As people gain freedom, they lose certainty. While this may be welcomed or met with suspicion, the response to uncertainty is often limitation.

Vacations offer a period of increasingly flexible identity shifts in a limited time and place. Vacations are at once the result of this increased flexibility and the prescription for it. They are bounded. The limitations are just as important as the freedoms for the success of the experience. Part of the appeal of a vacation is that it gives individuals an opportunity to do something different but with constraints built in that make it comfortable and predictable. The indulgences of a vacation are usually possible only for a short time and often only in a specific place.

On vacation individuals have expanded freedom, but they also make trade-offs that encroach on that autonomy. Constraints seep into a vacation when people conduct a cost-benefit analysis of what they want to do and what they can do. When traveling, there is a potential for a great deal of release from social time, for example. One does not need to conform to schedules or meet someone else's deadlines. On the other hand, this may mean traveling alone, which can be risky or require more effort. By joining a planned tour or attending an all-inclusive resort, vacationers pass on responsibility for themselves to someone else, but they also lose their autonomy, sometimes to a very high degree. Rigid schedules tell them where they must be and when, what and where they will eat, and the kinds of activities they can do. Alternatively, for the ambitious tourist, wanting to get the most out of a finite experience can turn into a quest to see and do as much as possible. Joining a tour to enjoy its access and security limits freedom of movement. Traveling with others provides company and the benefits of having someone to share the experience with but imposes the accommodation of someone else's wishes. Staying home can mean saving money but potentially comes at the expense of not feeling as if one has gotten a sufficient break.

The physical environments that people travel to and where they choose to stay also entail trade-offs. Hotels are designed with the intention of replicating the experience of home or at least introducing a feeling of security through familiarity and comfort. With the ubiquity of chain hotels and restaurants, a person can travel to virtually any major city and many smaller ones and find some experiential reminders of home. Sometimes their rooms are even tailored to their prestated preferences, down to the temperature when they walk in. The relief of having this escape route to a familiar place while exploring an unfamiliar environment is appealing to many. Although this increases comfort and reduces unease, it also diminishes spontaneity and discovery because one can come closer and closer to replicating the experience of home while away.

Communication technologies play a growing role in re-creating the comforts of home in a manner that is similar to these hotels and resorts. Instead of having a physical place to return to at the end of the day that is recognizable as homelike, an ever-present mental realm of home is created by phone calls, text messages, pictures, videos, television shows, movies, and other media that travel easily via the internet or a portable device. This creates a cognitive effect similar to staying at the Hilton or Marriot. People never have to leave the known behind when they remain just as engaged in a favorite television show or responsive to a family crisis as they would be at home. The younger volunteer tourists in China went back to the lodgings almost every day and watched DVDs of pirated American television shows that were available in any of the local markets. They could also download them to their computers and smartphones. They were navigating familiar devices to consume familiar media and interact with familiar people in familiar settings. It was possible to spend a day viewing Tang dynasty relics and then return to the hotel to watch a full season of the American television show *Arrested Development*. These technologies allow people to bring home along with them in the form of unlimited books, television shows, movies, music, and photographs.

This familiarity is maintained not just through the consumption of media but also through the active presentation of self to friends and relatives. Communication devices maintain links with home audiences, allowing people to take them into the vacation with them. Using social media sites, an afternoon spent on the beach with friends can be shared and shown off to a broad audience from home. Nonpresent acquaintances can witness a trip as it happens and in as much detail as the traveler wishes to share. Many of the people interviewed for this book were keenly aware of their audience at home and spent considerable time cultivating an image to share with them. At all age levels, one of the first things people did after returning home, if they waited that long, was to post albums of photos on Facebook.

Others, mostly younger participants, devoted a significant portion of their time away to manicuring their online presentation of identity. That this was taken seriously is evidenced by respondents who paid careful attention to what they wore for pictures or who took the time to record events and even rerecord them to project a desired image. These travelers were very aware of their audience at home, who they assumed were paying close attention.

Valuing Vacations

Vacations continue to take a diminished place in American culture. The very language we use to describe them devalues them. "Time off" suggests they are time of nothing, a time not filled with the substance of our daily lives. This in itself suggests that they are somehow less. If we define ourselves and the substance of our lives only in terms of work, this may be the case, but I hope this book shows that vacation time is actually quite full. It is full of the things that make us ourselves, that feed into our identities, and make us who we are. They build the self, rather than offer an escape from it.

Perhaps unsurprisingly, people who use more of their vacation time report being happier. In a 2018 survey, four in ten full-time workers said that their companies encouraged taking vacation time. People who worked at these companies reported having higher levels of satisfaction with their company, job, physical health and well-being, and personal relationships.[8] However, 62 percent of employees said that their companies discourage, send mixed messages about, or say nothing about vacation time.[9] And while these demanding schedules seem to be dictated by culture, they are not necessarily the preference of American workers. While some are workaholics who want to work more, many say they wish they could have more time off. A 1991 survey by Hilton Hotels found that two-thirds of American workers would accept being paid less money if it meant they could have more time off.[10]

Identity work and play infuse motivations for taking vacations. In a 2018 study sponsored by the U.S. Travel Association, 85 percent of Americans said they travel because of the pleasure of seeing their child excited about the experience. They also travel to relax and reduce stress; to make memories; for fun, excitement, and adventure; to see or do something new; and to strengthen relationships with significant others or other family and friends. Among the 24 percent of Americans who reported they had not taken a vacation in the last year, 47 percent said they were missing out on fun, excitement, and adventure, and 40 percent said they were losing opportunities to make memories.[11]

It is worth considering, then, what we lose when we collectively devalue time off. If vacations and free time are a time to develop who we are as individuals, then who are we if we do not take that time off? If we work all the time, what happens to those other facets of our identity that get shifted to the background? Do we just wait until retirement to fulfill them? If so, why is this necessary? Other societies, such as in Europe, where vacation time is more plentiful and often government mandated, do not seem to feel a need for this deferment of self-fulfillment. We clearly value time off for the young. Children get summer vacations, spring breaks, winter breaks, and half days. College students get the summers off. When people switch from being developing members of society to contributing members of society, the willingness to offer them this free time disappears. Changing this mind-set requires an understanding that there is value in developing the self, of indulging in a passion, spending time with loved ones, or building new relationships.

Identity Shifts in Everyday Life

A vacation is just one kind of break for time off that introduces contrast into a daily, weekly, or annual rhythm and alters phenomenological experiences of time. A continuum of short- to long-term discontinuities, in which vacations fall in the middle, introduces multidimensionality to the experience of everyday life. Disruptions of the shortest duration include pauses for coffee and cigarette breaks, taking a deep breath, staring off into space, daydreaming, trips to the restroom, catnaps, sending text messages, or closing one's office door for a few minutes.[12] Pausing for a brief moment of enjoyment or doing something out of the ordinary can elicit a fleeting feeling of vacation by drawing on experience of contrast, indulgence, or rule breaking. The comedian Jerry Seinfeld describes eating junk food as "little mini vacations in your stressful day."[13] Such brief examples do not necessarily involve identity shifts, although they may, but they do introduce beneficial breaks and disruptions.

The slightly longer duration of a sick day, a snow day, or a long holiday weekend allows short-lived lapses in routine during which individuals momentarily absent themselves from their immediate social expectations or briefly redirect their attention. The result is a brief rejuvenation, relief, and momentary freedom. Stepping back from the course of action like this briefly jolts the linearity of experience.[14] Such periodic relief is not only enjoyable; it is necessary to maintain a standard for ongoing action.

Slightly further along the temporal scale are distracting activities that capture our attention for a sustained period. Pastimes such as hobbies, sports, and games not only entertain but draw on knowledge, intelligence, and experience to divert attention for hours or even days.[15] They pause the flow of action of everyday life for a rejuvenating diversion. Games that are particularly challenging or absorbing like chess can capture attention and introduce extended pauses.[16]

The vacation is just one example of a period during which people may alter or rearrange identities to suit a temporary situation that either provides more freedom or allows a different focus. Unemployment, retirement, or maternity and paternity leave, for example, allow or require an identity shift brought about by the temporary reorganization of the self. Long-term breaks, like a summer off from school or an academic sabbatical, similarly remove individuals from the expectations of the routinized life course. The degree of voluntariness, the resources one has to sustain it, and the temporal boundaries that delimit this time for identity shifts are central to defining the experience.

In many ways unemployment is structurally similar to a vacation. People enter a period of time that is often short lived in which the saliences of their everyday self-identity are rearranged. They also gain considerable freedom from the schedules of the workday and autonomy over how they spend their time. Identity facets are rearranged as work obligations are removed, and the salience of family obligations may increase with time spent at home. At the same time, a completely new and highly salient identity, that of being unemployed, is introduced to one's repertoire. But unemployment is fundamentally different from a vacation in that it is often not voluntary. However, if one has sufficient financial resources, the stress need not be as taxing, and one can even approach the situation as a break.

The ability to do this is contingent on being able to return to the working world. During the recession of 2008, the term "funemployment" was coined by people who had lost work and had the financial reserves to maintain a lifestyle that allowed them to enjoy the structural freedoms of unemployment.[17] Embracing funemployment in a way that shows some of its similarities to vacationing for identity work, a man says, "The rat race puts blinders on you and makes time fly, and then the next thing you know, you've missed the chance to be your more exciting self, or to push yourself in a gutsier direction."[18] Taking time free from work apparently helped him achieve this goal. While he may make unemployment sound appealing, his optimism could have occurred only with the certainty that joblessness would not be a permanent state.

Retirees also enter a period when their identities make a dramatic shift and facets of self become rearranged. While some people may be reluctant to retire, this shift is usually voluntary and welcomed and therefore qualitatively different from unemployment. Retirement also has structural similarities to the vacation in that obligatory work is removed and other facets of identity are rearranged in its absence. Again, time becomes one's own, and the rhythms introduced by the workday are removed. Family members and hobbies may be moved to more prominence. The increase in free time allows indulgence in activities for which previously there was no time. A key difference from vacations is that retirement is not a temporary state in the life course. It represents a change that will not be reversed by return to work. The identity of working person is removed and that of retiree is introduced.

Maternity and paternity leave, if one is lucky enough to have a job that offers them, is also a moment of release from particular obligations with the introduction of a major new obligation. It is also a period in which a highly salient new identity is introduced and must be mingled with the existing set. For the duration of the leave the parent identity is moved to the forefront. While work schedules organized around the conventions of the clock are removed, schedules organized around the more idiosyncratic demands of an infant are introduced. While the maternity leave will end, the new identity will not and will be carried on throughout the life course.

Perhaps demonstrating the importance of a change in location and routine for relief, one study found service in a military reserve force to be an effective respite from daily work; people who did reserve duty experienced a decline in job stress and burnout compared with those who did not take a similar leave.[19] Although they were not taking a break but instead shifting from one type of labor to another, they were moving to a different place to do a different kind of work and taking a short period to develop a different kind of work identity from their everyday one.

Increasingly, some jobs also offer sabbaticals from work, similar to academic sabbaticals in which people take a few months to a year off from their job with the promise of return. Such a break offers something similar to children's summer vacation in its extended duration, a rarity once an adult reaches working life. These can be an opportunity to take ex-

tended time off to fill as desired or needed but only if one has the resources, because these are often unpaid. A person can travel, take time off
for family, develop a hobby, or as academics often do, use the time to focus
on some other aspect of work without the distraction of day-to-day work
responsibilities.

On a much shorter scale, an evening out offers some the opportunity
for identity play, such as suburbanites who regularly go to blues clubs in
the city. They temporarily play up a cosmopolitan identity as they go to
restaurants, cocktail bars, and dance clubs to listen to music. They fashion
themselves as "sexy divas and drink-swilling hipsters, dazzling sophisti-
cates and bewitching bombshells,"[20] if only for one night, and then return
to their more mundane everyday selves once they get home. Key, though,
is that these partyers are not creating a brand-new identity when they go
out; they are playing up an aspect of their everyday selves that gets pushed
to the back a little more than they might like in their everyday life of work
and family.

People who are amateurs at some profession or activity can take a
night off or a weekend to engage that activity more directly,[21] such as an
office worker who does stand-up comedy in his free time and goes to an
open mic night, a member of a band who plays occasionally on evenings
and weekends for the fun of it, an actor who does community theater, or
a singer who goes out to sing karaoke. These amateurs may take very seriously what they do, and it may be an important part of their self-identity,
but for whatever reason, perhaps financial or their level of talent, it is not
primary.

Throughout everyday life people are balancing their desire for freedom
and autonomy with both external and self-imposed constraint in ways
that are revealed and put to the test in their identity shifts. The trade-offs
and cost-benefit analyses discussed in this book permeate everyday life. A
person may take a work-related call at home or spend time on the weekends answering emails, integrating work into home at the expense of leisure time, to make the work week go more smoothly. A parent may go out
for the evening and leave the kids with a sitter but then check in to make
sure everything is going all right. Although a person may attempt to temporarily rearrange priorities, this salient facet of self will remain dominant.

Vacationers must juggle issues of salience and commitment as they
construct and bound a personally meaningful identity shift while moder-
ating the degree to which they connect to home and work. Rather than
seeing their trip as a break from day-to-day experience during which they

could leave it all behind and then return home, many of the people in this study actively controlled interactions with home through cell phones, email, and social networking sites while still marking their time away as special. They shaped their identity performance in response to an additional audience that although not present made demands on their time. Such connection and the sense of responsibility it brings certainly is not limited to vacation time. Daily, people struggle with boundaries blurring between work, play, family, friends, home, obligations, responsibilities, and personal interests.

Vacations are an extended period during which the organization of identity has some freedom, but people grasp for and take shorter moments throughout the course of their day. Limitations that control and maintain stability are always present, and people are continually looking for ways to usurp them, even if these means are small and short lived. Whether people subvert limitations by acting in ways that contrast with their daily experience or by staying true to themselves in some way that matches their preferences, they find moments of autonomy through identity work. In finding these moments, they bring agency, self-direction, and a little bit of freedom into the course of everyday life.

Appendix

Methodological Note

Vacationing and vacation behavior include a broad variety of actions; I thus chose representative groups on the basis of where people spent their time off and what they chose to do with it. In doing so I emphasized distance, temporalities, and the presence of others, because these are primary factors in shaping identities. I investigated three categories of vacationers, defined by their break from everyday life: volunteer tourists in China, beach vacationers in Hawaii, and stay-home vacationers. Because vacation activities are so broad, I supplemented these groups with a narrative analysis of vacation blogs to capture more diversity of experience across a broader range of examples.

I divided my sample target into those who stayed at home for their vacation and those who left. Those who stayed home, or took "staycations," did so usually for economic or family reasons and worked hard to create a novel or relaxing experience in their everyday environment. Although staying home has long been a use of vacation time that has largely been overlooked or not acknowledged as a proper vacation, the staycation achieved popular legitimacy as a valid use of time off in the recession of 2008–2009, during which this research was largely conducted. The majority of vacations taken in the United States do involve travel, and because of the diversity of experience and activity, I further divided traveling vacationers into two subgroups that follow culturally and historically patterned uses of vacation time: those who travel for culture and learning and those who travel for rest and relaxation. While many vacations involve both of these aspects—a trip to the beach that includes a tour of a historic city center, for example—I treated all my categories as ideal types. Volunteer tourists who traveled to China for two or three weeks used their vacation time in what they saw as a culturally enriching or educational manner. In this sense their leisure was productive.

They further represent a growing portion of Americans who value international travel and use it as a marker of status and skill. Alternatively, beach vacationers travel primarily for rest and relaxation. This form of leisure is not a means for productivity in itself but a respite from and reward for it during the rest of the year.

For each group, I examined the meanings people gave to their specific vacation and to vacations in general, how they contrasted it with their everyday life, and how they maintained or limited connections with their day-to-day experience. Qualitative research methods, and in-depth interviews in particular, are well suited to uncover such perspectives. I completed forty-five in-depth interviews: ten with stay-home vacationers, fifteen with beach vacationers, and twenty with tourists in China. Each answered the same set of questions about vacation meanings and events, definitions, and favored and ideal experiences; about how they maintained contact with home; and about their typical routines for preparing for and returning from vacations. They also answered a set of questions specific to their experience to understand why they chose that particular type of vacation and how it related to prior experiences.

Ethnographic research provides a deeper immersion into the experience of other people to better understand what they consider important or meaningful.[1] With shared experience, the researcher can see from the inside what people do and how they do it. By integrating ethnographic work, I was not depending solely on interviews but, when possible, combining them with periods of observation to capture both stated intent and concrete action. I could record both attitudes and behaviors.[2] My research question requires understanding how people shape identities in response to social contexts and specifically how they are influenced by the milieus of space and time. I traveled to the vacation destinations of interviewees to observe environmental cues shaping action that respondents themselves could not sufficiently describe through interviews alone. I therefore supplemented interviews with two periods of participant observation: three months as a volunteer tourist in Xi'an, China, and four months working at a resort in Waikiki, Hawaii. In this way I could locate the identities of vacationers within cultural and spatial contexts as they were doing them.

A potential limitation of this methodology was that I had no information about how people exited this specific identity, because they had not yet done so. I countered this by asking questions about their usual experience returning home from a vacation. Because all subjects had already participated in multiple vacations before the current one, they had a large base of prior experiences to share and expectation of what they would do to leave behind their current identity work. To the degree possible, I conducted interviews at the end of the respondents' trip to capture the majority of their experience.

A difficulty of ethnographic research is that the researcher must immerse herself in the experience of the subject to gain insight into his or her perspective but at the same time maintain objectivity and not lose impartiality. There is value in observing behaviors from both the inside and the outside. Working as a resort employee at one research site and participating as a fellow tourist in another al-

lowed me this emic and etic perspective on my subject.[3] I was able to view vacationers from both the inside as one of them and the outside as a staff member in
the industry designed around them.

In China, interviewees were selected by their length of stay, being limited to
a two-to-three-week trip, and from those who self-identified the trip as a vacation. Participants ranged in age from eighteen to seventy-five, with ten of the
interviewees being college students and the other ten ages twenty-three and
above. Most respondents were Americans, but there were also several British
and Canadians. Of this group, seventeen had traveled to China by themselves and
three were there with family members. Four had been to China before, while for
the other sixteen it was a new experience; sixteen had prior experience with international travel in general, while for four it was their first time leaving their
country.

Because of the high degree of interaction in the tour groups, I was able to build
a strong rapport with subjects, despite their short stay. I introduced myself and
my study to them upon their arrival and to subsequent groups as they arrived. I
did not find any objection to my presence there as a researcher, no requests for
interviews were denied, and many offered opinions and observations outside interviews. In fact, conversations usually extended beyond the confines of the interview and into the trip because people were eager to talk about their experiences. I obtained permission from the organization operating the trips before I
arrived, and local staff members were informed of my purpose there and were
supportive.

Interview subjects in Hawaii were recruited on beaches and in other public
areas. To overcome their reluctance to give up leisure time, subjects were offered
a five-dollar Starbucks gift card in exchange for their participation. Only two out
of seventeen subjects I approached refused participation. I found that most were,
again, eager to share their vacation experiences with someone who wanted to
listen, and subjects gave detailed accounts of their activities. One challenge, however, was maintaining their attention during interviews of people whose priorities
were often not focused on someone else's work. As a result, some interviews were
short. Of the fifteen interviewees, fourteen were traveling with relatives or
friends and one was traveling alone. Nine had been to Hawaii before, while six had
not. All had been to a beach on a prior vacation.

To gain additional connections with transient vacationers, I worked at a coffee
shop in the lobby of a large resort hotel in Waikiki. The resort was a part of a large
international chain of hotels and attracted clientele from primarily the United
States, Japan, and Australia. During the time I was employed, about 50 percent of
the customers at the resort were Japanese. This is a standard figure for Waikiki,
which attracts many Japanese tourists. About 43.9 percent of all visitors to
Oahu at the same time in the prior year were Japanese.[4] Although they made up
at least half my customers on any given day, I elected not to include this population in my study because of linguistic limitations. Their English was usually ex-
tremely limited, as was my Japanese. I also hold inadequate cultural knowledge
about Japan.

I took advantage of other opportunities to speak with vacationers. Most of my accommodations were in short-term budget lodgings where I could speak with other inhabitants. I also volunteered in the gift shop of a popular tourist spot that drew a variety of visitors to the island. The result was access to a diverse group of visitors. While Hawaii is an upscale destination, it is also an idealized one, and people from across the American socioeconomic spectrum make a trip to Hawaii a personal priority. These people include snowbirds traveling from colder states, military spouses and family members or people who formerly served in the military, and college students.

Data for stay-home vacationers come from ten in-depth interviews with individuals who chose not to leave their hometown for more than one night during their vacation. Respondents lived in New Jersey, Virginia, and Hawaii and were interviewed during the two-year period of 2009–2010. Recruitment was done through ads posted on online forums, in public libraries, on Facebook, and at a local community college. Participants were asked if they knew anyone else who vacationed at home, and additional respondents were recruited through a snowball sample. Five respondents were graduate students, three were working parents with young children, and two were working professionals. Because of the nature of their vacation I could not supplement interviews with participant observation.

A narrative analysis of eighty blogs posted publicly on the internet about vacations further supplemented the targeted in-depth interviews with a broad sample of vacation destinations from a variety of perspectives. A kind of public journal or diary, these blogs record details and memories of trips that individuals share with others back home. The blogs offered detailed and rich accounts of peoples' vacations, often beginning before departure and ending after return. This time period had the further advantage of providing information on planning and performance at all stages of the trip that the in-person interviews with vacationers did not provide.

Blogs and similar internet formats were particularly useful for my research question because they are increasingly used by people as a form of presentation of self. Individuals use these outlets to project an image to others and a particular perspective of their trip that they wish people to see. Internet forums, social networking sites, and other online networks that allow one to convey images of oneself to others aid in the construction and presentation of multiple, ongoing identities.[5]

People similarly provide brief snapshots of their vacation identities on other internet outlets like Facebook and Twitter, but I selected blogs because they are more thoughtfully constructed by users to present their vacation and provide much more detail. Blogs were selected from websites that specifically host travel accounts and were searched using the terms "vacation," "staycation," "family vacation," "camping," "cruise," "resort," and "road trip." Some blog authors gave little data or posted only photographs. To ensure richness of data, only those blogs with at least the equivalent of two typewritten pages when transferred to Microsoft Word pages were selected for inclusion.

Travel blogs are a way for people to present identity and interact with people back home while away. I do not have an accurate number of how many exist, because the internet is vast, and often people include accounts of their trips in their personal, everyday blogs. The sites that offer a specific travel-blogging platform, however, including TravelPod.com, LonelyPlanet.com, and TravelBlog.org, host thousands of individual blogs directly related to travel. A search for blogs posted on TravelPod.com, once the largest of such platforms but no longer in operation, and a primary source of data for this portion of the study, generated approximately 150,000 results.

As with any blog, these were written as part of an intentional presentation of an identity to others. While they may not always be representative of the authors' true experience, they are an excellent example of how the authors' wish their identity to be perceived and interpreted by others and how the authors go about presenting their identity to a general audience. For this reason, while blogs are an excellent source of data on the presentation of self, they are in themselves a construction of the identity that vacationers wish others to see, and data must be used selectively for understanding the actual experience of the authors, especially vacations, which tend to be thought of and presented as a positive experience. People want to project a positive identity. Unfortunately, then, blogs completely obscure those moments that their authors wish to hide, moments that would have been valuable for addressing my research question. There is no way to know what occurred but was purposefully not shared or was not deemed important enough to write about. What blogs do demonstrate is a high degree of social desirability bias, which can be useful when trying to answer questions about impression management and identity. Certain accounts are more reliable or useful than others, therefore, such as when the authors complain or describe mishaps, because these potentially represent a more sincere presentation than glowing and pleasant descriptions of experience.

The blogs selected for this study were written for two audiences. The first is acquaintances, friends, and family, who often interact with the authors and leave comments throughout. In some cases these people are referred to specifically by the authors as they write. The other is a more general, open-ended audience of people browsing travel-blogging websites. Authors have the option of either keeping a private blog, which only those granted access may see, or keeping a public blog, which anyone may read. All blogs used for this study were set to public access and thus were intended for a general audience. Authors occasionally make references to a more generalized audience with suggestions and advice, which suggests that they know that strangers will be reading their work.

Notes

INTRODUCTION

1. "Momcations Become Latest Travel Industry Trend," *eTN*, May 12, 2008, available at https://www.eturbonews.com/4843/momcations-becomes -latest-travel-trend; Sue Shellenbarger, "Guys Just Want to Have Fun," *Wall Street Journal*, June 15, 2010, available at http://online.wsj.com/article/ SB10001424052748703685404575306783337815438.html.

2. Cindy Sondik Aron, *Working at Play: A History of Vacations in the United States* (New York: Oxford University Press, 1999), 2.

3. Unless otherwise noted, all quotations are from interviews I conducted between 2008 and 2010 in the three locations described later in the chapter. All names are pseudonyms.

4. Alma Gottlieb, "Americans' Vacations," *Annals of Tourism Research* 9 (1982): 165–187.

5. Christena E. Nippert-Eng, *Home and Work: Negotiating Boundaries through Everyday Life* (Chicago: University of Chicago Press, 1996).

6. John Kelly, *Leisure Identities and Interactions* (London: George Allen and Unwin, 1983), 9.

7. Wayne Brekhus, "A Sociology of the Unmarked: Redirecting Our Focus," *Sociological Theory* 16, no. 1 (1998): 38.

8. Murray S. Davis, "That's Interesting! Towards a Phenomenology of Sociology and a Sociology of Phenomenology," *Philosophy of the Social Sciences* 1, no. 4 (1971): 310–311.

9. Liah Greenfeld, "When the Sky Is the Limit: Busyness in Contemporary American Society," *Social Research* 72, no. 2 (2005): 4–5, 17–18.

10. Richard Sennet, *The Corrosion of Character* (New York: Norton, 1998).

11. Anthony Giddens, *Modernity and Self-Identity: Self and Society in the Late Modern Age* (Stanford, CA: Stanford University Press, 1991), 5–6.

12. Roy Baumeister and Mark Muraven, "Identity as Adaptation to Social, Cultural and Historical Context," *Adolescence* 19 (1996): 408.

13. See, for example, Edward Bruner, "Transformation of Self in Tourism," *Annals of Tourism Research* 18, no. 2 (1991): 238–250; Luke Desforges, "Traveling the World: Identity and Travel Biography," *Annals of Tourism Research* 27 (2000): 926–945; Torun Elsrud, "Risk Creation in Traveling: Backpacker Adventure Narration," *Annals of Tourism Research* 28 (2001): 597–617; Asia Friedman, "Toward a Sociology of Perception: Sight, Sex, and Gender. *Cultural Sociology* 5, no. 2 (2010): 187–206; Vasiliki Galani-Moutafi, "The Self and the Other: Traveler, Ethnographer, Tourist," *Annals of Tourism Research* 27 (2000): 262; Gottlieb, "Americans' Vacations"; Scott McCabe and Elizabeth Stokoe, "Place and Identity in Tourists' Accounts," *Annals of Tourism Research* 31, no. 3 (2004): 601–622; Ian Munt, "The 'Other' Postmodern Tourism: Culture, Travel and the New Middle Classes," *Theory, Culture and Society* 11 (1994): 101–123; Chaim Noy, "This Trip Really Changed Me: Backpackers' Narratives of Self Change," *Annals of Tourism Research* 31, no. 1 (2004): 78–102; Hazel Tucker, "Narratives of Place and Self: Differing Experiences of Package Coach Tours in New Zealand," *Tourist Studies* 5, no. 3 (2005): 267–282; Stephen Wearing, "Re-centering the Self in Volunteer Tourism," in *The Tourist as a Metaphor of the Social World*, ed. Graham M. S. Dann (New York: CABI, 2002), 237–262; and Naomi Rosh White and Peter B. White, "Home and Away: Tourists in a Connected World," *Annals of Tourism Research* 34 (2007): 88–104.

14. Sheldon Stryker, *Symbolic Interactionism: A Social Structural Version* (Menlo Park, CA: Benjamin Cummings, 1980); Jan Stets and Peter Burke, "A Sociological Approach to Self and Identity," in *Handbook of Self and Identity*, ed. Mark Leary and June Price (New York: Guilford Press, 2003), 132.

15. Gregory Stone, "Appearance and the Self," in *Human Behavior and Social Processes: An Interactionist Approach*, ed. Arnold Rose (Boston: Houghton Mifflin, 1962), 93; Kevin Vryan, Patricia Adler, and Peter Adler, "Identity," in *Handbook of Symbolic Interactionism*, ed. L. T. Reynolds and Nancy J. Herman-Kinney (Lanham, MD: AltaMira Press, 2003), 368.

16. Shelley Budgeon, "Identity as an Embodied Event," *Body and Society* 9, no. 1 (2003): 35–55.

17. Vryan, Adler, and Adler, "Identity," 368–371.

18. Ibid.

19. Ibid.

20. Ibid., 368.

21. Wayne Brekhus, *Peacocks, Chameleons, Centaurs: Gay Suburbia and the Grammar of Social Identity* (Chicago: University of Chicago Press, 2003), 22–23.

22. Iddo Tavory, "Of Yarmulkes and Categories: Delegating Boundaries and the Phenomenology of Interactional Expectation, *Theory and Society* 39, no. 1 (2010): 50; Richard Jenkins, *Social Identity* (London: Routledge, 2014), 14.

23. Brekhus, *Peacocks, Chameleons, Centaurs*, 16–20.

24. Eviatar Zerubavel, *The Fine Line: Making Distinctions in Everyday Life* (Chicago: University of Chicago Press, 1991), 7.

25. Sheldon Stryker, "Identity Salience and Role Performance," *Journal of Marriage and the Family* 4 (1968): 558–564.

26. Nippert-Eng, *Home and Work*.

27. Brekhus, *Peacocks, Chameleons, Centaurs*, 20–27.

28. Ibid., 16–20.

29. Ibid., 24–27.

30. David Snow and Leon Anderson, "Identity Work among the Homeless: The Verbal Construction and Avowal of Personal Identities," *American Journal of Sociology* 92, no. 6 (1987): 1136–1371.

31. Herminia Ibarra and Jennifer Petriglieri, "Identity Work and Play," *Journal of Organizational Change Management* 23, no. 1 (2010): 10–25.

32. Ibid.

33. See Louis Zurcher, "Social-Psychological Functions of Ephemeral Roles: A Disaster Work Crew," *Human Organization* 27, no. 4 (1968): 281–297; Louis Zurcher, "The 'Friendly' Poker Game: A Study of an Ephemeral Role," *Social Forces* 49 (1970): 173–186; Louis Zurcher, "The Naval Reservist: An Empirical Assessment of Ephemeral Role Enactment," *Social Forces* 55, no. 3 (1977): 753–768.

34. Zurcher, "The 'Friendly' Poker Game," 185.

35. Stanley Cohen and Laurie Taylor, *Escape Attempts: The Theory and Practice of Resistance to Everyday Life* (London: Allen Lane, 1992); Nelson Graburn, "The Anthropology of Tourism," *Annals of Tourism Research* 10 (1983): 9–13; Patricia Adler and Peter Adler, "Transience and the Postmodern Self: The Geographic Mobility of Resort Workers," *Sociological Quarterly* 40, no. 1 (1999): 31–58.

36. *Oxford English Dictionary*, s.v. "vacation," available at http://www.oed.com.

37. J. W. Lounsbury and L. L. Hoopes, "A Vacation from Work: Changes in Work and Nonwork Outcomes," *Journal of Applied Psychology* 71 (1986): 392–401.

38. Nelson Graburn, "Tourism: The Sacred Journey," in *Hosts and Guests: The Anthropology of Tourism*, ed. Valene Smith (Philadelphia: University of Pennsylvania Press, 1977), 20–23; John Urry, *The Tourist Gaze: Leisure and Travel in Contemporary Societies* (London: Sage, 2002), 2–10.

39. Aron, *Working at Play*, 162.

40. Jane Desmond, *Staging Tourism: Bodies on Display from Waikiki to Sea World* (Chicago: University of Chicago Press, 1999), 8.

41. Ron Eyerman and Orvar Löfgren, "Romancing the Road: Road Movies and Images of Mobility," *Theory, Culture and Society* 12 (1995): 53–79; Mike Featherstone, "Automobilities: An Introduction," *Theory, Culture and Society* 21, nos. 4–5 (2004): 2.

42. Ann Swidler, "Culture in Action: Symbols and Strategies," *American Sociological Review* 51 (1986): 273–286.

43. Aron, *Working at Play*.

44. Ibid., 9.

45. Chris Rojek, *Ways of Escape: Modern Transformation in Leisure and Travel* (Lanham, MD: Rowman and Littlefield, 1993).

46. Chris Rojek, *The Labour of Leisure: The Culture of Free Time* (London: Sage, 2010), 89–91.

47. Aron, *Working at Play*, 69–71.

48. Ibid.

49. Phil Brown, *Catskill Culture: A Mountain Rat's Memories of the Great Jewish Resort Area* (Philadelphia: Temple University Press, 1998), 11.

50. Orvar Löfgren, *On Holiday: A History of Vacationing* (Berkeley: University of California Press, 1999), 252–253.

51. Brown, *Catskill Culture*, 186–189; Susan Sessions Rugh, *Are We There Yet? The Golden Age of American Family Vacations* (Lawrence: University Press of Kansas, 2008), 173–174.

52. Rugh, *Are We There Yet?*, 70–77.

53. Ibid., 168.

54. Aron, *Working at Play*, 118–119.

55. Francis Green and Michael Potepan, "Vacation Time and Unionism in the U.S. and Europe," *Industrial Relations* 27, no. 2 (1988): 180–194.

56. Rugh, *Are We There Yet?*, 6–16.

57. Aron, *Working at Play*, 157–175; Rugh, *Are We There Yet?*, 121–130.

58. Adrian Franklin, *Tourism: An Introduction* (London: Sage, 2003), 218–219.

59. Löfgren, *On Holiday*, 58–63.

60. Eyerman and Löfgren, "Romancing the Road," 56–57.

61. Daniel Boorstin, *The Image: A Guide to Pseudo-events in America* (New York: Atheneum, 1961), 80–84; Eric Leed, *The Mind of the Traveler: From Gilgamesh to Global Tourism* (New York: Basic Books, 1991).

62. Judith Adler, "Travel as a Performed Art," *American Journal of Sociology* 94, no. 6 (1989): 1366–1391.

63. Rojek, *Ways of Escape*, 98, 114.

64. Leed, *The Mind of the Traveler*, 7–14.

65. Löfgren, *On Holiday*, 160.

66. Adler, "Travel as a Performed Art," 1371.

67. Jodi Ellen Brodsky, "Intellectual Snobbery: A Socio-historical Perspective" (Ph.D. diss., Columbia University), 371–372.

68. Michelle Lamont and Annette Lareau, "Cultural Capital: Allusions, Gaps, and Glissandos in Recent Theoretical Developments," *Sociological Theory* 6, no. 2 (1988): 153–168.

69. Joe Gaspard, "Top Five Study Abroad Destinations from Let's Go Travel Guides," *Cision*, April 18, 2011, available at https://www.prweb.com/releases/letsgo/studyabroad2011/prweb8309358.htm.

70. Dean MacCannell, "Staged Authenticity: Arrangements of Social Space in Tourist Settings," *American Journal of Sociology* 79, no. 3 (1973): 589–603; Dean MacCannell, *The Tourist: A New Theory of the Leisure Class* (New York: Schocken Books, 1976).

71. Löfgren, *On Holiday*, 269.

72. David Grazian, *Blue Chicago: The Search for Authenticity in Urban Blues Clubs* (Chicago: University of Chicago Press, 2003), 10–11.

73. Eviatar Zerubavel, "Generally Speaking: The Logic and Mechanics of Social Pattern Analysis," *Sociological Forum* 22 (2007): 131–145.

74. Associated Press–NORC Center for Public Affairs Research, "Americans' Plans for Summer Vacation," 2017, available at http://www.apnorc.org/projects/Pages/HTML%20Reports/Americans%E2%80%99-Plans-for-Summer-Vacation.aspx.

75. Project: Time Off, "State of American Vacation, 2018," 2018, available at https://projecttimeoff.com/wp-content/uploads/2018/05/StateofAmericanVacation2018.pdf.

76. Rebecca Ray, Milla Sanes, and John Schmitt, *No-Vacation Nation Revisited* (Washington, DC: Center for Economic and Policy Research, 2013).

77. Ibid.

CHAPTER 1

1. Jean-Didier Urbain, *At the Beach*, trans. Catherine Porter (Minneapolis: University of Minnesota Press, 2003).

2. Jane Desmond, *Staging Tourism: Bodies on Display from Waikiki to Sea World* (Chicago: University of Chicago Press, 1999), 8.

3. Ibid., 6.

4. Ibid., 4.

5. John Kelly, *Leisure Identities and Interactions* (London: George Allen and Unwin, 1983), 99–104.

6. Ibid.

7. Barry Schwartz, "The Social Psychology of Privacy," *American Journal of Sociology* 73, no. 6 (1968): 741–752.

8. Diana Meyers, "Personal Autonomy and the Paradox of Feminine Socialization," in *Being Yourself: Essays on Identity, Action and Social Life* (Lanham, MD: Rowman and Littlefield, 2004), 8.

9. Robert Snow and Dennis Brissett, "Pauses: Explorations in Social Rhythm," *Symbolic Interaction* 9, no. 1 (1986): 1–18.

10. Erving Goffman, *Asylums: Essays on the Social Situations of Mental Patients and Other Inmates* (Oxford: Doubleday, 1961), 319–320.

11. Stanley Cohen and Laurie Taylor, *Escape Attempts: The Theory and Practice of Resistance to Everyday Life* (London: Allen Lane, 1992), 119.

12. David Diekema, "Aloneness and Social Form," *Symbolic Interaction* 15, no. 4 (1992): 481–500.

13. Barry Schwartz, "Notes on the Sociology of Sleep," *Sociological Quarterly* 11, no. 4 (1970): 485–499.

14. Cited in Anne Doquet and Olivier Evrard, "An Interview with Jean Didier Urbain: Tourism Beyond the Grave; A Semiology of Culture," *Tourist Studies* 8, no. 2 (2008): 176.

15. The name of the town has been changed to respect the respondent's privacy.

16. Arnold Van Gennep, *The Rites of Passage* (Chicago: University of Chicago Press, 1960). Victor Witter Turner, "Betwixt and Between: The Liminal Period in *Rites de Passage*," in *The Forest of Symbols: Aspects of Ndembu Ritual* (Ithaca, NY: Cornell University Press, 1967), 93–111; Victor Witter Turner, *The Ritual Process: Structure and Anti-structure* (Ithaca, NY: Cornell University Press, 1969).

17. Turner, *The Ritual Process*, 97.

18. V. Turner, "Liminal to Liminoid, in Play, Flow, and Ritual: An Essay in Comparative Symbology," *Rice University Studies* 60, no. 3 (1974): 53–92. Parallels with the religious ritual or pilgrimage in the tourist experience have been well addressed by anthropologists. Specifically in relation to the Caribbean, see Nelson Graburn, "The Anthropology of Tourism," *Annals of Tourism Research* 10 (1983): 9–13; Denison Nash and Valene Smith, "Anthropology of Tourism," *Annals of Tourism Research* 18 (1991): 17–18; and James Lett Jr., "Ludic and Liminoid Aspects of Charter Yacht Tourism in the Caribbean," *Annals of Tourism Research* 10 (1983): 35–56; and in relation to Disney World, see Alexander Moore, "Walt Disney World: Bounded Ritual Space and the Playful Pilgrimage Center," *Anthropological Quarterly* 53, no. 4 (1980): 207–218. Turner (1974) argued that play was implicit in liminoid periods.

19. George Herbert Mead, *Mind, Self and Society* (Chicago: University of Chicago Press, 1967); Norman Denzin, "Play, Games and Interaction: The Contexts of Childhood Socialization," *Sociological Quarterly* 16, no. 4 (1975): 458–478.

20. Johan Huizinga, *Homo Ludens: A Study of the Play-Element in Culture* (New York: Harper and Row, 1955), 26–30.

21. Dorothy Holland, William Lachicotte Jr., Debra Skinner, and Carole Cain, *Identity and Agency in Cultural Worlds* (Cambridge, MA: Harvard University Press, 1998), 236.

22. Gregory Stone, "Appearance and the Self," in *Human Behavior and Social Processes: An Interactionist Approach*, ed. Arnold Rose (Boston: Houghton Mifflin, 1962), 86–116; Lisa Kjolsrod, "Adventure Revisited: On Structure and Metaphor in Specialized Play," *Sociology* 37, no. 3 (2003): 459–476.

23. Gregory Bateson, "A Theory of Play and Fantasy," in *Steps to an Ecology of Mind* (Chicago: University of Chicago Press, 1972), 179.

24. Georg Simmel, "Sociability," in *On Individuality and Social Forms*, ed. Donald Levine (Chicago: University of Chicago Press, 1971), 127–140.

25. Ibid., 133–134.

26. Graham Dann, "Writing Out the Tourist in Space and Time," *Annals of Tourism Research* 26, no. 1 (1999): 159–187.

27. See, for example, Yaniv Belhassen, Carla Almeida Santos, and Natan Uriely, "Cannabis Usage in Tourism: A Sociological Perspective," *Leisure Studies* 26 (2007): 303–319; Susy Kruhse-Montburton, "Sex Tourism and the Traditional Male Identity," in *International Tourism: Identity and Change*, ed. Marie-Francoise Lanfant, John Allcock, and Edward Bruner (London: Sage, 1995), 192–204; Orvar

Löfgren, *On Holiday: A History of Vacationing* (Berkeley: University of California Press, 1999); Bulent Diken and Carsten Bagge Lausten, "Sea, Sun, Sex and the Discontents of Pleasure," *Tourist Studies* 4 (2004): 99–114; Maurice J. Kane and Hazel Tucker, "Adventure Tourism: The Freedom to Play with Reality," *Tourist Studies* 4 (2004): 217–234; Torun Elsrud, "Risk Creation in Traveling: Backpacker Adventure Narration," *Annals of Tourism Research* 28 (2001): 597–617.

28. Lisa Kjolsrod, "Adventure Revisited: On Structure and Metaphor in Specialized Play," *Sociology* 37, no. 3 (2003): 459–476; Al Gini, *The Importance of Being Lazy: In Praise of Play, Leisure and Vacations* (New York: Routledge, 2005).

29. Erving Goffman, "Where the Action Is," in *Interaction Ritual: Essays in Face-to-Face Behavior* (New Brunswick, NJ: Transaction, 2005), 161–169.

30. Ibid., 155–156.

31. Cohen and Taylor, *Escape Attempts*, 133–134.

32. Urbain, *At the Beach*, 269.

33. James Lett Jr., "Ludic and Liminoid Aspects of Charter Yacht Tourism in the Caribbean," *Annals of Tourism Research* 10 (1983): 35–56.

34. Desmond, *Staging Tourism*, 12.

35. Kruhse-Mountburton, "Sex Tourism and the Traditional Male Identity," 197; Jacqueline Sanchez-Taylor, "Dollars Are a Girl's Best Friend: Female Tourists' Sexual Behavior in the Caribbean," *Sociology* 35, no. 3 (2001): 749–764.

36. Eviatar Zerubavel, *The Fine Line: Making Distinctions in Everyday Life* (Chicago: University of Chicago Press, 1991), 11.

37. Erving Goffman, *Frame Analysis: An Essay on the Organization of Experience* (Cambridge, MA: Harvard University Press, 1974), 10–11.

38. Ibid., 21.

39. R. N. Ross, "Ellipsis and the Structure of Expectation," *San Jose Occasional Papers in Linguistics* 1 (1975): 183–191; Deborah Tannen, *Framing in Discourse* (New York: Oxford University Press, 1993), 5–6.

40. Asia Friedman, "Toward a Sociology of Perception: Sight, Sex, and Gender," *Cultural Sociology* 5, no. 2 (2010): 190.

41. Lilian Jonas, "Making and Facing Danger: Constructing Strong Character on the River," *Symbolic Interaction* 22, no. 3 (1999): 247–267.

42. Carol Rambo Ronai and Carolyn Ellis, "Turn-Ons for Money: Interactional Strategies of the Table Dancer," *Journal of Contemporary Ethnography* 18, no. 3 (1989): 272.

43. Susan Davis, *Spectacular Nature: Corporate Culture and the Sea World Experience* (Berkeley: University of California Press, 1997), 77–78.

44. Philip Pearce, *Tourist Behavior: Themes and Conceptual Schemes* (Clevedon, UK: Channel View, 2005), 143.

45. Hal Rothman, *Devil's Bargains: Tourism in the Twentieth-Century American West* (Lawrence: University of Kansas Press, 1998), 2.

46. Ann Swidler, "Culture in Action: Symbols and Strategies," *American Sociological Review* 51 (1986): 276.

47. Peter Bearman, *Doormen* (Chicago: University of Chicago Press, 2005), 102.

48. Alfred Schutz, *Collected Papers I* (The Hague: M. Nijhoff, 1962), 11–12.

49. Mary Chayko, *Connecting: How We Form Social Bonds and Communities in the Internet Age* (Albany: State University of New York Press, 2002), 25–26.

50. Patricia Adler and Peter Adler, *Paradise Laborers: Hotel Work in the Global Economy* (Ithaca, NY: Cornell University Press, 2004), 225–227.

51. Erving Goffman, *The Presentation of Self in Everyday Life* (New York: Random House, 1959).

CHAPTER 2

1. Robert Stebbins, "Serious Leisure: A Conceptual Statement," *Pacific Sociological Review* 25, no. 2 (1982): 251–272.

2. Ian Munt, "The 'Other' Postmodern Tourism: Culture, Travel and the New Middle Classes," *Theory, Culture and Society* 11 (1994): 110.

3. Ibid., 116.

4. Dean MacCannell, "Staged Authenticity: Arrangements of Social Space in Tourist Settings," *American Journal of Sociology* 79, no. 3 (1973): 589–603; Dean MacCannell, *The Tourist: A New Theory of the Leisure Class* (New York: Schocken Books, 1976).

5. Orvar Löfgren, *On Holiday: A History of Vacationing* (Berkeley: University of California Press, 1999), 269.

6. Stephen Wearing and John Neil, "Refiguring Self and Identity through Volunteer Tourism," *Society and Leisure* 23 (2000): 389–419; Stephen Wearing, "Re-centering the Self in Volunteer Tourism," in *The Tourist as a Metaphor of the Social World*, ed. Graham M. S. Dann (New York: CABI, 2002), 237–262.

7. David Martinez-Robles, "The Western Representation of Modern China: Orientalism, Culturalism and Historiographical Criticism," *Digithum* 10 (2008), available at https://digithum.uoc.edu/articles/abstract/10.7238/d.v0i10.511.

8. Shelley Jiang, *Let's Go China* (New York: St. Martin's Press, 2005).

9. See Edward Bruner, "Transformation of Self in Tourism," *Annals of Tourism Research* 18, no. 2 (1991): 238–250; Luke Desforges, "Traveling the World: Identity and Travel Biography," *Annals of Tourism Research* 27 (2000): 926–945; Torun Elsrud, "Risk Creation in Traveling: Backpacker Adventure Narration," *Annals of Tourism Research* 28 (2001): 597–617; Vasiliki Galani-Moutafi, "The Self and the Other: Traveler, Ethnographer, Tourist," *Annals of Tourism Research* 27 (2000): 203–224; Alma Gottlieb, "Americans' Vacations," *Annals of Tourism Research* 9 (1982): 165–187; Scott McCabe and Elizabeth Stokoe, "Place and Identity in Tourists' Accounts," *Annals of Tourism Research* 31, no. 3 (2004): 601–622; Munt, "The 'Other' Postmodern Tourism"; Chaim Noy, "This Trip Really Changed Me: Backpackers' Narratives of Self Change," *Annals of Tourism Research* 31, no. 1 (2004): 78–102; Hazel Tucker, "Narratives of Place and Self: Differing Experiences of Package Coach Tours in New Zealand," *Tourist Studies* 5, no. 3 (2005): 267–282; Wearing, "Re-centering the Self in Volunteer Tourism"; Naomi Rosh White and Peter B. White, "Home and Away: Tourists in a Connected World," *Annals of Tourism Research* 34 (2007): 88–104.

10. Desforges, "Traveling the World"; Elsrud, "Risk Creation in Traveling."

11. Robert Stebbins, *Serious Leisure: A Perspective for Our Time* (New Brunswick, NJ: Transaction, 2007), 79–80.

12. Judith Adler, "Travel as a Performed Art," *American Journal of Sociology* 94, no. 6 (1989): 1368.

13. Pierre Bourdieu and Jean-Claude Passeron, *Reproduction in Education, Society and Culture*, vol. 4 (London: Sage, 1990); Paul DiMaggio, "Cultural Entrepreneurship in Nineteenth Century Boston: The Creation of an Organizational Base for High Culture in America," *Media, Culture, and Society* 4 (1982): 35.

14. Michelle Lamont and Annette Lareau, "Cultural Capital: Allusions, Gaps, and Glissandos in Recent Theoretical Developments," *Sociological Theory* 6, no. 2 (1988): 156.

15. David Grazian, *Blue Chicago: The Search for Authenticity in Urban Blues Clubs* (Chicago: University of Chicago Press, 2003), 10–11.

16. John Urry, *Consuming Places* (New York: Routledge, 1995), 140.

17. MacCannell, "Staged Authenticity."

18. Erik Cohen, "Authenticity and Commoditization in Tourism," *Annals of Tourism Research* 15, no. 3 (1988): 371–386.

19. Gary Alan Fine, *Everyday Genius: Self-Taught Art and the Culture of Authenticity* (Chicago: University of Chicago Press, 2004).

20. Elsrud, "Risk Creation in Traveling"; Hamzah Muzaini, "Backpacking Southeast Asia: Strategies of 'Looking Local,'" *Annals of Tourism Research* 33, no. 1 (2006): 145.

21. Quoted in Arnie Weissmann, "'Authenticity' and the Travel Industry," *Travel Weekly*, February 12, 2012, available at http://www.travelweekly.com/arnie-weissmann/authenticity-and-the-travel-industry.

22. Löfgren, *On Holiday*, 262–264.

23. Philip Pearce, *Tourist Behavior: Themes and Conceptual Schemes* (Clevedon, UK: Channel View, 2005), 21.

24. Edward Bruner, "Tourism, Creativity and Authenticity," *Studies in Symbolic Interaction* 10 (1989): 109–114.

25. Adler, "Travel as a Performed Art."

26. Howard Saul Becker, *Art Worlds* (Berkeley: University of California Press, 1984).

27. Ibid., 226–227.

28. Eviatar Zerubavel, *The Fine Line: Making Distinctions in Everyday Life* (Chicago: University of Chicago Press, 1991), 14.

29. DiMaggio, "Cultural Entrepreneurship in Nineteenth Century Boston," 35.

30. Fine, *Everyday Genius*.

31. Seth Kugel, "An Insider's Tour of Chongqing Yields Frugal Gems," *New York Times*, March 20, 2013, available at http://frugaltraveler.blogs.nytimes.com/2013/03/20/an-insiders-tour-of-chongqing-yields-frugal-gems/?src=dayp.

32. Chris Rojek, *Ways of Escape: Modern Transformation in Leisure and Travel* (Lanham, MD: Rowman and Littlefield, 1993), 175.

33. Karen Stein, "Getting Away from It All: The Construction and Management of Temporary Identities on Vacation," *Symbolic Interaction* 34, no. 2 (2011): 290–308.

34. Michelle Callanan and Sarah Thomas, "Volunteer Tourism: Deconstructing Volunteer Activities within a Dynamic Environment," in *Niche Tourism: Contemporary Issues, Trends and Cases*, ed. M. Novelli (Oxford, UK: Butterworth-Heinemann, 2005), 183–200.

35. Ibid., 189.

36. Staff members used English names in place of their real Chinese names when interacting with Western tourists, explaining that these names are easier for visitors to remember and pronounce. "Jane" and "Marie" are pseudonyms for their chosen English names.

CHAPTER 3

1. Ron Eyerman and Orvar Löfgren, "Romancing the Road: Road Movies and Images of Mobility," *Theory, Culture and Society* 12 (1995): 53.

2. John Urry, "Mobility and Proximity," *Sociology* 36, no. 2 (2002): 257.

3. Nelson Graburn, "Tourism: The Sacred Journey," in *Hosts and Guests: The Anthropology of Tourism*, ed. Valene Smith (Philadelphia: University of Pennsylvania Press, 1977), 23.

4. Cindy Sondik Aron, *Working at Play: A History of Vacations in the United States* (New York: Oxford University Press, 1999), 10.

5. Eviatar Zerubavel, *The Fine Line: Making Distinctions in Everyday Life* (Chicago: University of Chicago Press, 1991), 16.

6. Graburn, "Tourism," 22–23.

7. John Urry, *The Tourist Gaze: Leisure and Travel in Contemporary Societies* (London: Sage, 2002), 4.

8. Vanessa Smith and Howard Hughes, "Disadvantaged Families and the Meaning of the Holiday," *International Journal of Tourism Research* 1 (1999): 128.

9. Rosemary Deem, "No Time for a Rest? An Exploration of Women's Work, Engendered Leisure and Holidays," *Time and Society* 5, no. 1 (1996): 5–25.

10. "Why Don't Americans Have Longer Vacations?" *New York Times*, August 4, 2010, available at http://www.nytimes.com/roomfordebate/2010/08/04/why-dont-americans-have-longer-vacations.

11. Rebecca Ray, Milla Sanes, and John Schmitt, *No-Vacation Nation Revisited* (Washington, DC: Center for Economic and Policy Research, 2013); Robert Levine, *A Geography of Time: The Temporal Misadventures of a Social Psychologist, or How Every Culture Keeps Time Just a Little Bit Differently* (New York: Basic Books, 1997), 144.

12. Sarah Sharma, "The Great American Staycation and the Risk of Stillness," *M/C Journal* 12, no. 1 (2009), available at http://journal.media-culture.org.au/index.php/mcjournal/article/viewArticle/122.

13. U.S. Patent and Trademark Office, "Staycation," Trademark Status and Document Retrieval, 2009, available at http://tsdr.uspto.gov/#caseNumber= 77475410&caseType=SERIAL_NO&searchType=statusSearch.

14. Deirdre Boden and Harvey Molotch, "The Compulsion of Proximity," in *Nowhere: Space, Time and Modernity*, ed. R. Friedland and D. Boden (Berkeley: University of California Press, 1994), 258–259.

15. Matt Wixon, *The Great American Staycation: How to Make a Vacation at Home Fun for the Whole Family (and Your Wallet!)* (Avon, MA: Adam's Media, 2009), 11.

16. Ibid. (emphasis added).

17. Elisabeth Leamy, "Tips for Planning a Great 'Staycation,'" *ABC News*, May 23, 2008, available at http://abcnews.go.com/GMA/Parenting/story?id= 4919211.

18. Roger Barker and Herbert Wright, *Midwest and Its Children* (Hamdon, CT: Archon Books, 1955).

19. John Falk and Lynn Dierking, *Learning from Museums: Visitor Experiences and the Making of Meaning* (Lanham, MD: AltaMira Press, 2000), 54–57.

20. Deem, "No Time for a Rest?"

21. "Mom Spends Beach Vacation Assuming All Household Duties in Closer Proximity to Ocean," *The Onion*, August 9, 2013, available at https://www .theonion.com/mom-spends-beach-vacation-assuming-all-household-duties -1819575406.

22. Barker and Wright, *Midwest and Its Children*, 7.

23. James Durston, "In Defense of Staying Home," *CNN*, July 4, 2013, available at http://travel.cnn.com/defense-staying-home-289606.

24. Stanley Cohen and Laurie Taylor, *Escape Attempts: The Theory and Practice of Resistance to Everyday Life* (London: Allen Lane, 1992), 115.

25. Zerubavel, *The Fine Line*, 7.

26. Cohen and Taylor, *Escape Attempts*, 116.

27. Steven Gelber, *Hobbies: Leisure and the Culture of Work in America* (New York: Columbia University Press, 1999), 2–3.

28. Robert Stebbins, "Serious Leisure: A Conceptual Statement," *Pacific Sociological Review* 25, no. 2 (1982): 253.

29. Ibid., 257–258.

30. Mihaly Csikszentmihalyi, *Beyond Boredom and Anxiety* (San Francisco: Jossey-Bass, 1975).

31. Ibid., 83.

CHAPTER 4

Portions of this chapter were previously published as Karen Stein, "Getting Away from It All: The Construction and Management of Temporary Identities on Vacation," *Symbolic Interaction* 34, no. 2 (2011): 290–308. Reprinted with permission by John Wiley and Sons.

1. Karen Stein, "Getting Away from It All: The Construction and Management of Temporary Identities on Vacation," *Symbolic Interaction* 34, no. 2 (2011): 290–308.

2. Ibid.

3. Ibid.

4. Eviatar Zerubavel, "Horizons: On the Sociomental Foundations of Relevance," *Social Research* 60, no. 2 (1993): 398.

5. Christena E. Nippert-Eng, *Home and Work: Negotiating Boundaries through Everyday Life* (Chicago: University of Chicago Press, 1996).

6. Celia Lurie, "The Objects of Travel," in *Touring Cultures: Transformations of Travel and Theory*, ed. Chris Rojek and John Urry (London: Routledge, 1997), 75–95.

7. Hazel Andrews, "Feeling at Home: Embodying Britishness in a Spanish Charter Tourist Resort," *Tourist Studies* 5 (2005): 247–266; Jørgen Ole Bærenholdt, Michael Haldrup, Jonas Larsen, and John Urry, *Performing Tourist Places* (Burlington, VT: Ashgate, 2004); David Crouch and Luke Desforges, "The Sensuous in the Tourist Encounter: Introduction—the Power of the Body in Tourist Studies," *Tourist Studies* 3 (2003): 5–22.

8. George Herbert Mead, *Mind, Self and Society* (Chicago: University of Chicago Press, 1967), 278–280.

9. M. Pagis, "Religious Self-Constitution: A Relational Perspective," in *Religion on the Edge: De-centering and Re-centering the Sociology of Religion*, ed. Courtney Bender (Oxford: Oxford University Press, 2012), 109–111; Colin Jerolmack and Iddo Tavory, "Molds and Totems: Nonhumans and the Constitution of the Social Self," *Sociological Theory* 32, no. 1 (2014): 64–77.

10. Jerolmack and Tavory, "Molds and Totems," 67.

11. Erving Goffman, *Stigma: Note on the Management of Spoiled Identity* (New York: Simon and Schuster, 1963); Iddo Tavory, "Of Yarmulkes and Categories: Delegating Boundaries and the Phenomenology of Interactional Expectation," *Theory and Society* 39, no. 1 (2010): 49–68.

12. Gregory Stone, "Appearance and the Self," in *Human Behavior and Social Processes: An Interactionist Approach*, ed. Arnold Rose (Boston: Houghton Mifflin, 1962), 91–93.

13. Nippert-Eng, *Home and Work*, 36.

14. Barry Brown, "Working the Problems of Tourism," *Annals of Tourism Research* 34, no. 2 (2007): 364–383.

15. Jerolmack and Tavory, "Molds and Totems," 68.

16. Ibid., 69–70.

17. M. Pagis, "Religious Self-Constitution: A Relational Perspective," in *Religion on the Edge: De-centering and Re-centering the Sociology of Religion*, ed. Courtney Bender (Oxford: Oxford University Press, 2012), 110.

18. Iddo Tavory, "Of Yarmulkes and Categories: Delegating Boundaries and the Phenomenology of Interactional Expectation, *Theory and Society* 39, no. 1 (2010): 65.

19. Jonas Larsen, "De-exoticizing Tourist Travel: Everyday Life and Sociality on the Move," *Leisure Studies* 27 (2008): 21–34.

20. Jerolmack and Tavory, "Molds and Totems," 67.

21. Edward Bruner, "Tourism, Creativity and Authenticity," *Studies in Symbolic Interaction* 10 (1989): 112.

22. Lurie, "The Objects of Travel," 76–77; Adrian Franklin, *Tourism: An Introduction* (London: Sage, 2003), 111.

23. Susan Stewart, *On Longing: Narratives of the Miniature, the Gigantic, the Souvenir, the Collection* (Baltimore: Johns Hopkins University Press, 1984), 137–138.

24. Lurie, "The Objects of Travel," 97; Nigel Morgan and Annette Pritchard, "On Souvenirs and Metonymy: Narratives of Memory, Metaphor and Materiality," *Tourist Studies* 5 (2005): 44.

25. Orvar Löfgren, *On Holiday: A History of Vacationing* (Berkeley: University of California Press, 1999), 87.

26. Henry Glassie, *Passing the Time in Ballymenon: Culture and History of an Ulster Community* (Philadelphia: University of Pennsylvania Press, 1982), 369–370.

27. Ira Silver, "Role Transitions, Objects and Identity," *Symbolic Interaction* 19 (1996): 2.

28. Barry Schwartz, "The Social Psychology of the Gift," *American Journal of Sociology* 73, no. 1 (1967): 2.

29. Jerolmack and Tavory, "Molds and Totems," 67.

30. Erving Goffman, *Frame Analysis: An Essay on the Organization of Experience* (Cambridge, MA: Harvard University Press, 1974), 45.

31. Stein, "Getting Away from It All."

32. Ronda Kaysen, "Yes, It Is Possible to Take a Weekend Family Getaway for $500," *Business Insider*, June 6, 2013, available at https://www.businessinsider .com/my-familys-500-weeklong-getaway-2013-6.

33. Stein, "Getting Away from It All."

34. Karen Cerulo, "Identity Construction: New Issues, New Directions," *Annual Review of Sociology* 23 (1997): 386.

35. Jonas Larsen, "Families Seen Sightseeing: Performativity of Tourist Photography," *Space and Culture* 8, no. 4 (2005): 416–434.

36. Naomi Rosh White and Peter B. White, "Home and Away: Tourists in a Connected World," *Annals of Tourism Research* 34 (2007): 100.

37. Lewis A. Coser, *Greedy Institutions: Patterns of Undivided Commitment* (New York: Free Press, 1974).

38. Christina Nippert-Eng, *Islands of Privacy* (Chicago: University of Chicago Press, 2010).

39. Ronda Kaysen, "My $500 Family Getaway: How a Staycation Saved Us Big," *The Week*, June 8, 2013, available at https://theweek.com/articles/463458/ 500-family-getaway-how-staycation-saved-big.

CHAPTER 5

1. Wayne Brekhus, *Peacocks, Chameleons, Centaurs: Gay Suburbia and the Grammar of Social Identity* (Chicago: University of Chicago Press, 2003), 17 (emphasis in original).

2. Ibid.

3. David Grazian, *Blue Chicago: The Search for Authenticity in Urban Blues Clubs* (Chicago: University of Chicago Press, 2003), 21–22.

4. Ibid., 64.

5. Brekhus, *Peacocks, Chameleons, Centaurs*, 19.

6. Thomas Gieryn, "What Buildings Do," *Theory and Society* 31, no. 1 (2002): 65.

7. N. J. Habraken, *The Structures of the Ordinary: Form and Control in the Built Environment* (Cambridge, MA: MIT Press, 1998), 17.

8. Eviatar Zerubavel, *The Fine Line: Making Distinctions in Everyday Life* (Chicago: University of Chicago Press, 1991), 7.

9. Ibid., 24–28.

10. Brekhus, *Peacocks, Chameleons, Centaurs*, 53.

11. Thomas Gieryn, "A Space for Place in Sociology," *Annual Review of Sociology* 26 (2000): 463–465; Yi-fu Tuan, *Space and Place: The Perspective of Experience* (Minneapolis: University of Minnesota Press, 1977), 6, 12–17.

12. Philip Pearce, *Tourist Behavior: Themes and Conceptual Schemes* (Clevedon, UK: Channel View, 2005), 149–150.

13. Jane Desmond, *Staging Tourism: Bodies on Display from Waikiki to Sea World* (Chicago: University of Chicago Press, 1999), 12–13.

14. Edward Bruner, "Slavery and the Return of the Black Diaspora: Tourism in Ghana," in *Culture on Tour: Ethnographies of Travel* (Chicago: University of Chicago Press, 2005), 102–106.

15. Rob Shields, *Places on the Margin: Alternative Geographies of Modernity* (London: Routledge, 1991), 30–32.

16. John Urry, *Consuming Places* (New York: Routledge, 1995), 26.

17. Susan Davis, *Spectacular Nature: Corporate Culture and the Sea World Experience* (Berkeley: University of California Press, 1997); Adrian Franklin, *Tourism: An Introduction* (London: Sage, 2003), 214.

18. Roderick Nash, *Wilderness and the American Mind* (New Haven, CT: Yale University Press, 1973).

19. Daniel Boorstin, *The Image: A Guide to Pseudo-events in America* (New York: Atheneum, 1961), 103.

20. *Oxford English Dictionary*, s.v. "destination," available at http://www.oed.com.

21. George S. Kanahele, *Waikiki 100 B.C. to 1900 A.D.: An Untold Story* (Honolulu: University of Hawaii Press, 1995).

22. Robert Sack, *Place, Modernity, and the Consumer's World* (Baltimore: Johns Hopkins University Press, 1992), 3–4.

23. Harvey Molotch, William Freudenberg, and Krista Paulsen, "History Repeats Itself, but How? City Character, Urban Tradition, and the Accomplishment of Place," *American Sociological Review* 65 (2000): 679–698.

24. Brekhus, *Peacocks, Chameleons, Centaurs*, 15.

25. Sack, *Place, Modernity, and the Consumer's World*, 159.

26. "About Chaa Creek" available at https://www.chaacreek.com (accessed November 12, 2018); "About Chaa Creek," available at https://www.chaacreek .com/about (accessed November 12, 2018).

27. Tom Salanniemi, "Pale Skin on the Playa del Anywhere: Finnish Tourists in the Liminoid South," in *Hosts and Guests Revisited: Tourism Issues in the 21st Century*, ed. Valene Smith and Maryann Brent (Elmsford, NY: Cognizant Communication, 2001), 91–92.

28. Mark Gottdiener, *The Theming of America: Dreams, Visions and Commercial Spaces* (Boulder, CO: Westview Press, 1997), 98.

29. Sharon Zukin, *Landscapes of Power: From Detroit to Disneyland* (Berkeley: University of California Press, 1991), 237–238.

30. Hamzah Muzaini, "Backpacking Southeast Asia: Strategies of 'Looking Local,'" *Annals of Tourism Research* 33, no. 1 (2006): 157.

31. Hazel Andrews, "Feeling at Home: Embodying Britishness in a Spanish Charter Tourist Resort," *Tourist Studies* 5 (2005): 247–266.

32. Boorstin, *The Image*, 80.

33. Ibid., 98.

34. Ibid.

35. Zygmunt Bauman, "From Pilgrim to Tourist—or a Short History of Identity," in *Questions of Cultural Identity*, ed. Stuart Hall and Paul Du Gay (London: Sage, 1996), 29–30.

36. Ibid., 30–31.

37. Erik Cohen, "Toward a Sociology of International Tourism," *Social Research* 39, no. 1 (1972): 175.

38. Edward Bruner, "Travel Stories Told and Retold," in *Culture on Tour: Ethnographies of Travel* (Chicago: University of Chicago Press, 2005), 13–17.

39. Danielle Contray, "Personalized Hotel Perks," *AOL*, January 17, 2010, available at https://www.aol.com/2010/01/17/personalized-hotel-perks.

40. Desmond, *Staging Tourism*, 13.

41. Chris Rojek, *Ways of Escape: Modern Transformation in Leisure and Travel* (Lanham, MD: Rowman and Littlefield, 1993), 62; Gottdiener, *The Theming of America*, 73; Tim Edensor, "Performing Tourism, Staging Tourism: (Re)Producing Tourist Space and Practice," *Tourist Studies* 1 (2000): 52.

42. Jean Baudrillard, *Simulations and Simulacra* (Ann Arbor: University of Michigan Press, 1985); Patricia Adler and Peter Adler, *Paradise Laborers: Hotel Work in the Global Economy* (Ithaca, NY: Cornell University Press, 2004), 14.

43. Adler and Adler, *Paradise Laborers*, 14–16.

44. Eviatar Zerubavel, *Social Mindscapes: An Invitation to Cognitive Sociology* (Cambridge, MA: Harvard University Press, 1997), 46–47.

45. John Urry, *The Tourist Gaze: Leisure and Travel in Contemporary Societies* (London: Sage, 2002), 88.

46. Tim Edensor, *Tourists at the Taj: Performance and Meaning at a Symbolic Site* (London: Routledge, 1998), 54.

47. Chelsea Fagan, "Paris Syndrome: A First-Class Problem for a First-Class Vacation," *The Atlantic*, October 18, 2011, available at https://www.theatlantic .com/health/archive/2011/10/paris-syndrome-a-first-class-problem-for-a-first -class-vacation/246743.

48. Pirkko Markula, "As a Tourist in Tahiti: An Analysis of Personal Experience," *Journal of Contemporary Ethnography* 26, no. 2 (1997): 203.

49. Zukin, *Landscapes of Power*, 231.

50. Ann Swidler, *Talk of Love: How Culture Matters* (Chicago: University of Chicago Press, 2001), 36.

CHAPTER 6

Portions of this chapter were previously published as Karen Stein, "Time Off: The Social Experience of Time on Vacation," *Qualitative Sociology* 35 (2012): 335–353. Reprinted by permission of Springer Nature.

1. Karen Stein, "Time Off: The Social Experience of Time on Vacation," *Qualitative Sociology* 35 (2012): 335.

2. Michael Flaherty, *A Watched Pot: How We Experience Time* (New York: New York University Press, 1999); Robert Lauer, *Temporal Man: The Meaning and Uses of Social Time* (New York: Praeger, 1981).

3. Patricia Adler and Peter Adler, *Paradise Laborers: Hotel Work in the Global Economy* (Ithaca, NY: Cornell University Press, 2004), 126.

4. Georg Simmel, *On Individuality and Social Forms*, ed. Donald Levine (Chicago: University of Chicago Press, 1971), 188.

5. Robert Levine, *A Geography of Time: The Temporal Misadventures of a Social Psychologist, or How Every Culture Keeps Time Just a Little Bit Differently* (New York: Basic Books, 1997), xix–xx.

6. Pitrim Sorokin and Robert Merton, "Social Time: A Methodological and Functional Analysis," *American Journal of Sociology* 42, no. 5 (1937): 623.

7. Robert Snow and Dennis Brissett, "Pauses: Explorations in Social Rhythm," *Symbolic Interaction* 9, no. 1 (1986): 3.

8. Dennis Brissett and Robert Snow, "Boredom: Where the Future Isn't," *Symbolic Interaction* 16, no. 3 (1993): 245.

9. Edward Hall, *The Dance of Life: The Other Dimension of Time* (New York: Doubleday, 1983).

10. Eviatar Zerubavel, "The Language of Time: Toward a Semiotics of Temporality," *Sociological Quarterly* 28 (1987): 343–356.

11. Ibid.

12. Barry Schwartz, "Notes on the Sociology of Sleep," *Sociological Quarterly* 11, no. 4 (1970): 485–486.

13. Brissett and Snow, "Boredom," 247.

14. Eviatar Zerubavel, *The Seven Day Circle: The History and Meaning of the Week* (New York: Free Press, 1985), 113–120.

15. Stein, "Time Off."

16. Wayne Brekhus, *Peacocks, Chameleons, Centaurs: Gay Suburbia and the Grammar of Social Identity* (Chicago: University of Chicago Press, 2003), 24–25.

17. Eviatar Zerubavel, "Private Time and Public Time: The Temporal Structure of Social Accessibility and Professional Commitments," *Social Forces* 58, no. 1 (1979): 39.

18. Georg Simmel, "The Metropolis and Mental Life," in *The Sociology of Georg Simmel*, ed. and trans. Kurt Wolff (Glencoe, IL: Free Press, 1950), 409–424.

19. Zerubavel, "Private Time and Public Time," 41.

20. Ibid.

21. Émile Durkheim, *The Elementary Forms of Religious Life* (New York: Free Press, 1965), 345–347.

22. Zerubavel, "The Language of Time," 348–349.

23. Stein, "Time Off."

24. Zerubavel, *The Seven Day Circle*, 136–138.

25. Henri Hubert, "A Brief Study of the Representation of Time in Religion and Magic," in *Essay on Time* (Oxford: Durkheim Press, 1999), 51–53.

26. Edmund Leach, "Two Essays concerning the Symbolic Representation of Time," in *Rethinking Anthropology* (New York: Athlone Press, 1961), 132–134.

27. Stein, "Time Off."

28. Ibid.

29. Orvar Löfgren, *On Holiday: A History of Vacationing* (Berkeley: University of California Press, 1999), 166.

30. Susan Sessions Rugh, *Are We There Yet? The Golden Age of American Family Vacations* (Lawrence: University Press of Kansas, 2008), 181.

31. Stein, "Time Off."

32. Witold Rybczynski, *Waiting for the Weekend* (New York: Penguin, 1991), 233.

33. Stein, "Time Off."

34. Stanford Lyman and Marvin Scott, *A Sociology of the Absurd* (New York: Appleton-Century-Crofts, 1970), 198.

35. Eviatar Zerubavel, *Hidden Rhythms: Schedules and Calendars in Social Life* (Chicago: University of Chicago Press, 1981), 6.

36. Levine, *A Geography of Time*, 25–26.

37. Jerry Jacobs and Kathleen Gerson, *The Time Divide: Work, Family, and Gender Inequality* (Cambridge, MA: Harvard University Press, 2004), 120.

38. Stein, "Time Off."

39. Michael Flaherty, *The Textures of Time: Agency and Temporal Experience* (Philadelphia: Temple University Press, 2011).

40. Zerubavel, "The Language of Time," 344.

41. David Maume, "Gender Differences in Taking Vacation Time," *Work and Occupations* 33, no. 2 (2006): 166.

42. Robert Merton, *Sociological Ambivalence and Other Essays* (New York: Free Press, 1976), 24–25.

43. Stein, "Time Off."

44. Ibid.

45. Ibid.

46. Graham Dann, "Writing Out the Tourist in Space and Time," *Annals of Tourism Research* 26, no. 1 (1999): 168; Mark Cocker, *Loneliness and Time: British Travel Writing in the Twentieth Century* (London: Secker and Warburg, 1992), 2.

47. Thomas Hylland Eriksen, *Tyranny of the Moment: Fast and Slow Time in the Information Age* (London: Pluto Press, 2001), 57.

48. William A. Reese and Michael A. Katovitch, "Untimely Acts: Extending the Interactionist Conception of Deviance," *Sociological Quarterly* 30 (1989): 159–184.

49. Zerubavel, *The Seven Day Circle*, 136–138.

50. Mark Neumann, "Living on Tortoise Time: Alternative Travel as the Pursuit of Lifestyle," *Symbolic Interaction* 16, no. 3 (1983): 209.

51. Erving Goffman, "The Underlife of a Public Institution," in *Asylums* (Garden City, NY: Doubleday, 1961), 171–320.

52. Adler and Adler, *Paradise Laborers*, 132.

53. Stephanie Rosenbloom, "Single in the Caribbean," *New York Times*, February 3, 2012, available at http://travel.nytimes.com/2012/02/05/travel/single-in-the-caribbean-sun.html.

54. Murray Melbin, "Night as Frontier," *American Sociological Review* 43, no. 1 (1978): 3–22; Adler and Adler, *Paradise Laborers*, 123–125.

55. Gary Alan Fine, *Kitchens* (Berkeley: University of California Press, 2009), 56.

56. Erving Goffman, *The Presentation of Self in Everyday Life* (New York: Random House, 1959).

57. Zerubavel, "Private Time and Public Time," 39.

58. Edward Bruner, "Travel Stories Told and Retold," in *Culture on Tour: Ethnographies of Travel* (Chicago: University of Chicago Press, 2005), 13–15.

59. Melbin, "Night as Frontier."

60. Levine, *A Geography of Time*, 6.

61. Ibid., 149.

CONCLUSION

1. Wayne Brekhus, *Peacocks, Chameleons, Centaurs: Gay Suburbia and the Grammar of Social Identity* (Chicago: University of Chicago Press, 2003), 204–205.

2. Christena E. Nippert-Eng, *Home and Work: Negotiating Boundaries through Everyday Life* (Chicago: University of Chicago Press, 1996); Karen Stein, "Getting Away from It All: The Construction and Management of Temporary Identities on Vacation," *Symbolic Interaction* 34, no. 2 (2011): 290–308.

3. Jonas Larsen, "De-exoticizing Tourist Travel: Everyday Life and Sociality on the Move," *Leisure Studies* 27 (2008): 25.

4. John Kelly, *Leisure Identities and Interactions* (London: George Allen and Unwin, 1983), 99.

5. Karen Cerulo, "Mining the Intersections of Cognitive Sociology and Neuroscience," *Poetics* 38, no. 2 (2010): 125.

6. Judith Howard, "Social Psychology of Identities," *Annual Review of Sociology* 26 (2000): 369.

7. Daniel Renfrow, "A Cartography of Passing in Everyday Life," *Symbolic Interaction* 27, no. 4 (2004): 493.

8. Project: Time Off, "State of American Vacation, 2018," 2018, p. 6, available at https://projecttimeoff.com/wp-content/uploads/2018/05/Stateof AmericanVacation2018.pdf.

9. Ibid., 7.

10. Robert Levine, *A Geography of Time: The Temporal Misadventures of a Social Psychologist, or How Every Culture Keeps Time Just a Little Bit Differently* (New York: Basic Books, 1997), 145.

11. Project: Time Off, "State of American Vacation."

12. Barry Schwartz, "Notes on the Sociology of Sleep," *Sociological Quarterly* 11, no. 4 (1970): 485–586; Robert Snow and Dennis Brissett, "Pauses: Explorations in Social Rhythm," *Symbolic Interaction* 9, no. 1 (1986): 7.

13. Jerry Seinfeld, "Feces Are My Purview," *Comedians in Cars Getting Coffee*, Netflix, January 30, 2014.

14. Snow and Brissett, "Pauses," 7.

15. Roger Caillois, *Man, Play and Games* (New York: Free Press of Glencoe, 1960), 33; Mihaly Csikszentmihalyi, "Some Paradoxes in the Definition of Play," in *Play as Context*, ed. Alyce Cheska (West Point, NY: Leisure Press, 1981), 14–46.

16. Csikszentmihalyi, "Some Paradoxes in the Definition of Play."

17. Kimi Yoshimo, "'Funemployed' Revel in Freedom from Work," *San Francisco Chronicle*, June 7, 2009, available at https://www.sfgate.com/business/article/Funemployed-revel-in-freedom-from-work-3228311.php.

18. Ibid.

19. D. Etziot, D. Eden, and Y. Lapidot, "Active Reserve Duty as an Ameliorative Respite from Civilian Job-Stress and Burnout" (paper presented at the Fifth International Conference on Social Stress Research, Honolulu, HI, June 1994).

20. David Grazian, *Blue Chicago: The Search for Authenticity in Urban Blues Clubs* (Chicago: University of Chicago Press, 2003), 63.

21. Robert Drew, "Embracing the Role of Amateur: How Karaoke Bar Patrons Become Regular Performers," *Journal of Contemporary Ethnography* 25, no. 4 (1997): 449–468.

APPENDIX

1. Robert Emerson, Rachel Fretz, and Linda Shaw, *Writing Ethnographic Fieldnotes* (Chicago: University of Chicago Press, 1995), 2.

2. Colin Jerolmack and Shamus Khan, "Talk Is Cheap: Ethnography and the Attitudinal Fantasy," *Sociological Methods and Research* 43, no. 2 (2014): 178–209.

3. Kenneth Pike, *Language in Relation to a Unified Theory of the Structure of Human Behavior*, 2nd ed. (The Hague: Mouton, 1967).

4. Hawaii Tourism Authority, "2009 Annual Visitor Research Report," 2009, available at http://files.hawaii.gov/dbedt/visitor/visitor-research/2009-annual -visitor.pdf.

5. Sherry Turkle, *Life on the Screen: Identity in the Age of the Internet* (New York: Simon and Schuster, 1995); Lori Kendall, "Meaning and Identity in 'Cyber-space': The Performance of Gender, Class, and Race Online," *Symbolic Interaction* 21, no. 2 (1998): 129–153.

Bibliography

"About Chaa Creek." Available at https://www.chaacreek.com (accessed November 12, 2018).

"About Chaa Creek." Available at https://www.chaacreek.com/about (accessed November 12, 2018).

Adler, Judith. "Travel as a Performed Art." *American Journal of Sociology* 94, no. 6 (1989): 1366–1391.

Adler, Patricia, and Peter Adler. *Paradise Laborers: Hotel Work in the Global Economy.* Ithaca, NY: Cornell University Press, 2004.

———. "Transience and the Postmodern Self: The Geographic Mobility of Resort Workers." *Sociological Quarterly* 40, no. 1 (1999): 31–58.

Associated Press–NORC Center for Public Affairs Research. "Americans' Plans for Summer Vacation." 2017. Available at http://www.apnorc.org/projects/Pages/HTML%20Reports/Americans%E2%80%99-Plans-for-Summer-Vacation.aspx.

Andrews, Hazel. 2005. "Feeling at Home: Embodying Britishness in a Spanish Charter Tourist Resort." *Tourist Studies* 5 (2005): 247–266.

Aron, Cindy Sondik. *Working at Play: A History of Vacations in the United States.* New York: Oxford University Press, 1999.

Bærenholdt, Jørgen Ole, Michael Haldrup, Jonas Larsen, and John Urry. *Performing Tourist Places.* Burlington, VT: Ashgate, 2004.

Barker, Roger, and Herbert Wright. *Midwest and Its Children.* Hamdon, CT: Archon Books, 1955.

Bateson, Gregory. "A Theory of Play and Fantasy." In *Steps to an Ecology of Mind*, 177–193. Chicago: University of Chicago Press, 1972.

Baudrillard, Jean. *Simulations and Simulacra*. Ann Arbor: University of Michigan Press, 1985.

Bauman, Zygmunt. "From Pilgrim to Tourist—or a Short History of Identity." In *Questions of Cultural Identity*, edited by Stuart Hall and Paul Du Gay, 18–36. London: Sage, 1996.

Baumeister, Roy, and Mark Muraven. "Identity as Adaptation to Social, Cultural and Historical Context." *Adolescence* 19 (1996): 405–416.

Bearman, Peter. *Doormen*. Chicago: University of Chicago Press, 2005.

Becker, Howard Saul. *Art Worlds*. Berkeley: University of California Press, 1984.

Belhassen, Yaniv, Carla Almeida Santos, and Natan Uriely. "Cannabis Usage in Tourism: A Sociological Perspective." *Leisure Studies* 26 (2007): 303–319.

Boden, Deirdre, and Harvey Molotch. "The Compulsion of Proximity." In *Nowhere: Space, Time and Modernity*, edited by R. Friedland and D. Boden, 1–60. Berkeley: University of California Press, 1994.

Boorstin, Daniel. *The Image: A Guide to Pseudo-events in America*. New York: Atheneum, 1961.

Bourdieu, Pierre, and Jean-Claude Passeron. *Reproduction in Education, Society and Culture*. Vol. 4. London: Sage, 1990.

Brekhus, Wayne. *Peacocks, Chameleons, Centaurs: Gay Suburbia and the Grammar of Social Identity*. Chicago: University of Chicago Press, 2003.

———. "A Sociology of the Unmarked: Redirecting Our Focus." *Sociological Theory* 16, no. 1 (1998): 34–51.

Brissett, Dennis, and Robert Snow. "Boredom Where the Future Isn't." *Symbolic Interaction* 16, no. 3 (1993): 237–256.

Brodsky, Jodi Ellen. "Intellectual Snobbery: A Socio-historical Perspective." Ph.D. diss., Columbia University, 1987.

Brown, Barry. "Working the Problems of Tourism." *Annals of Tourism Research* 34, no. 2 (2007): 364–383.

Brown, Phil. *Catskill Culture: A Mountain Rat's Memories of the Great Jewish Resort Area*. Philadelphia: Temple University Press, 1998.

Bruner, Edward. "Slavery and the Return of the Black Diaspora: Tourism in Ghana." In *Culture on Tour: Ethnographies of Travel*, 101–188. Chicago: University of Chicago Press, 2005.

———. "Tourism, Creativity and Authenticity." *Studies in Symbolic Interaction* 10 (1989): 109–114.

———. "Transformation of Self in Tourism." *Annals of Tourism Research* 18, no. 2 (1991): 238–250.

———. "Travel Stories Told and Retold." In *Culture on Tour: Ethnographies of Travel*, 1–29. Chicago: University of Chicago Press, 2005.

Budgeon, Shelley. "Identity as an Embodied Event." *Body and Society* 9, no. 1 (2003): 35–55.

Caillois, Roger. *Man, Play and Games*. New York: Free Press of Glencoe, 1960.

Callanan, Michelle, and Sarah Thomas. "Volunteer Tourism: Deconstructing Volunteer Activities within a Dynamic Environment." In *Niche Tourism: Contem-*

porary Issues, Trends and Cases, edited by M. Novelli, 183–200. Oxford, UK: Butterworth-Heinemann, 2005.

Cerulo, Karen. "Identity Construction: New Issues, New Directions." *Annual Review of Sociology* 23 (1997): 385–409.

———. "Mining the Intersections of Cognitive Sociology and Neuroscience." *Poetics* 38, no. 2 (2010): 115–132.

Chayko, Mary. *Connecting: How We Form Social Bonds and Communities in the Internet Age*. Albany: State University of New York Press, 2002.

Cocker, Mark. *Loneliness and Time: British Travel Writing in the Twentieth Century*. London: Secker and Warburg, 1992.

Cohen, Erik. "Authenticity and Commoditization in Tourism." *Annals of Tourism Research* 15, no. 3 (1988): 371–386.

———. "Toward a Sociology of International Tourism." *Social Research* 39, no. 1 (1972): 164–182.

Cohen, Stanley, and Laurie Taylor. *Escape Attempts: The Theory and Practice of Resistance to Everyday Life*. London: Allen Lane, 1992.

Contray, Danielle. "Personalized Hotel Perks." *AOL*, January 17, 2010. Available at https://www.aol.com/2010/01/17/personalized-hotel-perks.

Coser, Lewis A. *Greedy Institutions: Patterns of Undivided Commitment*. New York: Free Press, 1974.

Crouch, David, and Luke Desforges. "The Sensuous in the Tourist Encounter: Introduction—the Power of the Body in Tourist Studies." *Tourist Studies* 3 (2003): 5–22.

Csikszentmihalyi, Mihaly. *Beyond Boredom and Anxiety*. San Francisco: Jossey-Bass, 1975.

———. "Some Paradoxes in the Definition of Play." In *Play as Context*, edited by Alyce Cheska, 14–26. West Point, NY: Leisure Press, 1981.

Dann, Graham. "Writing Out the Tourist in Space and Time." *Annals of Tourism Research* 26, no. 1 (1999): 159–187.

Davis, Murray S. "That's Interesting! Towards a Phenomenology of Sociology and a Sociology of Phenomenology." *Philosophy of the Social Sciences* 1, no. 4 (1971): 309–344.

Davis, Susan. *Spectacular Nature: Corporate Culture and the Sea World Experience*. Berkeley: University of California Press, 1997.

Deem, Rosemary. "No Time for a Rest? An Exploration of Women's Work, Engendered Leisure and Holidays." *Time and Society* 5, no. 1 (1996): 5–25.

Denzin, Norman. "Play, Games and Interaction: The Contexts of Childhood Socialization." *Sociological Quarterly* 16, no. 4 (1975): 458–478.

Desforges, Luke. "Traveling the World: Identity and Travel Biography." *Annals of Tourism Research* 27 (2000): 926–945.

Desmond, Jane. *Staging Tourism: Bodies on Display from Waikiki to Sea World*. Chicago: University of Chicago Press, 1999.

Diekema, David. "Aloneness and Social Form." *Symbolic Interaction* 15, no. 4 (1992): 481–500.

Diken, Bulent, and Carsten Bagge Lausten. "Sea, Sun, Sex and the Discontents of Pleasure." *Tourist Studies* 4 (2004): 99–114.

DiMaggio, Paul. "Cultural Entrepreneurship in Nineteenth Century Boston: The Creation of an Organizational Base for High Culture in America." *Media, Culture, and Society* 4 (1982): 33–50.

Doquet, Anne, and Olivier Evrard. "An Interview with Jean Didier Urbain: Tourism beyond the Grave: A Semiology of Culture." *Tourist Studies* 8, no. 2 (2008): 175–191.

Drew, Robert. "Embracing the Role of Amateur: How Karaoke Bar Patrons Become Regular Performers." *Journal of Contemporary Ethnography* 25, no. 4 (1997): 449–468.

Durkheim, Émile. *The Elementary Forms of Religious Life*. New York: Free Press, 1965.

Durston, James. "In Defense of Staying Home." *CNN*, July 4, 2013. Available at http://travel.cnn.com/defense-staying-home-289606.

Edensor, Tim. "Performing Tourism, Staging Tourism: (Re)Producing Tourist Space and Practice." *Tourist Studies* 1 (2000): 59–81.

———. *Tourists at the Taj: Performance and Meaning at a Symbolic Site*. London: Routledge, 1998.

Elsrud, Torun. "Risk Creation in Traveling: Backpacker Adventure Narration." *Annals of Tourism Research* 28 (2001): 597–617.

Eriksen, Thomas Hylland. *Tyranny of the Moment: Fast and Slow Time in the Information Age*. London: Pluto Press, 2001.

Emerson, Robert, Rachel Fretz, and Linda Shaw. *Writing Ethnographic Fieldnotes*. Chicago: University of Chicago Press, 1995.

Etziot, D., D. Eden, and Y. Lapidot. "Active Reserve Duty as an Ameliorative Respite from Civilian Job-Stress and Burnout." Paper presented at the Fifth International Conference on Social Stress Research, Honolulu, HI, June 1994.

Eyerman, Ron, and Orvar Löfgren. "Romancing the Road: Road Movies and Images of Mobility." *Theory, Culture and Society* 12 (1995): 53–79.

Fagan, Chelsea. "Paris Syndrome: A First-Class Problem for a First-Class Vacation." *The Atlantic*, 2011. Available at https://www.theatlantic.com/health/archive/2011/10/paris-syndrome-a-first-class-problem-for-a-first-class-vacation/246743.

Falk, John, and Lynn Dierking. *Learning from Museums: Visitor Experiences and the Making of Meaning*. Lanham, MD: AltaMira Press, 2000.

Featherstone, Mike. "Automobilities: An Introduction." *Theory, Culture and Society* 21, nos. 4–5 (2004): 1–24.

Fine, Gary Alan. *Everyday Genius: Self-Taught Art and the Culture of Authenticity*. Chicago: University of Chicago Press, 2004.

———. *Kitchens*. Berkeley: University of California Press, 2009.

Flaherty, Michael. *The Textures of Time: Agency and Temporal Experience*. Philadelphia: Temple University Press, 2011.

———. *A Watched Pot: How We Experience Time*. New York: New York University Press, 1999.

Franklin, Adrian. *Tourism: An Introduction*. London: Sage, 2003.

Friedman, Asia. "Toward a Sociology of Perception: Sight, Sex, and Gender." *Cultural Sociology* 5, no. 2 (2010): 187–206.

Galani-Moutafi, Vasiliki. "The Self and the Other: Traveler, Ethnographer, Tourist." *Annals of Tourism Research* 27 (2000): 203–224.

Gaspard, Joe. "Top Five Study Abroad Destinations from Let's Go Travel Guides." April 18, 2011. Available at https://www.prweb.com/releases/letsgo/study abroad2011/prweb8309358.htm.

Gelber, Steven. *Hobbies: Leisure and the Culture of Work in America*. New York: Columbia University Press, 1999.

Giddens, Anthony. *Modernity and Self-Identity: Self and Society in the Late Modern Age*. Stanford, CA: Stanford University Press, 1991.

Gieryn, Thomas. "A Space for Place in Sociology." *Annual Review of Sociology* 26 (2000): 463–496.

———. "What Buildings Do." *Theory and Society* 31, no. 1 (2002): 35–74.

Gini, Al. *The Importance of Being Lazy: In Praise of Play, Leisure and Vacations*. New York: Routledge, 2005.

Glassie, Henry. *Passing the Time in Ballymenon: Culture and History of an Ulster Community*. Philadelphia: University of Pennsylvania Press, 1982.

Goffman, Erving. *Frame Analysis: An Essay on the Organization of Experience*. Cambridge, MA: Harvard University Press, 1974.

———. "On the Characteristics of Social Institutions." In *Asylums: Essays on the Social Situations of Mental Patients and Other Inmates*, 1–124. Oxford: Doubleday, 1961.

———. *The Presentation of Self in Everyday Life*. New York: Random House, 1959.

———. *Stigma: Note on the Management of Spoiled Identity*. New York: Simon and Schuster, 1963.

———. "The Underlife of a Public Institution." In *Asylums*, 171–320. Garden City, NY: Doubleday, 1961.

———. "Where the Action Is." In *Interaction Ritual: Essays in Face-to-Face Behavior*, 149–270. New Brunswick, NJ: Transaction, 2005.

Gottdiener, Mark. *The Theming of America: Dreams, Visions and Commercial Spaces*. Boulder, CO: Westview Press, 1997.

Gottlieb, Alma. "Americans' Vacations." *Annals of Tourism Research* 9 (1982): 165–187.

Graburn, Nelson. "The Anthropology of Tourism." *Annals of Tourism Research* 10 (1983): 9–13.

———. "Tourism: The Sacred Journey." In *Hosts and Guests: The Anthropology of Tourism*, edited by Valene Smith, 17–31. Philadelphia: University of Pennsylvania Press, 1977.

Grazian, David. *Blue Chicago: The Search for Authenticity in Urban Blues Clubs*. Chicago: University of Chicago Press, 2003.

Green, Francis, and Michael Potepan. "Vacation Time and Unionism in the U.S. and Europe." *Industrial Relations* 27, no. 2 (1988): 180–194.

Greenfield, Liah. "When the Sky Is the Limit: Busyness in Contemporary American Society." *Social Research* 72, no. 2 (2005): 1–24.

Habraken, N. J. *The Structures of the Ordinary: Form and Control in the Built Environment.* Cambridge, MA: MIT Press, 1998.

Hall, Edward. *The Dance of Life: The Other Dimension of Time.* New York: Doubleday, 1983.

Hawaii Tourism Authority. "2009 Annual Visitor Research Report." 2009. Available at http://files.hawaii.gov/dbedt/visitor/visitor-research/2009-annual -visitor.pdf.

Holland, Dorothy, William Lachicotte Jr., Debra Skinner, and Carole Cain. *Identity and Agency in Cultural Worlds.* Cambridge, MA: Harvard University Press, 1998.

Howard, Judith. "Social Psychology of Identities." *Annual Review of Sociology* 26 (2000): 367–393.

Hubert, Henri. "A Brief Study of the Representation of Time in Religion and Magic." In *Essay on Time,* 43–92. Oxford: Durkheim Press, 1999.

Huizinga, Johan. *Homo Ludens: A Study of the Play Element in Culture.* New York: Harper and Row, 1955.

Ibarra, Herminia, and Jennifer Petriglieri. "Identity Work and Play." *Journal of Organizational Change Management* 23, no. 1 (2010): 10–25.

Jacobs, Jerry, and Kathleen Gerson. *The Time Divide: Work, Family, and Gender Inequality.* Cambridge, MA: Harvard University Press, 2004.

Jenkins, Richard. *Social Identity.* London: Routledge, 2014.

Jerolmack, Colin, and Shamus Khan. "Talk Is Cheap: Ethnography and the Attitudinal Fantasy." *Sociological Methods and Research* 43, no. 2 (2014): 178–209.

Jerolmack, Colin, and Iddo Tavory. Molds and Totems: Nonhumans and the Constitution of the Social Self. *Sociological Theory* 32, no. 1 (2014): 64–77.

Jiang, Shelley. *Let's Go China.* New York: St. Martin's Press, 2005.

Jonas, Lilian. "Making and Facing Danger: Constructing Strong Character on the River." *Symbolic Interaction* 22, no. 3 (1999): 247–267.

Kanahele, George S. *Waikiki 100 B.C. to 1900 A.D.: An Untold Story.* Honolulu: University of Hawaii Press, 1995.

Kane, Maurice J., and Hazel Tucker. "Adventure Tourism: The Freedom to Play with Reality." *Tourist Studies* 4 (2004): 217–234.

Kelly, John. *Leisure Identities and Interactions.* London: George Allen and Unwin, 1983.

Kendall, Lori. "Meaning and Identity in 'Cyberspace': The Performance of Gender, Class, and Race Online." *Symbolic Interaction* 21, no. 2 (1998): 129–153.

Kjolsrod, Lisa. "Adventure Revisited: On Structure and Metaphor in Specialized Play." *Sociology* 37, no. 3 (2003): 459–476.

Kruhse-Montburton, Susy. "Sex Tourism and the Traditional Male Identity." In *International Tourism: Identity and Change,* edited by Marie-Francoise Lanfant, John Allcock, and Edward Bruner, 192–204. London: Sage, 1995.

Kugel, Seth. "An Insider's Tour of Chongqing Yields Frugal Gems." *New York Times,* March 20, 2013. Available at http://frugaltraveler.blogs.nytimes.com/2013/03/20/an-insiders-tour-of-chongqing-yields-frugal-gems/?src=dayp.

Lamont, Michelle, and Annette Lareau. "Cultural Capital: Allusions, Gaps, and Glissandos in Recent Theoretical Developments." *Sociological Theory* 6, no. 2 (1988): 153–168.

Larsen, Jonas. "De-exoticizing Tourist Travel: Everyday Life and Sociality on the Move." *Leisure Studies* 27 (2008): 21–34.

———. "Families Seen Sightseeing: Performativity of Tourist Photography." *Space and Culture* 8, no. 4 (2005): 416–434.

Lauer, Robert. *Temporal Man: The Meaning and Uses of Social Time.* New York: Praeger, 1981.

Leach, Edmund. "Two Essays concerning the Symbolic Representation of Time." In *Rethinking Anthropology*, 124–136. New York: Athlone Press, 1961.

Leamy, Elisabeth. "Tips for Planning a Great 'Staycation.'" *ABC News*, May 23, 2008. Available at http://abcnews.go.com/GMA/Parenting/story?id=4919211.

Leed, Eric. *The Mind of the Traveler: From Gilgamesh to Global Tourism.* New York: Basic Books, 1991.

Lencek, Lena, and Gideon Bosker. *The Beach.* New York: Viking, 1998.

Lett, James, Jr. "Ludic and Liminoid Aspects of Charter Yacht Tourism in the Caribbean." *Annals of Tourism Research* 10 (1983): 35–56.

Levine, Robert. *A Geography of Time: The Temporal Misadventures of a Social Psychologist, or How Every Culture Keeps Time Just a Little Bit Differently.* New York: Basic Books, 1997.

Löfgren, Orvar. *On Holiday: A History of Vacationing.* Berkeley: University of California Press, 1999.

Lounsbury, J. W., and L. L. Hoopes. "A Vacation from Work: Changes in Work and Nonwork Outcomes." *Journal of Applied Psychology* 71 (1986): 392–401.

Lurie, Celia. "The Objects of Travel." In *Touring Cultures: Transformations of Travel and Theory*, edited by Chris Rojek and John Urry, 75–95. New York: Routledge, 1997.

Lyman, Stanford, and Marvin Scott. *A Sociology of the Absurd.* New York: Appleton-Century-Crofts, 1970.

MacCannell, Dean. "Staged Authenticity: Arrangements of Social Space in Tourist Settings." *American Journal of Sociology* 79, no. 3 (1973): 589–603.

———. *The Tourist: A New Theory of the Leisure Class.* New York: Schocken Books, 1976.

Markula, Pirkko. "As a Tourist in Tahiti: An Analysis of Personal Experience." *Journal of Contemporary Ethnography* 26, no. 2 (1997): 202–224.

Martinez-Robles, David. "The Western Representation of Modern China: Orientalism, Culturalism and Historiographical Criticism." *Digithum* 10 (2008). Available at https://digithum.uoc.edu/articles/abstract/10.7238/d.v0i10.511.

Maume, David. "Gender Differences in Taking Vacation Time." *Work and Occupations* 33, no. 2 (2006): 161–190.

McCabe, Scott, and Elizabeth Stokoe. "Place and Identity in Tourists' Accounts." *Annals of Tourism Research* 31, no. 3 (2004): 601–622.

Mead, George Herbert. *Mind, Self and Society*. Chicago: University of Chicago Press, 1967.

Melbin, Murray. "Night as Frontier." *American Sociological Review* 43, no. 1 (1978): 3–22.

Merton, Robert. *Sociological Ambivalence and Other Essays*. New York: Free Press, 1976.

Meyers, Diana. "Personal Autonomy and the Paradox of Feminine Socialization." In *Being Yourself: Essays on Identity, Action and Social Life*, 3–12. Lanham, MD: Rowman and Littlefield, 2004.

Molotch, Harvey, William Freudenberg, and Krista Paulsen. "History Repeats Itself, but How? City Character, Urban Tradition, and the Accomplishment of Place." *American Sociological Review* 65 (2000): 679–698.

"Momcations Become Latest Travel Industry Trend." *eTN*, May 12, 2008. Available at https://www.eturbonews.com/4843/momcations-becomes-latest-travel-trend.

"Mom Spends Beach Vacation Assuming All Household Duties in Closer Proximity to Ocean." *The Onion*, August 9, 2013. Available at https://www.theonion.com/mom-spends-beach-vacation-assuming-all-household-duties-1819575406.

Moore, Alexander. "Walt Disney World: Bounded Ritual Space and the Playful Pilgrimage Center." *Anthropological Quarterly* 53, no. 4 (1980): 207–218.

Morgan, Nigel, and Annette Pritchard. "On Souvenirs and Metonymy: Narratives of Memory, Metaphor and Materiality." *Tourist Studies* 5 (2005): 29–53.

Munt, Ian. "The 'Other' Postmodern Tourism: Culture, Travel and the New Middle Classes." *Theory, Culture and Society* 11 (1994): 101–123.

Muzaini, Hamzah. "Backpacking Southeast Asia: Strategies of 'Looking Local.'" *Annals of Tourism Research* 33, no. 1 (2006): 144–161.

Nash, Denison, and Valene Smith. "Anthropology of Tourism." *Annals of Tourism Research* 18 (1991): 12–25.

Nash, Roderick. *Wilderness and the American Mind*. New Haven, CT: Yale University Press, 1973.

Neumann, Mark. "Living on Tortoise Time: Alternative Travel as the Pursuit of Lifestyle." *Symbolic Interaction* 16, no. 3 (1983): 201–235.

Nippert-Eng, Christena E. *Home and Work: Negotiating Boundaries through Everyday Life*. Chicago: University of Chicago Press, 1996.

———. *Islands of Privacy*. Chicago: University of Chicago Press, 2010.

Noy, Chaim. "This Trip Really Changed Me: Backpackers' Narratives of Self Change." *Annals of Tourism Research* 31, no. 1 (2004): 78–102.

Pagis, M. "Religious Self-Constitution: A Relational Perspective." In *Religion on the Edge: De-centering and Re-centering the Sociology of Religion*, edited by Courtney Bender, 92–114. Oxford: Oxford University Press, 2012.

Pearce, Philip. *Tourist Behavior: Themes and Conceptual Schemes*. Clevedon, UK: Channel View, 2005.

Pike, Kenneth. *Language in Relation to a Unified Theory of the Structure of Human Behavior*. 2nd ed. The Hague: Mouton, 1967.

Project: Time Off. "State of American Vacation, 2018." 2018. Available at https://projecttimeoff.com/wp-content/uploads/2018/05/StateofAmericanVacation2018.pdf.

Ray, Rebecca, Milla Sanes, and John Schmitt. *No-Vacation Nation Revisited*. Washington, DC: Center for Economic and Policy Research, 2013.

Reese, William A., and Michael A. Katovitch. "Untimely Acts: Extending the Interactionist Conception of Deviance." *Sociological Quarterly* 30 (1989): 159–184.

Renfrow, Daniel. "A Cartography of Passing in Everyday Life." *Symbolic Interaction* 27, no. 4 (2004): 485–506.

Rojek, Chris. *The Labour of Leisure: The Culture of Free Time*. Thousand Oaks, CA: Sage, 2010.

———. *Ways of Escape: Modern Transformation in Leisure and Travel*. Lanham, MD: Rowman and Littlefield, 1993.

Ronai, Carol Rambo, and Carolyn Ellis. "Turn-Ons for Money: Interactional Strategies of the Table Dancer." *Journal of Contemporary Ethnography* 18, no. 3 (1989): 271–298.

Rosenbloom, Stephanie. "Single in the Caribbean." *New York Times*, February 3, 2012. Available at http://travel.nytimes.com/2012/02/05/travel/single-in-the-caribbean-sun.html.

Ross, R. N. "Ellipsis and the Structure of Expectation." *San Jose Occasional Papers in Linguistics* 1 (1975): 183–191.

Rothman, Hal. *Devil's Bargains: Tourism in the Twentieth-Century American West*. Lawrence: University of Kansas Press, 1998.

Rugh, Susan Sessions. *Are We There Yet? The Golden Age of American Family Vacations*. Lawrence: University Press of Kansas, 2008.

Rybczynski, Witold. *Waiting for the Weekend*. New York: Penguin, 1991.

Sack, Robert. *Place, Modernity, and the Consumer's World*. Baltimore: Johns Hopkins University Press, 1992.

Salanniemi, Tom. "Pale Skin on the Playa del Anywhere: Finnish Tourists in the Liminoid South." In *Hosts and Guests Revisited: Tourism Issues in the 21st Century*, edited by Valene Smith and Maryann Brent, 80–92. Elmsford, NY: Cognizant Communication, 2001.

Sanchez-Taylor, Jacqueline. "Dollars Are a Girl's Best Friend: Female Tourists' Sexual Behavior in the Caribbean." *Sociology* 35, no. 3 (2001): 749–764.

Schutz, Alfred. *Collected Papers I*. The Hague: M. Nijhoff, 1962.

Schwartz, Barry. "Notes on the Sociology of Sleep." *Sociological Quarterly* 11, no. 4 (1970): 485–499.

———. "The Social Psychology of the Gift." *American Journal of Sociology* 73, no. 1 (1967): 1–11.

———. "The Social Psychology of Privacy." *American Journal of Sociology* 73, no. 6 (1968): 741–752.

Seinfeld, Jerry. "Feces Are My Purview." *Comedians in Cars Getting Coffee*. Netflix, January 30, 2014.

Sennet, Richard. *The Corrosion of Character*. New York: Norton, 1998.

Sharma, Sarah. "The Great American Staycation and the Risk of Stillness." *M/C Journal* 12, no. 1 (2009). Available at http://journal.media-culture.org.au/index.php/mcjournal/article/viewArticle/122.

Shellenbarger, Sue. "Guys Just Want to Have Fun." *Wall Street Journal*, June 15, 2010. Available at http://online.wsj.com/article/SB10001424052748703685404575306783337815438.html.

Shields, Rob. *Places on the Margin: Alternative Geographies of Modernity*. London: Routledge, 1991.

Silver, Ira. "Role Transitions, Objects and Identity." *Symbolic Interaction* 19 (1996): 1–20.

Simmel, Georg. "The Metropolis and Mental Life." In *The Sociology of Georg Simmel*, edited and translated by Kurt Wolff, 409–424. Glencoe, IL: Free Press, 1950.

———. "Sociability." In *On Individuality and Social Forms*, edited by Donald Levine, 127–140. Chicago: University of Chicago Press, 1971.

Smith, Vanessa, and Howard Hughes. "Disadvantaged Families and the Meaning of the Holiday." *International Journal of Tourism Research* 1 (1999): 123–133.

Snow, David, and Leon Anderson. "Identity Work among the Homeless: The Verbal Construction and Avowal of Personal Identities." *American Journal of Sociology* 92, no. 6 (1987): 1336–1371.

Snow, Robert, and Dennis Brissett. "Pauses: Explorations in Social Rhythm." *Symbolic Interaction* 9, no. 1 (1986): 1–18.

Sorokin, Pitrim, and Robert Merton. "Social Time: A Methodological and Functional Analysis." *American Journal of Sociology* 42, no. 5 (1937): 615–629.

Stebbins, Robert. "Serious Leisure: A Conceptual Statement." *Pacific Sociological Review* 25, no. 2 (1982): 251–272.

———. *Serious Leisure: A Perspective for Our Time*. New Brunswick, NJ: Transaction, 2007.

Stein, Karen. "Getting Away from It All: The Construction and Management of Temporary Identities on Vacation." *Symbolic Interaction* 34, no. 2 (2011): 290–308.

———. "Time Off: The Social Experience of Time on Vacation." *Qualitative Sociology* 35 (2012): 335.

Stets, Jan, and Peter Burke. "A Sociological Approach to Self and Identity." In *Handbook of Self and Identity*, edited by Mark Leary and June Price, 128–152. New York: Guilford Press, 2003.

Stewart, Susan. *On Longing: Narratives of the Miniature, the Gigantic, the Souvenir, the Collection*. Baltimore: Johns Hopkins University Press, 1984.

Stone, Gregory. "Appearance and the Self." In *Human Behavior and Social Processes: An Interactionist Approach*, edited by Arnold Rose, 86–116. Boston: Houghton Mifflin, 1962.

Stryker, Sheldon. "Identity Salience and Role Performance." *Journal of Marriage and the Family* 4 (1968): 558–564.

———. *Symbolic Interactionism: A Social Structural Version*. Menlo Park, CA: Benjamin Cummings, 1980.

Swidler, Ann. "Culture in Action: Symbols and Strategies." *American Sociological Review* 51 (1986): 273–286.

———. *Talk of Love: How Culture Matters*. Chicago: University of Chicago Press, 2001.

Tannen, Deborah. *Framing in Discourse*. New York: Oxford University Press, 1993.

Tavory, Iddo. "Of Yarmulkes and Categories: Delegating Boundaries and the Phenomenology of Interactional Expectation." *Theory and Society* 39, no. 1 (2010): 49–68.

Tuan, Yi-fu. *Space and Place: The Perspective of Experience*. Minneapolis: University of Minnesota Press, 1977.

Tucker, Hazel. "Narratives of Place and Self: Differing Experiences of Package Coach Tours in New Zealand." *Tourist Studies* 5, no. 3 (2005): 267–282.

Turkle, Sherry. *Life on the Screen: Identity in the Age of the Internet*. New York: Simon and Schuster, 1995.

Turner, Victor Witter. "Betwixt and Between: The Liminal Period in *Rites de Passage*." In *The Forest of Symbols: Aspects of Ndembu Ritual*, 93–111. Ithaca, NY: Cornell University Press, 1967.

———. "Liminal to Liminoid, in Play, Flow, and Ritual: An Essay in Comparative Symbology." *Rice University Studies* 60, no. 3 (1974): 53–92.

———. *The Ritual Process: Structure and Anti-structure*. Ithaca, NY: Cornell University Press, 1969.

Urbain, Jean-Didier. *At the Beach*. Translated by Catherine Porter. Minneapolis: University of Minnesota Press, 2003.

Urry, John. *Consuming Places*. New York: Routledge, 1995.

———. "Mobility and Proximity." *Sociology* 36, no. 2 (2002): 255–274.

———. *The Tourist Gaze: Leisure and Travel in Contemporary Societies*. London: Sage, 2002.

U.S. Patent and Trademark Office. "Staycation." Trademark Status and Document Retrieval. 2009. Available at http://tsdr.uspto.gov/#caseNumber=77475410&caseType=SERIAL_NO&searchType=statusSearch.

Van Gennep, Arnold. *The Rites of Passage*. Chicago: University of Chicago Press, 1960.

Vryan, Kevin, Patricia Adler, and Peter Adler. "Identity." In *Handbook of Symbolic Interactionism*, edited by L. T. Reynolds and N. J. Merman-Kinney, 367–390. Lanham, MD: AltaMira Press, 2003.

Wearing, Stephen. "Re-centering the Self in Volunteer Tourism." In *The Tourist as a Metaphor of the Social World*, edited by Graham Dann and Jens Kristian Steen Jacobsen, 237–262. Oxon, UK: CABI, 2002.

Wearing, Stephen, and John Neil. "Refiguring Self and Identity through Volunteer Tourism." *Society and Leisure* 23 (2000): 389–419.

Weissman, Arnie. "'Authenticity' and the Travel Industry." *Travel Weekly*, February 13, 2012. Available at http://www.travelweekly.com/arnie-weissmann/authenticity-and-the-travel-industry.

White, Naomi Rosh, and Peter B. White. "Home and Away: Tourists in a Connected World." *Annals of Tourism Research* 34 (2007): 88–104.

"Why Don't Americans Have Longer Vacations?" *New York Times*, August 4, 2010. Available at http://www.nytimes.com/roomfordebate/2010/08/04/why-dont -americans-have-longer- vacations.

Wixon, Matt. *The Great American Staycation: How to Make a Vacation at Home Fun for the Whole Family (and Your Wallet!)*. Avon, MA: Adam's Media, 2009.

Yoshimo, Kimi. "'Funemployed' Revel in Freedom from Work." *San Francisco Chronicle*, June 7, 2009. Available at https://www.sfgate.com/business/ article/Funemployed-revel-in-freedom-from-work-3228311.php.

Zerubavel, Eviatar. *The Fine Line: Making Distinctions in Everyday Life*. Chicago: University of Chicago Press, 1991.

———. "Generally Speaking: The Logic and Mechanics of Social Pattern Analysis." *Sociological Forum* 22 (2007): 131–145.

———. *Hidden Rhythms: Schedules and Calendars in Social Life*. Chicago: University of Chicago Press, 1981.

———. "Horizons: On the Sociomental Foundations of Relevance." *Social Research* 60, no. 2 (1993): 397–413.

———. "The Language of Time: Toward a Semiotics of Temporality." *Sociological Quarterly* 28 (1987): 343–356.

———. "Private Time and Public Time: The Temporal Structure of Social Accessibility and Professional Commitments." *Social Forces* 58, no. 1 (1979): 38–58.

———. *The Seven Day Circle: The History and Meaning of the Week*. New York: Free Press, 1985.

———. *Social Mindscapes: An Invitation to Cognitive Sociology*. Cambridge, MA: Harvard University Press, 1997.

Zukin, Sharon. *Landscapes of Power: From Detroit to Disneyland*. Berkeley: University of California Press, 1991.

Zurcher, Louis. "The 'Friendly' Poker Game: A Study of an Ephemeral Role." *Social Forces* 49 (1970): 173–186.

———. *The Mutable Self*. Beverly Hills, CA: Sage, 1977.

———. "The Naval Reservist: An Empirical Assessment of Ephemeral Role Enactment." *Social Forces* 55, no. 3 (1977): 753–768.

———. "Social-Psychological Functions of Ephemeral Roles: A Disaster Work Crew." *Human Organization* 27, no. 4 (1968): 281–297.

Index